Living with Dyslexia
Second edition

What is it like living with dyslexia on a day-to-day basis?

Based on interviews with dyslexic children and their families, this insightful book presents first-hand accounts of how dyslexia affects the children themselves and the people around them.

Living with Dyslexia places the original fascinating findings within the context of current research and practice in the UK, Europe, Australia and the US. The author:

- examines issues of confidence and self-esteem;
- explores the coping strategies adopted by children and adults with dyslexia;
- investigates the concept of dyslexia-friendly schools;
- studies how children were first identified as having dyslexia, and the social and emotional difficulties they encountered;
- offers guidance on how teachers and parents can best support children with specific learning difficulties;
- considers the cognitive, educational, social and emotional perspectives in order for teachers and parents to gain a better understanding of dyslexia.

This new edition provides an updated account of cognitive research and examines important changes in relation to special educational needs policy and practice in the last ten years, including the Revised SEN Code of Practice (2001), Removing Barriers to Achievement (2004) and the National Literacy Strategy (2006).

Living with Dyslexia recognises that the voices of children with dyslexia are increasingly important in developing good educational practice and makes an important contribution to the literature on dyslexia.

Barbara Riddick is PhD Programme Director at the School of Education, University of Durham, UK.

nasen
Helping Everyone Achieve

Other titles published in association with the National Association for Special Educational Needs (nasen):

Dyspraxia 5–14: Identifying and Supporting Young People with Movement Difficulties
Christine Macintyre
978-0-415-54397-2 (hbk)
978-0-415-54396-5 (pbk)

Teaching Foundation Mathematics: A Guide for Teachers of Older Students with Learning Disabilities
Nadia Naggar-Smith
978-0-415-45164-2

Language for Learning: A Practical Guide for Supporting Pupils with Language and Communication Difficulties across the Curriculum
Sue Hayden
978-1-84312-468-9

The Rob Long Omnibus Edition of Better Behaviour
Rob Long
978-1-84312-470-2

The Special School's Handbook
Michael Farrell
978-0-415-41685-6 (hbk)
978-0-415-41686-3 (pbk)

The SEN Handbook for Trainee Teachers, NQTs and Teaching Assistants
Wendy Spooner
978-1-84312-404-7

The New nasen A–Z of Reading Resources
Suzanne Baker and Lorraine Petersen
978-1-84312-441-2

Beating Bureaucracy in Special Educational Needs
Jean Gross
978-0-415-44114-8

P Levels in Mainstream Settings: Meeting the Needs of all Pupils
Lorraine Petersen and Ann Fergusson
(forthcoming)
978-0-415-43791-2

Diversity and Personalised Learning
John Visser
(forthcoming)
978-0-415-46752-0

Living with Dyslexia

uences
abilities

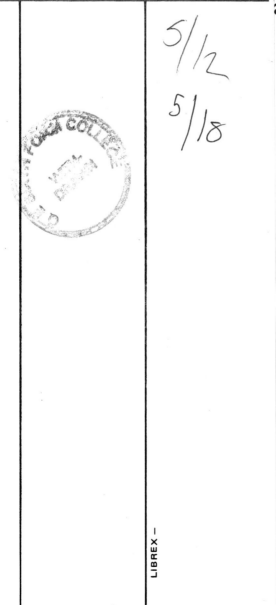

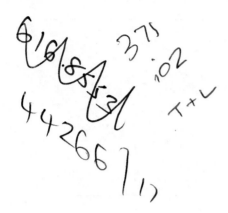

First published 1996
by David Fulton Publishers

This edition published 2010
by Routledge
2 Park Square, Milton Park, Abingdon, Oxon OX14 4RN

Simultaneously published in the USA and Canada
by Routledge
270 Madison Avenue, New York, NY 10016

Routledge is an imprint of the Taylor & Francis Group, an informa business

Typeset in Garamond by Prepress Projects Ltd, Perth, UK
Printed and bound in Great Britain by TJ International Ltd, Padstow, Cornwall

British Library Cataloguing in Publication Data
A catalogue record for this book is available from the British Library

Library of Congress Cataloging in Publication Data
Riddick, Barbara
Living with Dyslexia: the social and emotional consequences of specific learning difficulties/
disabilities/Barbara Riddick.—2nd ed.
p. cm.
Includes bibliographical references and index.
1. Dyslexic children—Education. 2. Dyslexia—Social aspects. 3. Dyslexia—Psychological
aspects.
I. Title.
LC4708.R54 2010
371.91'44–dc22
2009009263

ISBN 10: 0–415–47758–1 (pbk)
ISBN 10: 0–203–86457–3 (ebk)

ISBN 13: 978–0–415–47758–1 (pbk)
ISBN 13: 978–0–203–86457–9 (ebk)

nasen is a professional membership association which supports all those who work with or care for children and young people with special and additional educational needs. Members include teachers, teaching assistants, support workers, other educationalists, students and parents.

nasen supports its members through policy documents, journals, its magazine *Special!*, publications, professional development courses, regional networks and newsletters. Its website contains more current information such as responses to government consultations. nasen's published documents are held in very high regard both in the UK and internationally.

This book is dedicated to Tom and all the other children who have struggled with dyslexia.

Contents

Tables

Foreword

It is a very great pleasure to be asked to provide a foreword to the second edition of *Living with Dyslexia*, following in the footsteps of Baroness Warnock, who contributed the preface to the first edition. I have followed Barbara Riddick's work for some years and delighted in her concern for the well being of the dyslexic child, which is so often overlooked in research which concentrates solely on literacy outcomes for these children. The 12 years since the previous edition was published have seen substantial changes in the approach to dyslexia, with the UK in my view, leading the field in provision, with the 1994 Code of Practice leading to an emphasis on earlier identification, inclusion and moves towards the dyslexia-friendly school. This period has seen the publication of a range of screening tests to identify children at risk for dyslexia, and new developments in methods of support, including the US concept of response to intervention. It has also seen the development of new theories of dyslexia, which recognise the wider context within which dyslexic children may struggle. It is clear that all of these changes must impact on the outcome for children with dyslexia, and they are outlined clearly here. However, one of the most important changes which the previous edition of this book was instrumental in achieving has been the acknowledgement that the social and emotional consequences of dyslexia can be the most difficult to overcome. This has led to further research in the areas of self-efficacy and self-esteem in dyslexia. This book reinforces the need for understanding and support for children with dyslexia from parents and teachers, but also the importance of the children's own understanding of their strengths and weaknesses in order to fulfil their potential. It should be recommended reading for all those involved in dyslexia.

Angela Fawcett
Director of the Centre for Child Research, Swansea University

Preface

Why a book on living with dyslexia? A simple answer is that this is still a relatively neglected area. At a more complicated level the reasons for this can be suggested. Much of the early work on dyslexia was carried out by interested clinicians such as Orton and Hinshelwood. Their approach had both the strengths and the weaknesses of the clinical approach. They made careful detailed observations of their clients' difficulties, but inevitably their primary focus was the clinical setting and not the day-to-day world that their clients lived in. More recently there has been an enormous expansion in experimental research trying to identify the cognitive (thinking) deficits/differences underlying dyslexia. Whilst this research has greatly increased our knowledge of dyslexia its focus has been largely on looking at these deficits in the experimental setting and not on how these deficits are dealt with on an everyday basis. Turning to recent educational research much of this has focused on comparing different methods of intervention or teaching. These have generally been evaluated in terms of specific learning outcomes such as reading ages and not broader measures of educational and personal well being. This is not to deny that many vivid accounts of the personal difficulties encountered by both children and adults with dyslexia exist. These range from individual biographies to collections of case histories. The problem with these is that because of their piecemeal nature they are open to criticisms of bias, unrepresentativeness and lack of generalisability. One of the major aims of this book is to look at how information on living with dyslexia can be collected in a systematic manner and integrated with other forms of research to increase our overall understanding of dyslexia. Another aim has been to let children and their parents speak for themselves as far as possible so we can gain a clearer understanding of how living with dyslexia appears from their perspective. It is also hoped that in doing this the information presented will be of help to all those working with dyslexic children and will enable them to review or reflect on the nature of the support that they are offering both to dyslexic children and their families. Because the cognitive deficits/differences underlying dyslexia are an integral and pervasive part of children's experience some understanding of these is necessary in order to appreciate what 'living with dyslexia' entails so a brief review of current thinking has been included. In a similar vein it was considered that as dyslexia is part of the wider construct of special educational needs (or children with additional needs), this wider perspective should also be reviewed. It is hoped that by doing this, the experiences of living with dyslexia can be placed within this wider context.

Despite the controversy in educational circles about the term 'dyslexia', this term was chosen because it was the one that the overwhelming majority of children and parents who were interviewed said that they found most helpful in understanding their specific difficulties. One of the aims of this book is to look at the advantages and disadvantages of using the label 'dyslexia' and to examine how it relates to other terms such as 'specific learning disability'. The intention is not to be dogmatic but to raise constructive debate about this and a number of other issues surrounding dyslexia. A major argument of this book is that we do need to take seriously the views of children and their parents on living with dyslexia if we are to have a comprehensive and properly informed understanding of the condition.

Update

Being asked to write a new edition of a book on living with dyslexia after a gap of 12 years is an instructive experience. It has allowed me to take stock of what has changed in that time in terms of both theory and practice and to consider how those changes may impact on the lives and education of children now. Initially the entire preface was going to be re-written but on reading it through I thought that what was originally written was still relevant and that it was more helpful to provide an update summarising some of the major developments or changes. These will be discussed in more detail in the main body of the book.

1   In the UK the term 'dyslexia' has become more widely acceptable to the education system and is enshrined in legislation such as the SEN Revised Code of Practice.
2   In England and Wales the adoption of a national literacy strategy has lead to a more systematic approach to the teaching of reading with an emphasis on phonological skills.
3   In the US the notion of 'response to instruction' is seen by some as the key to defining reading disability/dyslexia and providing effective intervention.
4   International comparisons have given a much clearer picture of how different types of languages present different levels and types of difficulty for dyslexic learners.
5   Globally there has been more emphasis on an inclusive approach to education that pays attention to how children learn and the barriers that education establishments present.
6   Within the context of a more inclusive approach to education there has been interest in developing 'dyslexia-friendly' mainstream schools particularly, but not exclusively, in the UK.
7   Although still relatively few in comparison with cognitive research studies, many more studies have been carried out on the social and emotional aspects of dyslexia and the general issues of how people learn to live with cognitive differences.

Over the past 12 years I've had the privilege of spending time in North America, Australia, Europe, the Far East and Russia discussing, lecturing on and meeting children, parents, educationalists and researchers with an interest in dyslexia. This has helped develop my understanding of the issues that are fundamental to living with dyslexia across cultures and languages and how these intersect with specific cultural expectations and practices.

Acknowledgements

The research described in this book was supported by a grant from the Nuffield Foundation.

Many thanks must go to all the children and parents who were interviewed as part of the study. A big thank you must also go to all the teachers and especially to Pat Evans at the Newcastle Branch of the Dyslexia Action, who provided help and support and also agreed to be interviewed.

Thanks to the publishers John Wiley & Sons for allowing reproduction of three tables from a paper written by the author entitled 'Dyslexia and development: an interview study'. Thanks also to Carfax Publishing Company (PO Box 25, Abingdon, Oxfordshire, OX14 3UE) for permission to reproduce material from a paper by the author published in *Disability and Society*.

Introduction

At a very general level research and writing on dyslexia can be put under three major headings. First, there is the large body of cognitive research, some of which will be briefly summarised in the first chapter of this book. Second, there is a broad band of educational research and writing, and finally there is a small but increasing body of research on the social and personal consequences of dyslexia. Inevitably there is considerable overlap between these areas and, for example, some of the studies on intervention have been derived directly from cognitive research but have clear educational implications.

Despite the overlaps there is a case to be made for suggesting there is still a lack of engagement between these various areas of research. The major concern thus far of cognitive psychologists has been to identify the processing deficits underlying dyslexia. They have been less concerned with looking at how these deficits/differences might interact with broader everyday influences such as a child's view of herself as a learner. In contrast much mainstream educational research and writing has ignored or denied the existence of dyslexia as a concept and it has therefore not been directly researched or written about. Many educationalists would argue that they have included many so-called dyslexic children within a different conceptual framework which sees them as part of the continuum of children with specific learning difficulties/disabilities within the broader category of children with special needs. From this perspective there has been a considerable amount of research especially on children who have had difficulties learning to read. The problem is that, because some cognitive and educational researchers have started from different perspectives with different approaches to defining and identifying children with a difficulty, it is hard to compare and draw meaningful conclusions from their relative research.

As stated before, there is less research at present on the social and personal consequences of dyslexia. Much of what exists comes from outside the mainstream of academic research and consists of personal accounts in the form of autobiographies or collections of case studies. At this informal level there are also the opinions of clinicians and specialist teachers on the personal consequences of dyslexia. At a more general level there is research on children's self-concept as learners (Marsh and O'Mara 2008, Elbaum and Vaughan 2003) and the personal development of a range of children with special needs. This area is examined in more detail in Chapter 3 of this book. In Britain the steady stream of research and writing by Professor Tim Miles (1982, 1987, 1993, 1997, 2006, 2007; Miles and Miles 1990, 1999) at Bangor University has consistently drawn on and integrated research and writing from all three areas. In the US Stanovich (2005, Cunningham and Stanovich 1997, Stanovich and Stanovich 2006) has commented particularly on the interface between cognitive and educational research and thinking.

Chapter 1

Defining dyslexia

An overview of dyslexia and specific learning difficulties

'When *I* use a word,' Humpty Dumpty said in a rather scornful tone, 'it means just what I choose it to mean – neither more nor less.'

'The question is,' said Alice, 'whether you *can* make words mean so many different things.'

'The question is,' said Humpty Dumpty, 'which is to be master – that's all.'

(Lewis Carroll, *Through the Looking Glass,* 1865)

In the UK the terms 'dyslexia' and 'specific learning difficulties' are often used synonymously although most authorities would see 'specific learning difficulties' (splds) as an umbrella term for a range of learning difficulties of which 'dyslexia' is one variant (Teachernet 2009). At a very general level educationalists and particularly educational psychologists tend to prefer the term 'specific learning difficulties' and clinicians, voluntary organisations and concerned lay people the term 'dyslexia'. These differences of opinion can be seen as partly due to the different perspectives that educationalists and clinicians are likely to have. As the purpose of this book is to look at the views of people who have chosen to live with the term 'dyslexia', this is the term that has been used predominantly, although where quoted research or writing has used other terms such as 'specific learning difficulties' or 'learning disabilities' these terms have been included.

At a common sense everyday level dyslexia is often defined as an unexpected difficulty in learning to read, write and spell. But like many definitions as soon as it is examined more closely it becomes more difficult to pin down and a number of problems and ambiguities arise. Who decides that the difficulty is unexpected, and on what basis? How behind does a child have to be for it to be counted as a difficulty and how is the difficulty judged or quantified? Do all children need to show the same sort of difficulty or can they show different types of difficulties and still be called dyslexic? In examining definitions of dyslexia it becomes apparent that different definitions highlight different aspects or levels of the problem. Frith (1992) has proposed that in looking at learning disabilities such as autism and dyslexia it is important to look at the links between the different levels of explanation so that we can begin to see the links between biological causation, cognitive impairments, and behaviours such as poor reading and spelling. The following definition, put forward by the World Federation of Neurology (1968) (cited in Critchley 1970), was widely used in the past and formed a platform for more recent definitions:

> Dyslexia is a disorder manifested by difficulty in learning to read despite con-
> ventional instruction, adequate intelligence and socio-cultural opportunity. It is
> dependant upon fundamental cognitive disabilities which are frequently of consti-
> tutional origin.

It can be seen that a definition like this includes behaviour, cognition and cause. Definitions like this are often referred to as exclusion definitions because it suggests that a child can be defined as dyslexic only if a number of factors are excluded. Critics would argue that this type of approach tends to favour the identification of middle-class children and may have led to the fallacious assumption that dyslexia is a 'middle-class disorder'. To look at the problem another way it suggests that socially disadvantaged children or mildly learning disabled children cannot be defined as dyslexic. But the evidence we have so far suggests that the cognitive impairments underlying dyslexia are evenly spread across the population and are as likely to occur in these groups as any other groups. What has not been researched extensively yet is how the specific cognitive impairments underlying dyslexia interact with other impairments such as a hearing disability or with environmental factors such as lack of exposure to the printed word. It may for example be the case that, whereas under optimal conditions children can compensate for a certain degree of specific cognitive impairment, these same impairments coupled with an unfavourable environment may lead to considerable difficulties in learning to read and write. Similar problems exist with what are known as discrepancy definitions of dyslexia. In this case it is the child's poor performance in learning to read and write in relation to their age and level of intelligence that is stressed. Critics would again argue that this tends to favour more intelligent and more middle-class children where it is supposed that the gap between their expected performance and their actual performance is more apparent. Another difficulty is that obvious discrepancies between reading and spelling scores tend to diminish as children get older so that by adolescence this approach will exclude many children who do have the specific cognitive impairments underlying dyslexia such as poor short-term memory. Korhonen (1995) found for example in a longitudinal study that children who had reading difficulties at 9 years of age had a significantly worse digit span at 18 years of age, were significantly worse on a word fluency task and were slower and more error prone on a spelling task in comparison with a control group. Research such as this underlines that older dyslexic children and adults still have difficulties which put them at a disadvantage especially in situations such as written examinations. So although discrepancy definitions may be good at identifying some children with dyslexia they may well lead to bias in who is identified and the underidentification of some groups of children. It should be pointed out that fewer practising psychologists now work on the basis of discrepancy definitions and even when IQ tests form part of a dyslexia assessment they are there to add information to the overall profile rather than to exclude children with lower IQs from being identified as dyslexic. Part of the reason for the reluctance of some educationalists to recognise dyslexia in the past may have been connected to their underlying disquiet about the way it was defined and the implications that this had for the identification of children and allocation of resources.

Another problem with some of the earlier definitions of dyslexia is that they defined dyslexia largely or exclusively in terms of a reading problem. Although learning to read is invariably a problem, the majority of dyslexic children do eventually learn to read. In order to deal with these kinds of criticisms modern definitions of dyslexia have tried to specify the cognitive impairments underlying dyslexia and the range of skills affected by such impairments. The following definition is given by the British Dyslexia Association (BDA 2009):

> Dyslexia is a specific learning difficulty which mainly affects the development of literacy and language related skills. It is likely to be present at birth and to be life long in its effects. It is characterised by difficulties with phonological processing, rapid naming, working memory, processing speed and the automatic development of skills that may not match up to an individual's other cognitive abilities. It tends to be resistant to conventional teaching methods, but its effects can be mitigated by appropriately specific intervention, including the application of information technology and supportive counselling.

Although critics might disagree with the specific details of this definition few would disagree with the need to have a definition that draws on the considerable body of cognitive research. One point that emerges more clearly from this type of definition is that dyslexia should be regarded as a complex phenomenon with different individuals showing different combinations or expressions of these underlying difficulties. Another point is that it is the underlying problems in short-term memory and speech sound recognition that should be emphasised. It may be that like autism, where the term 'autistic spectrum disorder' is often used, we will move in the future to talking about a dyslexia spectrum.

International perspectives

In the US and Canada the term 'learning disability' (LD) is roughly equivalent to the UK term 'specific learning difficulty'. The Learning Disabilities Association of America (2009) describes learning disabilities as

> neurologically based processing problems. These processing problems can interfere with learning basic skill such as reading, writing or mathematics. They can also interfere with higher-level skills such as organization, time planning, and abstract reasoning.

They point out that this term covers a wide variety of specific cognitive difficulties which are not the result of inadequate instruction or low intelligence. It is estimated by the association that 6 per cent of the school population have an identified LD for which they receive support. There is a broad consensus that 70–80 per cent of the children classified as LD in North America are identified as having a specific reading disability (RD). It is also the case that a high proportion of children classified as reading disabled would meet the criteria for prevailing UK and US definitions of dyslexia. In the US the International Dyslexia Association (IDA 2007) defines dyslexia as

> characterized by difficulties with accurate and/or fluent word recognition and by poor spelling and decoding abilities. These difficulties typically result from a deficit

in the phonological component of language that is often unexpected in relation to other cognitive abilities and the provision of effective classroom instruction.

Siegel (2003) in a paper on reading disabilities in North America says that she thinks the terms 'reading disability' and 'dyslexia' are synonymous. She also observes that 'fear and disdain of the term "dyslexia" is common in North America' and that as a consequence it is less often used than in some other parts of the world.

Because of the move away from discrepancy definitions in the US the Individual with Disabilities Education Act (IDEA 2004) has stipulated that a significant discrepancy between intellectual ability and achievement must not be required in order to identify a specific learning disability. In the US in particular the notion of response to intervention has been suggested as the way forward in defining reading disabilities/dyslexia (Fuchs and Fuchs 2006). The general argument is that particularly in less advantaged social groups up to 30–40 per cent of children may make a slow start in reading because of lack of sufficient exposure to reading and in some cases lack of appropriate scientifically based reading instruction. When such children are provided with appropriate reading experience and instruction many of them make considerable progress and would no longer be seen as having a reading problem. It is those children who have made relatively little or no progress despite such intervention who would then be deemed to have a reading disability/dyslexia. In a sense this is a more explicit version of the phrase 'despite adequate instruction' added in one form or another to many definitions of dyslexia. Although there are criticisms of this approach (see Chapter 2) it does address the issue of how to distinguish between children with fundamental processing difficulties in learning to read and children with more transient difficulties related to lack of experience and practice.

The current situation

A misleading assumption has been passed down that there is no consensus on defining dyslexia. As Siegel and Smythe (2006) point out there is a convergence of opinions among leading dyslexia bodies and researchers that difficulty with the development of accurate and fluent word reading is fundamental to contemporary definitions of dyslexia. The definition recommended to educational psychologists in the UK (BPS 1999) exemplifies this point:

> Dyslexia is evident when accurate and fluent word reading and/or spelling develops very incompletely or with great difficulty. This focuses on literacy at the 'word level' and implies the problem is severe or persistent despite appropriate learning opportunities.

Siegel and Lipka (2008) in an overview of definitions of learning disability point out that although there is reasonably good agreement over theoretical definitions of learning disability the difficulty comes in agreeing how these definitions should be operationalised. In other words exactly what indicators and measures should be used to identify learning disability and by the same token dyslexia? Although defining dyslexia, and in particular operationalising it, can still be seen as work in progress, this is true of many labels and categorisations in that they all have to take account of new research findings and changing social attitudes. What is becoming apparent is that dyslexia is on a spectrum with a range of specific learning and language difficulties and that there is a continuum between good, average and poor readers. Snowling (2008) suggests we should conceive of dyslexia as a dimension rather than as a category.

As with many disabilities/differences, identifying the very severe or extreme examples is relatively easy; what is more difficult is deciding where to draw the line or even if it is appropriate to draw a line between individuals deemed to have a difficulty/difference and those deemed not to. If it is decided that drawing a line is inappropriate the issue then arises as to the best way to characterise the continuum between for example good and poor readers. It is also important that this does not send out signals that are erroneously interpreted by the wider world that dyslexia is after all, as widely believed in the past, a 'myth'.

The impact and purpose of labelling

One of the difficulties with definitions of dyslexia is that different groups of people require a definition for different purposes. Genetic researchers who want a representative sample of dyslexic children may be looking for a definition that gives high precision, whereas teachers may want a definition that includes both indicators they have ready access to and suggestions for intervention. As Reid (2001) puts it, in asking the question 'what is dyslexia' (p. 11) many classroom teachers are in essence asking for a working plan as much as a definition of dyslexia. Many individuals with dyslexia and campaigning groups want definitions that, as well as emphasising their positive attributes, include the full range of difficulties they encounter in everyday life, such as spelling, writing and some aspects of memorising. So, even if the fundamental aspects of dyslexia are agreed upon, the way these are expressed or the emphasis that is put on certain features may differ depending on the intended audience.

Dyslexia and labelling: a personal view

All labels tend to have advantages and disadvantages attached to them especially when they are trying to encapsulate a complex entity such as dyslexia (Riddick 2000, 2001). Although the children and adults I've interviewed and discussed the label with over the years have been biased towards those who endorse the label, I've come across a variety of views from the highly positive to the highly negative. Much appears to depend on the way in which the label is offered to individuals and the pre-existing beliefs they have about the label. It also depends on how an individual would fare without the label or with an alternative label. Many of the children and students I have interviewed argue that at least having the label dyslexia challenges people's incorrect assumptions about them and for example stops teachers calling them lazy or stupid (see Chapters 2, 5 and 10 for further discussion).

'Reading disabled' as used in North America may be a valid term especially with younger school children but there are problems with it. Nearly all the children correctly identified as reading disabled in the US and elsewhere will also have spelling, writing and working memory difficulties; a proportion will also have co-ordination difficulties. As children get older, with adequate support their reading will improve and for many their main difficulties by secondary age and beyond are in spelling and writing speed. The problem of having a label based on one process such as reading is that it only gives a partial representation of the difficulties an individual may face because of specific underlying cognitive difficulties/differences. It may also lead to less coherent long-term planning in terms of intervention and support. Some intensive reading intervention programmes have been 'successful' in improving children's reading but have reported spelling and writing difficulties in follow-up classroom evaluations, for which no specific support has been available. Reading disability also defines a person entirely in terms of a disability or deficit and does not suggest strengths as well as weaknesses. A few years ago in the US after a lecture I'd given on risk and protective factors for successfully coping with dyslexia at university a young man approached me. He looked pale and strained and blinked repeatedly as he spoke. He introduced himself by saying,

> Hi, I have a learning disability, a reading disability, a writing disability, a math disability, a co-ordination disability and attention deficit. Can you suggest how I can improve my really low self-esteem?

These can all be seen as features of dyslexia and, although it would be glib to suggest that simply calling himself dyslexic would solve all his problems, I couldn't help but feel that reciting this litany of disability and deficit was not a good starting point for improving his self-esteem. The advantage of the term 'dyslexia' is that it can allow for a more positive perspective with the suggestion of strengths as well as weaknesses and the idea of difference as much as disability or deficit. It also enables a developmental perspective to be taken, with varying skills highlighted at different ages ideally leading to a more coherent and comprehensive approach to long-term planning and intervention. Different people will have different constructions of dyslexia; in my mind it conjures up strengths, an alternative approach to learning and positive role models as well as difficulties with specific aspects of reading, spelling and working memory. In the UK the term 'dyslexia' can now confer legitimacy on someone's difficulties and also give them access to a 'culture' of dyslexia which challenges negative portrayals and also allows them to draw on a range of practical and social support including positive role models. Of course my views are formed by my own experiences, cultural setting and educational context in the UK; US-based researchers might equally argue that the term 'LD' (learning disability) or 'RD' (reading disability) has similar connotations in their culture to dyslexia in the UK, although it should be pointed out that there is a thriving International Dyslexia Organisation in the US, which suggests that there is still debate about this point. What is important is what a label or term denotes in a particular cultural setting and whether it is the most enabling and productive way to characterise a difficulty or difference in that setting, not only for professionals but for people who have to live with the label. What is surprising is that there is very little cross-cultural research on this issue.

An alternative perspective

Nearly all the definitions considered so far characterise dyslexia (or at least the processing skills thought to underlie dyslexia) as deficient or a problem in some way. It is noticeable that descriptions or definitions given by support organisations or campaigning groups are more likely to include or underline that dyslexics are as bright as other people and may have a number of skills and talents.

Some groups and individuals take this further and either argue that dyslexia should be seen as a difference rather than as a disability or argue that dyslexia is an unnecessary label because such individuals should be viewed as part of the ordinary range of human performance. Both cases are underpinned by a social model of disability perspective, which argues that it is the social environment that disables people and needs 'fixing' or altering rather than 'dyslexic' individuals (Riddick 2000, 2001). The social model has been important and powerful in challenging societies views and practices in relation to 'disability' and at its most extreme would argue there is no such thing as disability, only disabling environments. Although this perspective has been very helpful in bringing about change it also has its limitations and has been criticised by some disabled people for ignoring or underplaying the reality of the inherent physical or cognitive difficulties they have to deal with (Shakespeare 2006). Another approach is to adopt an interactional model (sometimes termed a bio-psycho-social model), which considers both the role of the environment and the individual and the interaction between them. Many researchers and practitioners would argue that this is what they do and more often the debate is where the emphasis should be put and what is the most productive way to combine these two perspectives.

As well as a contemporary cultural context labels also have an historical context and people may choose to live with a certain label not only to define who they are but also who they are not. Since the inception of mass literacy in many cultures, being literate has become inextricably linked to notions of being well educated and intelligent. Because people who have struggled with literacy have been persistently seen as 'stupid', lazy or careless it is not surprising that they want a label that challenges these assumptions and changes the erroneous attributions (reasons) given by others for their difficulties. In 2007 a leading journalist implied on one of the most popular and highly regarded current affairs programmes in Britain that dyslexia was just another word for 'stupid' (*Today* programme, cited in Dyslexia Action 2007). Although this remark has been dismissed as coming from an ill-informed individual it does underline the historical and cultural prejudices that individuals with dyslexia still have to contend with. One of the major issues anyone with severe dyslexia-type difficulties has to deal with is how they wish to view these differences/disabilities over their life-time and how they would like others to respond to them. In coming up with definitions of dyslexia there are issues of power and control and whose voice and concerns should be heard in formulating and promulgating them. Paradoxically, although biological and cognitive researchers in particular have been criticised by some groups for their perceived focus on deficits, it is this type of research that has helped legitimise dyslexia to a wider audience and has given people with dyslexia the authority to challenge environmental barriers and negative attitudes.

As stated before, there are many interested parties including dyslexic people and their families, academic researchers, educational practitioners such as class teachers, educational psychologists and education policy makers, and clinical practitioners such as speech and language therapists. All these groups may have differing views on how the difficulties some children encounter should be characterised and defined and even within groups there are differences of opinion. In a sense it comes back to Humpty Dumpty's question: 'which is to be master – that's all'.

Linking definition to identification

An important point about contemporary definitions of dyslexia is that they set out to say what dyslexia is rather than defining dyslexia largely in terms of what it isn't. Along with these more positive definitions of dyslexia researchers have also tried to list positive signs or indicators of dyslexia. Miles and Miles were early pioneers of this approach (1999) in suggesting the following as possible indicators of dyslexia in primary age children:

1   confuses left and right
2   difficulty in saying long words
3   difficulty in subtracting
4   difficulty in learning tables
5   difficulty in saying months of the year
6   confuses b and d for longer than most children
7   difficulty in recalling digits
8   family history of similar difficulties.

Miles and Miles emphasise that a dyslexic child won't necessarily show all these difficulties and that a non-dyslexic child may well have problems with some of the items. What they claim is important is the overall clinical picture which is obtained. So a dyslexic child for example may have difficulty with several of these items and show a marked delay in their reading and/or spelling age compared with their chronological age and be struggling at school. Miles has incorporated all these items into the Bangor Dyslexia Test (1997). In order to select items that do consistently distinguish between dyslexic and non-dyslexic children Miles (1983) has compared children from both groups across age ranges on 7 out of 12 items in the test. He found that, although no item on its own distinguished dyslexic from non-dyslexic children, dyslexic children did consistently receive a higher overall score on this test.

In devising the Bangor Dyslexia Test Miles addressed two important issues. The first was the need to check out whether signs picked out by clinicians really were reliable indicators of dyslexia. The second was to have a test that was based on theoretical assumptions about the cognitive deficits underlying dyslexia. In this case it was argued that problems with naming were brought about by deficits in short-term memory and difficulties in accessing long-term memory. Items such as digit span and subtraction test short-term memory and items such as naming months and saying multiplication tables test long-term memory. Although critics have pointed out the test's lack of comprehensiveness it does have the strong advantage of being quick (average 10 minutes) and easy to administer so that it can be used by classroom teachers. The disadvantage is that some items do involve clinical judgement. Miles acknowledges that the Bangor Dyslexia Test samples only a limited range of items and that some of these items need modification if it is to be used with children under 7 years of age. It is also the case that in the 20 years since its development cognitive research has considerably added to our understanding of dyslexia. Many leading researchers including Lyon (2006) Torgesen (2004), Lundberg and Hoien (2001) and Snowling (2002) have suggested that testing of phonological awareness should play an essential role in the identification of specific learning difficulties. Tests tend to be divided into screening tests, which may identify children at risk of dyslexia, and more comprehensive assessments comprising a number of independent tests which look in depth at a whole range of processing and literacy skills. Whereas some tests are specifically designed to identify children who are at risk of dyslexia others are designed to look at specific components of skills such as reading across the full range of children. They do not set out specifically to identify dyslexia but in providing a profile, for example of reading skills, highlight children with profiles commensurate with dyslexia. The use of computer-based assessment has become increasingly important with supporters pointing out that it can be used as a quick, efficient and cost-effective way of testing large numbers of children (Merrell and Tymms 2007). The tests and assessments that are developed and/or utilised tend to be related to the definition and underlying theory of dyslexia subscribed to by the constructors and/or assessors. As already indicated, proponents of a phonological theory of dyslexia (Snowling 2002, Torgesen 2004) emphasise the need for assessment of phonological skills whereas Fawcett and Nicolson (2008), who propose a cerebellar theory of dyslexia, also include some items that assess particular aspects of motor skills (see list in the next paragraph).

Early identification

One area in which there has been particular progress has been the identification of cognitive deficits/differences in infant and pre-school children (Bryant and Bradley 1985, Jorm *et al.* 1986). Bryant and Bradley, for example, found that children of 3 and 4 years of age who did relatively badly on a rhyming task were at higher risk of having subsequent difficulty in learning to read. Case studies also confirm that by 7 many dyslexic children feel they have failed in the classroom setting. Until relatively recently the received wisdom was that a child couldn't be diagnosed as dyslexic until about 7 years of age. This seemed to be based on the notion that a diagnosis could not be made until a measurable discrepancy between their reading age and their chronological age could be demonstrated; in other words, until they had failed at learning to read. This fits with the older discrepancy and exclusion approaches to defining dyslexia and illustrates the importance of having an approach to the condition that identifies positive signs and the cognitive deficits underlying it. This more recent approach suggests that, as the cognitive deficits that lead to difficulty in learning to read and spell are identifiable at a pre-reading stage, it should be possible to identify early on children who are at increased risk of having difficulty in learning to read. Singleton (2002) and Fawcett and Nicolson (2004) have put forward this point of view and both have developed early screening tests for 4- to 6-year-old children. Fawcett and Nicolson's (2004) Dyslexia Early Screening Test consists of the following 12 sub-tests:

- rapid naming
- bead threading
- phonological discrimination
- postural stability
- rhyme/alliteration
- forwards digit span
- digit naming

- letter naming
- sound order
- shape copying
- corsi frog (spatial memory)
- vocabulary (group/individual).

As can be seen this list includes items such as bead threading to test fine motor skills, a test of postural stability, and tests of spatial skills alongside a number of tests of phonological skills and short-term memory skills. In the US Lyon (2006) reports that kindergarten assessments of phoneme awareness, rhyming ability and rapid letter and number naming are all highly predictive of reading difficulties later on, especially in conjunction with a family history of dyslexia. On this basis he suggests that children at risk of dyslexia can be identified by the age of 5 years.

Incidence of dyslexia

Given the difficulties in defining and identifying dyslexia, it is hard to come up with a precise estimate of the number of individuals affected. The consensus among many researchers (Miles 2006) and organisations, such as the British Dyslexia Association (BDA 2008), is that at a conservative estimate 4 per cent of the population are severely dyslexic and another 6 per cent have mild to moderate dyslexia. It is often pointed out that on average this indicates that there will be one severely dyslexic child in each class. In the US the International Dyslexia Association (2009) estimate that of the 6–7 per cent of school age children deemed to have a learning disability around 85 per cent are identified as having a specific reading disability or dyslexia. Lyon (2006) reports that the prevalence of dyslexia in the school age population in the US is in the range of 5–10 per cent. UK and US estimates are thus similar but Smythe *et al.* (2004) found across 14 different countries that the reported incidence varied between 1 per cent and 11 per cent. Much of this may be related to differing national policies and practices but there is evidence that the literacy difficulties encountered by dyslexics do vary in nature depending on the language they are using.

In the past most researchers also reported a ratio of about three boys to every one girl with dyslexia. Shaywitz *et al.* (1990) questioned this ratio and presented evidence that in the US girls with reading disabilities were underidentified. It was suggested that girls might be less likely to draw attention to themselves with acting out behaviour and people were less likely to consider that a girl might have reading disabilities. Rutter *et al.* (2004) summarised much of the research on sex differences in reading disability and reported on new findings from four epidemiological studies. They reported that in all four studies there were higher rates of reading disabilities in boys. Although the ratios varied considerably between the studies they averaged out at about two boys to every one girl. At present more evidence is needed before anything clear cut can be said. But it does relate back to an earlier point about the dangers of setting up expectations that tend to preclude certain children from being defined as dyslexic for whatever reason. A number of researchers have pointed out (Ellis 1993, Siegel 2004) that the percentage of children who are defined as dyslexic is in some sense fairly arbitrary in that it depends on the particular criteria that are used. So for example the percentage of children with dyslexia will vary if a spelling age of 18 months below the norm is chosen as opposed to a spelling age of 24 months below the norm.

Genetics and heritability

A classic study by Hallgren in 1950 found that 88 per cent of individuals with dyslexia also had at least one close family member with the same condition. Finucci *et al.* (1976) also came up with a similar figure of 81 per cent. Critics could argue that these figures can be explained away by environmental factors, but closer examination of the figures suggests that this is unlikely. Children with an affected relative not living with them are just as likely to have difficulties and other siblings living at home may have no difficulties at all. Twin studies have also confirmed that there is a genetic component to dyslexia. The Colorado Twin Study (De Fries 1991) is one of the largest and best designed of these studies. This study involved 101 identical twins and 114 non-identical twins. For identical twins the concordance rate for reading problems was 70 per cent and for the non-identical twins it was 43 per cent. More recently the Colorado longitudinal twin study of reading disability has also reported that reading difficulties were highly stable over a 5–6 year period with shared genetic influences accounting for much of this stability (Wadsworth *et al.* 2007). Given that much recent research has focused on the cognitive impairments underlying dyslexia this suggests that what is inherited is not a reading disability per se but a defect or difference in one or more of the cognitive skills underlying language and reading. Olson *et al.* (1990) found that the phonological skills for breaking words down into syllables and for reading nonsense words were highly heritable whereas reading comprehension was not. This suggests that some children inherit specific phonological disabilities that can have a serious affect on their ability to learn to read. Schumacher *et al.* (2007) in a review of the genetics of dyslexia conclude that depending on what dimension of processing is investigated up to 80 per cent of dyslexia is accounted for by inherited factors. This does not mean that the environment is not important; in fact for high-risk individuals the environment is critically important in how any difficulties will be expressed and responded to. So far information on the heritability of dyslexia has largely been considered in relation to biological and cognitive research. One area that has not been explored is the possible personal implications for the child of having a parent or close relative with the same disability. This will be discussed in more detail in Chapter 9 of this book. Across a number of studies it is estimated that where a parent or older sibling has dyslexia an average of 40 per cent of subsequent children will also meet the criteria for dyslexia, whereas in families with no history of dyslexia type difficulties there is only a 5–6 per cent chance of a child meeting the criteria for dyslexia.

The history of dyslexia

It is only since literacy on a universal scale has become the norm that dyslexia has become a significant issue. The early literature on dyslexia was nearly all medical in origin and mainly focused on the clinical case study approach. In Britain in 1917 an ophthalmologist named James Hinshelwood published a book entitled *Congenital Word Blindness*. As the title implies, this book focused on the visual problems that were thought to underlie dyslexia. This early preoccupation with visual problems was hardly surprising given Hinshelwood's background and the fact that several of the striking characteristics of dyslexia appeared superficially to have a visual basis. The reversing of letters such as b and d, and words such as 'no' and 'on' and frequent omission of suffixes such as 'ing' all seemed to imply that a visual deficit underlay dyslexia. Orton (1937) in the US published an influential book entitled *Reading, Writing and Speech Problems in Children*. Orton also thought that visual problems underlay dyslexia. Perhaps because of his background as a psychiatrist Orton was very concerned with the emotional consequences of the repeated failure that dyslexic children encountered. It is sometimes suggested (Snowling 2000) that this early dominance by the medical model has led to some of the reservations expressed by educationalists. Although this may be the case it doesn't fully explain the degree of difficulty encountered in considering dyslexia in relation to other special needs. Until the mid-1970s school medical officers were involved in the identification of all children with special needs but, for example, in the case of sensory and physical impairments the transition to an educational model seems to have been relatively smooth. The difference with dyslexia appears to be that there are no clear physical markers, so that until recently dyslexia was defined almost entirely in terms of behaviour, i.e. difficulty in learning to read and spell. The problem with this approach was that all sorts of assumptions were made as to why a child was failing to learn to read. These included lack of parental interest, too much parental interest, emotional or behavioural problems, poor attention or motivation or that the child was immature and/or a slow learner. It was less often considered that the primary cause of the child's reading difficulties might be specific cognitive impairments and that if any of these other behaviours were observed these might be a secondary outcome of the child's difficulty in learning to read. This is not to deny that environmental factors may play an important part in the process and that for some children the way that reading is taught may be of critical importance. But research by Croll and Moses (1985) found that, when 428 primary school teachers were surveyed about children with learning difficulties including those with reading problems, in only 2.5 per cent of the cases were school factors thought to play a part. In 55 per cent of poor readers, low ability or IQ was implicated and in over 40 per cent of cases environmental factors outside the school, such as lack of parental interest, were given as the reason for children's poor performance. Alessi (1988) in a similar study in North America asked 50 school psychologists to comment on over 5,000 referrals. It was found that general within-child factors or home environmental factors were always seen as the cause of failure and failure was never attributed to the curriculum. Thus until recently it appears that reading failure was most commonly attributed at the within-child level to generalised slow learning and at the environmental level to adverse factors outside the school. This is the direct opposite to what it is proposed produces dyslexia/specific learning difficulties, which at the within-child level is specific as opposed to general impairments and at the environmental level is adverse factors within the school (i.e. poor teaching of reading). Given these very different perspectives it is perhaps not surprising that specific learning difficulties including dyslexia have been underidentified in the past and have led to some controversy and disagreement among educationalists.

Although far severer in outcome, the condition probably closest to dyslexia in terms of its lack of 'visibility' is autism. Frith (1992) argues that in both cases looking at behaviour alone is not sufficient in defining these disorders because behaviour is influenced by factors such as experience and motivation and is therefore constantly changing and varying. She argues that we need to identify the cognitive deficits/differences underlying the behaviour in order to come up with a clearer definition. The advantage of doing this is that behaviours that look very similar on the surface may be found to have very different roots. A child, for example, who doesn't say nursery rhymes might not do so because of simple lack of exposure to them or because they lack the phonological (sound) awareness.

Researching dyslexia

As already indicated, the first research on dyslexia was of a clinical case study approach. Three major criticisms are made of this type of research. One is that clinicians see a biased, often self-selected sample of the population; second, it can be misleading to generalise from a single case; and third, this type of research doesn't distinguish cause from effect. So for example in the case of letter reversals such as b/d, which are often noted by clinicians, it still doesn't indicate whether the reversals are simply the result of inexperience at reading or whether reversals hold reading up and therefore contribute to lack of reading experience. Despite the criticisms of the case study approach, authorities as diverse as Snowling (2000), Sternberg and Grigorenko (2004) and Miles (2006) have emphasised the important contribution that case studies can make. Case studies can suggest any commonalties, issues or hypotheses that need systematic testing. In turn findings from experimental research can be checked against case studies to see that they have real world or ecological validity. Finally case studies can flesh out and breathe life into experimental data and give more understanding of the complexities and wider context surrounding the data.

Much of the early research on dyslexia used control groups of non-dyslexic children of the same age. On the face of it this would seem a reasonable thing to do, but it does lead to difficulties in drawing interpretations from the data. If, for example, you do find a difference between the reading of dyslexic and non-dyslexic children how can you be sure that this is because of some fundamental difference between them and not simply because the dyslexic children are performing like children who are 2 years younger in their reading age? In order to get round this problem the more recent good quality research has also used where possible control groups of younger children matched in reading age to the dyslexic children. In this case it is argued that if any differences in reading performance are found these can't simply be put down to differences in reading experience. An important point that both Snowling (2000) and Frith (1997) made is that dyslexia is a developmental disorder and the way in which any underlying impairments were expressed would change with age and experience.

Theories of dyslexia

Phonological difficulties

The majority of researchers agree that phonological processing skills are directly related to children's ability to learn to read (Torgesen 2004, Snowling 2008) and this is the predominant theory used to explain dyslexia at the moment. Phonological processing skills involve listening to the sounds made in oral language and using knowledge of these in learning to decode written words. There have been three major areas of research on phonological skills: these have been on phonological awareness, phonological memory and accessing phonological information from long-term memory. Phonemes are the smallest sound elements that a word can be divided up into and much of the earlier work on phonological awareness focused on the relationship between single phonemes and single letters. Goswami and Bryant (1990) pointed out that children's knowledge of syllables and sensitivity to rhyme and alliteration are also an important part of phonological awareness. Several researchers had shown that before children can read they can pick out words that rhyme (Bradley and Bryant 1985, Gates 1992). So if for example a child was presented with the word 'sky' and asked which of 'rat', 'fly' and 'log' ended with the same sound they would successfully pick out 'fly'. The significance of this finding is that children who display good phonological awareness before they learn to read typically go on to learn to read more easily than children who have difficulty with this task. It has also been found that children who have significant difficulty learning to read often have poor phonological awareness. Snowling (1980) was one of the first to report that many dyslexic children had poor non-word (known as pseudo-words in the US) naming or spelling skills. This is one of the most reliable and consistent findings to emerge from this field of research. In these types of investigations children are asked to read out one by one a list of pronounceable made-up words such as 'pret' and 'mub' and 'clube'. What is found is that dyslexic children as a group do worse on this task than non-dyslexic children. This suggests that dyslexic children lack the necessary phonological skills to work out how to say the words correctly. Because these are words they have not encountered before they cannot use their visual memory as an alternative strategy. The importance of this phonological theory is that it underlines that the difficulty is with decoding single words, which in turn leads to difficulties with reading fluency and accuracy and also spelling. Commonly children with such difficulties do better on tests of reading comprehension when the text is read out to them rather than having to read it for themselves. In a sense they have difficulty with a vital but fairly low level technical aspect of reading and can have good high-order literacy skills. This explains why it is possible to have writers and poets like W.B. Yeats among those that are identified as dyslexic or as having weak spelling skills. Du Sautoy (2008), professor of mathematics at Oxford University, made the following comment in an interview:

> Times tables. You know, I'm not terribly fast at my times tables, because that's not what I think mathematics is about. I think it's the same as thinking that a good speller will make a great writer. Well, no actually – a great writer can be *crap* at spelling but have great vision and ways of bringing stories alive.

Snowling (2000) comments that one of the most consistent findings for children and adults with dyslexia is that of poor short-term verbal memory as opposed to normal short-term visual memory. The explanation given is that, as items are held in short-term verbal memory in the form of speech codes, the poor phonological representations of dyslexic children lead to impaired word representations and less efficient memory coding. Because only a restricted number of items can be stored in short-term memory the end result is that dyslexic individuals can store fewer items and are thus placed at a disadvantage when required to carry out tasks that make heavy demands on short-term or working memory. Other factors such as speech rate may also be implicated but the key point is that this explanation sees poor short-term verbal memory as an integral part of a phonological theory of dyslexia. This in turn helps to explain a number of observed features of dyslexia such as the difficulty in rote learning lists such as days of the week, and remembering new names and instructions. The particular importance of the phonological theory is that it has had considerable influence on educational intervention and on the teaching of reading in schools. It is also to date the most extensively researched theory with a considerable weight of evidence behind it

Longitudinal studies

An important point that emerges from research on early phonological skill development is the value of longitudinal studies. Cross-sectional studies which have looked at a group of children, at a particular point in time, have made a significant contribution but there are certain questions they cannot answer. Are, for example, the children who are identified as having reading difficulties at 6 years of age the same children who are identified as having reading difficulties at 5 years or 7 years of age? If a cross-sectional study finds that 7-year-olds with poor reading also have poor phonological skills are we to assume that the poor phonological skills have contributed to the poor reading or that the poor reading has contributed to the poor phonological skills? In Bradley and Bryant's (1985) study mentioned above on pre-reading children's detection of rhyme they followed the progress of these children in learning to read over a 3-year period and by doing so were able to show the links between phonological awareness and the development of reading. Torgesen, Wagner and Rashotte (1994) in the US also followed children from kindergarten through to second grade. They tested all children on phonological tasks and reading tasks at all three intervention points. They found that reading difficulties were associated with difficulties not only in phonological awareness but also in phonological working memory, and access to phonological information in long-term memory.

Long-term difficulties

Evidence is also mounting that in severer cases these early deficits in phonological processing skills persist over a number of years and in some cases into adulthood (Bruck 1992). Single case studies which have followed individuals over time and consistently tested their phonological skills, wider cognitive skills and literacy skills have also confirmed that for many individuals phonological processing deficits play an important role in their poor literacy development (Hulme and Snowling 1992, Funnell and Davison 1989). Hulme and Snowling describe the case of JM, a boy of 16 years of age who had been followed for the previous 8 years. When first seen at the age of 8 years, despite his obvious intelligence he was only beginning to learn to read and write. At this stage he could not read unfamiliar words or made up words and his spelling was often unphonetic; for example, 'CAP' was spelt 'GAD'.

Over the next 4 years JM learnt to read but it was thought he did this largely by visual strategies as his non-word reading and spelling still showed poor phonological skills. At 13 years he was asked to repeat 40 non-words and got 25 of these correct. This was well below the average of 35.5 correct answers given by reading age matched controls. On the basis of this and other similar findings it was suggested that the key problem that JM had was in output phonology. Lundberg (1994) compared 15-year-old dyslexic students with matched non-dyslexic controls and found that they performed far worse on a variety of tasks such as reading non-words and syllable reversal. Korhonen (1995) in a longitudinal study followed nine dyslexic children from 9 years of age to 18 years of age. It was found that many of the difficulties that the children had such as poor rapid naming and poor reading and spelling persisted over time. Korhonen argues that these results favour the idea that there are permanent underlying deficits in dyslexia which don't appreciably improve with age. A more recent study by Snowling, Muter and Carroll (2007) endorses this point of view. They followed up fifty 12- to 13-year-olds with a family history of dyslexia who had first been assessed at the age of 8 years and found that the 42 per cent who met their full criteria for dyslexia still displayed similar literacy problems in early adolescence. This means not that children with dyslexia can't develop compensatory strategies to deal with their problems but that their primary cognitive deficits are likely to persist over time.

Cerebellar difficulties

Fawcett and Nicolson (2004, 2008) have been leading proponents of the hypothesis that deficits/differences in cerebellar processing are fundamental to an explanation of dyslexia. They argue that because the cerebellum is involved in the control of rapid skilled movement it affects language dexterity, automatisation of skills and balance. They came to this conclusion after their earlier studies (1994) revealed that dyslexic children performed worse than other children on some tests of motor skills and automatisation and notably on a balance task in which they were asked to recite digits backwards whilst walking along a balance beam. They suggested that, because these skills were not as automatic as in non-dyslexic children, they required more concentration to perform them well and thus in situations in which they were required to concentrate on two skills at the same time this led to a deterioration in their performance. Whereas their early work was seen as a challenge to the phonological hypothesis, they propose that in fact the cerebellar hypothesis can be a unifying explanation that accounts for phonological processing difficulties and motor skill and automatisation difficulties. They acknowledge that at present phonological difficulties are central to identification and early intervention but they contend that a wider and more fundamental explanation of dyslexia may be more productive in the long run.

Magnocellular difficulties

Because of long-reported visual difficulties in relation to dyslexia Stein (1994, 2001, 2003) has carried out a series of studies on binocular instability and convergence difficulties in children with dyslexia. His early work on this led to research on the role of the magnocellular pathway in visual processing. There are two neural pathways involved in visual processing: the parvocellular, which deals with relatively static information, and the magnocellular, which detects rapid transitions in the incoming information. Stein argues that whereas the parvocellular pathway operates efficiently in dyslexics there are mild abnormalities in the magnocellular pathway that lead to less efficient processing. Stein proposes that this can account for a number of the visual difficulties linked to dyslexia. He also suggests that as these two neural pathways operate in relation to all incoming sensory information so auditory and motor information are similarly affected. This in Stein's view would account for phonological processing difficulties as well as some visual and motor difficulties. As Wolf and O'Brien (2001) pointed out, efficient reading involves detecting the rapid auditory frequency transitions between phonemes at very high speed. Steins magnocellular theory thus unites phonological, visual and motor explanations of dyslexia. This is a relatively recent theory and, although there is some evidence in support of it, findings are mixed and more evidence is needed before firmer conclusions can be drawn.

Are all dyslexics the same?

There are several reasons for considering this question. The first and most obvious is that it has implications for teaching and intervention. If there were distinct sub-types within dyslexia different types of teaching and intervention might be required to meet the needs of these different groups. Allied to this it might have implications for the kind of criteria by which dyslexics are identified. There are also implications for the kind of methodology used to research dyslexia. If group comparisons are made between dyslexic and non-dyslexic subjects with results averaged out over the group, individual differences will be lost and this may distort the way in which the results are interpreted. The reader might be forgiven for thinking that on the evidence produced so far all dyslexics have pretty much the same underlying cognitive processing difficulties. But many leading researchers over a long period of time (Johnson and Myklebust 1967, Coltheart *et al.* 1983, Manis and Bailey 2008) have argued that there are sub-types within dyslexia. Johnson and Myklebust (1967) first proposed a distinction between auditory and visual dyslexics. They were actually referring to relative strengths and weaknesses in relating sounds to words and not to visual perceptual difficulties as such. But their work was often taken to support a simplistic division between visual and auditory difficulties. Before going any further with this discussion there are some general issues to consider. If we talk about sub-types in dyslexia are we talking about differences in fundamental impairments or differences in the compensatory strategies that children use? We also need to know if different sub-types reflect genuine differences in the underlying impairments or differing degrees of the same impairment. Both Goswami and Bryant (1990) and Ellis (1993) have argued that we also need to look at the pattern of reading differences in ordinary readers. It may be that any differences found between dyslexic readers simply reflect the normal range of differences found between ordinary readers. According to Ellis ordinary readers can be placed on a continuum between those that rely heavily on visual whole-word strategies and those that rely heavily on phonic strategies. The former rely on visual whole-word recognition because they have poor phonic skills, whereas the latter rely on phonic skills because of their difficulty in accessing the visual lexicon and subsequent poor sight vocabulary. Ellis claims that the majority of children fall somewhere between the extremes of this continuum with a reasonable level of skill in both visual and phonic strategies. He goes on to conclude that if this is the case then we should expect the same distribution of difficulties among dyslexic children with some at either extreme, with severe phonic or visual difficulties, but the majority showing a mixture of visual and phonic impairments. There is debate at the moment as to whether the most productive way forward is to look at the continuum of variation within dyslexia or to try and research dyslexia on the basis of sub-groups.

Everatt (2002) gives a useful and balanced overview of the possible relationship between vision and reading. He concludes that general visual difficulties do not appear to play an important part in dyslexia but that there is more evidence for deficits in the visual neural pathways as indicated by Stein's work. A point of concern over a long period of time has been that a small percentage of dyslexic children do report problems such as print going fuzzy, blurring and moving round despite them having seemingly normal vision (Garzia 1993). One issue is whether this occurs in a percentage of non-dyslexic children and is therefore not of major significance or whether again it interacts with other factors or is a major source of difficulty in its own right. Two mothers out of the 22 interviewed in the main study to be described in this book said that their children often commented on what appeared to be visual problems. JA for example had commented several times to his mother that words seemed to jump out of the page at him and that sometimes they seemed to disappear off the page. His mother reported that he had been treated for several years for a severe squint. This may just be coincidence but it does stress the need to be aware that there may be multiple and complex causes for the difficulties displayed by individuals with dyslexia. At present there is debate between those researchers who think that dyslexia can be adequately explained by underlying phonological difficulties and those who argue that alternative or more comprehensive theories are required to adequately explain all the manifestations of dyslexia. There is also debate between those researchers who think that although there are individual differences between dyslexics it is not valid or productive to divide them into discrete sub-types (Snowling 2008, Siegel 2003) whereas other researchers argue that it is valid and productive to do so (Manis and Bailey 2008, Fletcher, Morris and Lyon 2003). From the point of view of those who live with a particular cognitive profile such as dyslexia, and those that teach or support them, the issue is whether a particular theory adequately explains and represents their everyday experiences of dealing with the world.

Rayner (1993) argues that we are wrong to assume that there is only one 'cause' underlying dyslexia and, although in the short run it makes research and intervention more difficult, in the long run we will get better results if we appreciate that dyslexia may have many causes and will in turn require intervention geared to these different causes. Whatever the final outcome of this debate, most researchers would agree that at a behavioural level there are considerable individual differences between individuals with dyslexia despite the striking commonalties. Even if only one specific cognitive impairment were found to underlie dyslexia this is hardly a surprising finding when the number of potential factors interacting with the primary deficit are taken into account. These can include:

1   other cognitive skills
2   early language experience
3   learning style
4   personality
5   formal teaching of reading
6   developmental stage
7   compensatory strategies
8   social experiences.

At present there is little research looking at how a primary deficit/difference might interact with factors such as the ones named above. What this does suggest is that at present we need to remain open-minded about the likely causes of dyslexia and that we mustn't prematurely advocate blanket approaches to intervention.

Interventions

In summarising interventions it is helpful to use Frith's three levels of explanation and characterise them as focusing on the biological, cognitive or behavioural although in reality it can be difficult to separate out cognitive and behavioural interventions as there is a high degree of overlap.

Interventions are usually related to the theory of dyslexia being subscribed to, although, as can be seen in the above example, it also depends on the level of explanation being focused on. In this example it could be argued that if magnocellular function is improved this should lead to better processing of phonological information and this in turn should lead to more fluent and accurate reading. Whereas there is a strong body of evidence for the efficacy of phonological interventions (see Chapter 2) other interventions at the biological level are newer and much less well researched and in many cases sound evidence of their efficacy is lacking so far. With an increase and diversification in research and theorising on dyslexia a wider range of interventions are on offer particularly in the private sector. The difficulty for people living with dyslexia and other concerned professionals is in weighing up the claims made for various forms of intervention. Stanovich and Stanovich (2003) in an article on how teachers can use research to inform their professional practice make the following comment: 'The current problem is how to sift through the avalanche of misguided and uninformed advice to find genuine knowledge. Our problem is not information; we have tons of information. What we need are quality control mechanisms' (p. 4).

Dyslexia: more than a reading problem

One of the dangers of discussing dyslexia is that it is easy to slip into discussing it largely as a reading problem. One reason for this is that the term 'dyslexia' has often been used in conjunction with other terms such as 'reading disabled', 'reading delayed' and 'specific learning disability (reading)'. Another reason is that research on dyslexia often compares dyslexic children with both ordinary readers and children considered to have other forms of reading difficulty. Allied to this there is a large body of research

Table 1.1 Types of intervention related to Frith's three-level model of dyslexia

	Level	Example of difference	Related intervention
Environment	Biological	Less efficient magnocellular processing	Sunflower oil to improve processing
	Cognitive	Poor phonological awareness	Specific phonological awareness training
	Behavioural	Poor reading fluency and accuracy	Integrated programme incorporating specific skills

on the reading process that research on dyslexia can draw on and relate to. Given that reading difficulties are for most dyslexic children the first obvious educational problem that they present with, the focus on reading is understandable. But, whereas most dyslexic children do eventually learn to read, the majority have long-term spelling difficulties (Miles 2007). Ellis (1993) says that 'The difficulties that developmental dyslexics experience in writing and spelling are often at least as severe, if not worse than their difficulties at reading.' Snowling (2008) also points out that in the long run it is easier to compensate for reading difficulties by relying on partial cues and semantic knowledge, whereas for spelling there has to be an exact mapping of sounds to written words. Riddick (1995b) found that by 10 years of age the majority of dyslexic children in her interview sample were far more concerned with their writing and spelling difficulties than their reading and that as they progressed into secondary school concerns over the speed and accuracy of their work increased. The problem with characterising dyslexia at the behavioural level (e.g. difficulty copying off the board, poor spelling, problems learning tables) is that you can end up with a list of seemingly unrelated difficulties. Cognitive psychologists would argue that by identifying the processing deficits underlying dyslexia it is possible to gain a more coherent picture of the types of learning problems that may be encountered. In the above case it could be argued that poor working memory skills could account for all three types of difficulty. McLoughlin *et al.* (2002) in considering adults with dyslexia argue that their fundamental difficulty should be seen as one of poor working or short-term memory. The advantage of this approach is that it is then possible to understand and anticipate the kind of tasks that will give them difficulties and to plan effective ways of compensating for these difficulties.

In addition to writing and spelling difficulties Miles and Miles (2004) claim that many dyslexics also have difficulties with some specific aspects of numeracy such as learning multiplication tables. In this case knowing about poor working memory in dyslexic children makes their difficulty in mental arithmetic and learning of number facts, and particularly times tables, much more understandable. As well as helping teachers devise appropriate teaching strategies it also indicates that dyslexic children are as competent as other children in many other aspects of mathematics. As with poor spellers it again demonstrates how you can have dyslexic children who are poor at mental arithmetic but go on to be exceptionally good at mathematics because of their good conceptual understanding of the subject. Because of concern over the performance of children with dyslexia in the educational setting most of the research so far has focused on the academic difficulties in reading, writing, spelling and to a lesser extent maths. But people with dyslexia and their families talk of a wide range of situations in which their underlying cognitive impairments can put them at a disadvantage or make the situation more difficult for them to cope with. Fawcett and Nicolson (1994) suggest there needs to be more research based on the everyday difficulties that people with dyslexia report that they have. As described earlier in this chapter they reported that in a series of studies not only were young children with dyslexia worse on short-term memory tasks and phonological skills but they were also worse on motor tasks such as bead threading and putting pegs in a board (Nicolson and Fawcett 1999). Rudel (1985) observed that there were difficulties in newly acquired motor skills although these were usually outgrown by the age of 9 or 10. Clinicians, educationalists and parents of children with dyslexia have consistently pointed to motor difficulties especially in sequenced activities such as tying shoelaces. Augur (1985) suggests that difficulties in dressing, doing up buttons, kicking or throwing a ball, hopping and skipping are all commonly observed in young dyslexic children. What is not clear at present is what proportion of children with dyslexia have these kinds of difficulties and what the range and extent of them might be. Chaix *et al.* (2007) reported that out of a sample of 58 children with phonological dyslexia 40–57 per cent (depending on how severity was classified) had motor difficulties with manual dexterity, co-ordination and balance. Miles (1993) reports that dyslexic children (76 per cent) are almost twice as likely to show confusion over left and right as non-dyslexic children (36 per cent). He cautions that we should take this kind of information as indication of a tendency and not overgeneralise this as something all dyslexic children will have problems with or something that is exclusive to dyslexic children. As Pollock *et al.* (2004) point out, for many children these kinds of difficulties may be put down to confusions in verbal labelling and such children do in fact seem to have quite a good sense of direction, whereas there does appear to be a smaller group of children who do have real difficulties with space and time. The area where there is least research at present is on the day-to-day implications of living with cognitive impairments such as a poor short-term memory. At a common sense level it's not difficult to imagine that a child who doesn't know the days of the week and cannot remember messages from school is likely to be more confused and disorganised in their daily life than a child who does have these skills. In the study to be described in this book a mother spoke about an instance when her son couldn't remember the name of his new teacher or the number of his class. On returning from the dentist's he needed to ask where he would find her, but was too afraid to do so because of not knowing her name. He was eventually found sitting in the cloakroom and received a telling off for not having joined his class. A student who was recently assessed for dyslexia spoke about the constant difficulties she got into because she couldn't remember people's names. She talked about a recent incident when she couldn't remember the names of some of her fellow course students after the summer vacation and they had taken offence at this. The difficulty in researching these kinds of experiences is in sorting out which of them are specifically related to dyslexia and which of them are common to people in general. It may well be the case that many of these experiences are not exclusive to individuals with dyslexia but that they are far more common.

Summary

1   Different definitions of dyslexia fulfil different purposes and reflect different perspectives.
2   We need to know about the cognitive deficits/differences underlying dyslexia in order to have a proper understanding of how it affects individuals.
3   The cognitive differences/deficits underlying dyslexia can be identified at an early age.
4   In the majority of cases there is a genetic component to dyslexia.
5   The cognitive differences/deficits underlying dyslexia are likely to remain.
6   Cognition as well as behaviour needs to be considered if children with dyslexia/specific learning difficulties are to be accurately assessed.

Chapter 2

The educational perspective

No one in the field of education would deny that there are myths surrounding dyslexia ... But this does not mean that dyslexia is a myth.

(Snowling 2005)

Special needs history and current practice

Trying to summarise current educational policy and practice in relation to dyslexia is complex as it involves a number of factors and the interaction between them. These include:

1   current overall education policy and practice particularly in relation to the teaching of reading and assessment and monitoring of basic educational attainments;
2   current special educational needs (SEN) policy and practice particularly in relation to the identification and support of children with specific learning difficulties through out their school career;
3   current initial and in-service professional development of teachers particularly in relation to reading and specific learning difficulties;
4   the level and nature of difficulty posed by a particular language in relation to reading and writing it;
5   the role of voluntary organisations in shaping or re-acting to educational policy and practice.

A point made by Gersten and Dimino (2006) is that 'the field of special education seems to lurch forward in a seemingly never ending series of reforms and initiatives'. This makes it difficult to summarise policy and practice in relation to dyslexia even within a particular administrative area. It's also uncertain what impact the plethora of policy initiatives have on teachers' actual classroom practice and attitudes and what the consequent impact on children might be. It's easy to get lost in the morass of official documentation and the minutia of specific policy initiatives and lose sight of the overall picture in relation to dyslexia. The important points are:

1   How well are pre-reading or early reading difficulties identified and attended to?
2   How well are children who either slip through the net or have persistent problems despite good early literacy intervention attended to as they progress through school?

Overall education policy

Even in a country such as England, which has a relatively centralised education policy with a national curriculum, national testing and a primary literacy hour, there are still considerable variations in practice in relation to dyslexia. How policy is interpreted and implemented differs at the level of local authorities, individual schools within an authority, and individual teachers within a school. So although national policy provides an important backdrop to the educational experiences of children the experiences of individual children with dyslexia differ considerably. In countries such as Canada and Australia, where education policy is formulated and implemented at the State or province level, there can be marked regional variations. In Canada for example Alberta came third and Quebec came twenty-third in the PIRLS 2006 international comparisons of reading competence in 9- to 10-year-olds.

In many English-speaking countries including the UK and the US there were concerns in the past over the poor reading, spelling and writing performance of their school age children in international comparisons. This has led to large-scale funding in the US to look at the scientific basis for effective teaching of reading and in England to the adoption of a National Literacy Strategy in 1998. This strategy in its original form was highly prescriptive with detailed guidelines for a 'literacy hour' every day in primary school classrooms. There was an emphasis on resource and training materials for teachers and on the explicit teaching of phonological skills as part of the reading process. The focus now in the UK is on how phonological skills can be most effectively integrated into wider reading skills and how best high-quality teaching of reading can be promoted (Rose 2006). Intuitively it seems plausible that approaches to reading which recognise the importance of phonological skills would be helpful to many children who struggle to learn to read. Although the government claims that the National Literacy Strategy (now known as primary national strategy) has been effective in improving overall reading performance, critics have raised particular concerns over a sub-group of children who have still lagged behind. In England this has been part of the movement to drive up educational standards and has been accompanied by national attainment testing of children with results for individual schools published in national league tables. Many teachers feel they are having to satisfy both a standards and an inclusion agenda and that this can create real tensions for them in terms of their priorities.

Introduction to current special educational needs policy

At a global level the past 10 years has seen an increasing emphasis on inclusive education and the idea that mainstream schools should adapt themselves to meet the needs of a diverse range of learners. In many countries this has been underpinned by new disability and/or education legislation which requires educationalists to monitor the progress of all children and identify and remove barriers to learning for those that are struggling. In the US the No Child Left Behind Act (NCLB 2001) was introduced with the specific aim of raising the educational attainments of those children at risk of failure. It states that 'NCLB's new provisions for assessment and accountability are designed to focus increased levels of attention on under-performing groups of students and to close the achievement gap between them and their peers'. NCLD mentions the 2.9 million students with learning disabilities as part of the group of children they are particularly concerned about.

In the UK the revised Special Educational Needs Code of Practice (DfES 2001) includes statutory duties set out by the Special Needs and Disability Act 2001. The DfES (Department for Education and Skills), now DCSF (Department for Children, Schools and Families), advises that all schools, local authorities and supporting services such as health and social services must have regard to the SEN Code of Practice and must not ignore it. Dyslexic children are named within the code under the umbrella of specific learning difficulties with the requirement that suitable programmes to aid their cognition and learning be put in place. In 2004 the DfES issued *Removing Barriers to Achievement* in which it set out its vision for improving education and support for children with special educational needs and disabilities. It named dyslexic children alongside children with speech language and communication difficulties as one of the four target groups it would be focusing on. The naming of dyslexia within official government documentation and in official advice to teachers has been important in legitimising the term within educational circles in the UK. When research was carried out in the mid-1990s for the first edition of this book (Riddick 1996) the author was told quite firmly by several schools that the term 'dyslexia' was not recognised or used within their school. Many of the parents interviewed at the time also commented that dyslexia was a taboo word within their child's school. In New Zealand dyslexia was officially recognised by the Ministry of Education in 2007 for the first time. The ministry ascribed this to mounting international research evidence on the nature of reading and writing difficulties although a high-profile campaign by the Dyslexia Foundation of New Zealand may well have contributed to the decision. It should be pointed out that, although other countries such as Australia, Canada and the US do not widely use the term 'dyslexia', they would contend that the needs of such children are met through general reading initiatives and targeted support for children with specific learning disabilities or reading disabilities.

Early intervention for reading difficulties

More important initially than the issue of what label is used is whether children's reading difficulties are correctly identified and responded to or more ideally whether children at risk of reading difficulties are identified early on and given adequate support and intervention. In England there is an intersection between a reading process approach, which identifies children who need additional levels of literacy support, and a more holistic SEN approach, which identifies an individual child's strengths and weaknesses on a broader basis and where necessary draws up an Individual Learning Plan or in some schools a personal learning plan. The DCSF conceives of three waves of literacy support: the first is high-standard literacy teaching delivered to all children, the second wave is catch-up literacy intervention in small groups planned and provided by the school, and only those children who still have literacy difficulties will participate in more specialist third-wave interventions, which might involve consultation with professionals outside the school. It is suggested that most children who require wave 2 literacy intervention should not be conceived of as having special educational needs and that they would be expected to catch up with their peers as a result of this intervention. When children go onto wave 3 support they are likely to be recorded as having a SEN that requires School Action or School Action Plus. This is similar to the US response to instruction (RTI) model, which also uses a graduated three-tier literacy support programme. The US approach emphasises that reading instruction should be scientifically based and should regularly monitor children's performance (IRA 2002). When children do not make the expected progress after high-quality initial reading instruction and second-tier catch-up instruction they move on to more intensive and individualised third-tier instruction and at this point are likely to be identified as reading disabled. There is considerable optimism about this model in the US but it does have its critics, who point out that although it is appealing there is not yet sound empirical evidence of its effectiveness. It can be argued that it still waits for children to fail before putting adequate support in place and in defining children as RD on the basis of response to intervention it assumes that all children will have received equivalent quality instruction. Critics such as Wagner (2008) therefore question the reliability and validity of the process used to define children as RD and argue that earlier identification of children at risk of reading difficulties is possible and desirable using improved standardised tests of print awareness etc. Many reading researchers (Wagner 2008, Torgesen 2004) have pointed out that it is vital to intervene as early as possible because children who are poor readers in the first grade remain poor readers throughout primary school if their difficulties are not addressed at this point. All agree that an important part of effective reading intervention is regular and well calibrated monitoring of children's reading. It may be that a combination of initial screening and/ or assessment with monitoring of how a child responds to instruction will prove the best approach to identification and appropriate support.

Special educational needs policy in the UK

Special needs policy in the UK can be traced back to the seminal Warnock Report in 1978. This advocated the abolition of rigid categories of handicap and a move towards a more relativistic and fluid notion of special educational needs. It introduced the idea of a social constructionist view of SENs, which stressed that whether a child would experience special educational needs would depend on how their differences were viewed and the educational environment they were put in. In making this statement it pointed out that schools varied considerably in their expertise, organisation, outlook and resources and that even within a single school the impact of a disability could vary depending on the child's personality, the degree of support and encouragement that they received from their family and the interests that they had outside school. This has clear relevance to dyslexia and suggests that the degree to which a child encounters difficulties will depend on the degree of support available to them.

From the educational perspective the problems of defining and identifying dyslexia are inextricably bound up with more general issues about defining and identifying special needs. A strong criticism the Warnock Report had of categories was that they led to stigma and negative labelling sometimes of a long-term nature. The Warnock Report was expressing a view widely held in the 1970s and 1980s (Szasz 1961, Goffman 1968) about the problems of labelling. Few would disagree about the negative connotations attached to certain labels and the harmful consequences that can ensue. But the danger is that this can lead to oversimplification and overgeneralisation of the argument. It can be argued that the nature, purpose and context in which a label is used all influence the degree of positive and negative outcomes associated in using it (Riddick 2000, 2001). A child with a visual impairment, for example, may not want to be publicly labelled as such within school, but may want teachers to know enough about the impairment so they can adapt teaching appropriately. The child may also want at a personal level to understand the visual difficulties that they have and be given some idea of whether any improvement or deterioration can be expected in their sight. This issue of categorisation or labelling in relation to dyslexia will be looked at in more detail in Chapter 6. As a general point it can be suggested that the concept of dyslexia was being debated during the 1970s and 1980s within a cultural context that was doubtful or sceptical of the value of labels. But it can be argued that in order to have a full and accurate picture of a child's learning difficulties we need to know how all the environmental factors which are in operation interact with the within-child factors to produce a particular outcome. Some special educationalists, in extending the thinking of the Warnock Report (DES 1978), were highly critical of explanations of learning disability that focused on within-child factors. Although they were correct to criticise the exclusive use of within-child factors the danger was that in some cases by denying the role of these factors they were adopting what could be called the 'without-child' approach.

One of the outcomes of the Warnock Report was that it recommended that any child who was having serious educational difficulty could if necessary and with family agreement be statemented. This statement was to involve a detailed assessment of a child's needs with a clear specification of the kind of special provision that was required. It was then legally binding for the local authority to deliver the provision set out in the statement. The Warnock Report envisaged that only a small proportion of children with the most severe and complex special educational needs would be statemented. Currently, although 18 per cent of children are deemed to have SENs at any one time, only 3 per cent of them currently have a statement. It would be expected that the needs of most dyslexic children could be met without a statement but there are a very small percentage of children with dyslexia/specific learning difficulties who do have a statement. This has been a contentious area because many parents have felt that their children's special educational needs have not been met and that they have had to resort to requesting a statement in order to obtain support for their child. Although statements are seen as outdated and troublesome, partly because they set up a division between children who do and do not have them, they are still in operation in England and Wales. From the point of view of local authorities and schools they are trying to deploy scarce resources as equitably as possible and do have to make difficult decisions about how resources will be allocated. The SEN Code of Practice (DfES 2001), with its emphasis on all teachers being responsible for children with SENs, was seen as part of the way to address these concerns. It was also argued that, with a more inclusive approach to education, SEN funding should support systemic changes to teaching and learning to meet the needs of a wide range of children. The requirement for schools to demonstrate how they are meeting special educational needs and the greater emphasis given by OFSTED to SEN provision in their school inspections are seen as important in raising the profile of SENs. The House of Commons Report (HCESC 2006) notes that SEN funding has increased in the last few years but because of serious prior underfunding it is still not sufficient to meet the special educational needs of a diverse group of children. At present the need for a balance between a more systemic whole-school support and specific individual support is one that runs throughout SEN provision.

It is interesting that Mary Warnock, who signalled the change to a more relative and less categorical approach to conceptualising special needs back in 1978, was in 1994 arguing that teachers should be aware of the signs that may indicate a specific learning difficulty or dyslexia:

> It is therefore of the greatest importance that teachers, even when quite young and inexperienced, should know what to look for as signs that a child has a specific learning difficulty or dyslexia, which may well not manifest itself until school work begins.
>
> (Warnock 1994)

But the 1978 Warnock Report expressed considerable concern over the needs of children with specific learning difficulties so Mary Warnock is showing consistency in still voicing these concerns. She says that what has changed is that we now have considerably more knowledge on the occurrence of such difficulties and the devastating effect that they can have on children's lives. She argues that on this basis it is essential that all teachers be presented with this information as part of their initial teacher training.

Models of good practice

Early pioneers

In the 1990s some mainstream schools, especially where there was good local authority support, started to develop a comprehensive approach to meeting the needs of children with dyslexia/specific learning disabilities. Cleveland Local Education Authority (England) for example had a policy of not statementing children with specific learning difficulties where possible, and instead providing them with a package of support (Stansfield 1994). This support included placement in an intensive reading class, access to a learning support service, information technology (IT) equipment and advice on this equipment for parents and schools. The intensive reading classes for primary school children involved both withdrawal and within-class support from a team of 10 specialist teachers. At secondary level there were four learning support teachers whose aim it was to move away from supporting specific children to supporting and training teachers within the secondary schools to meet the needs of their own pupils. Information technology support was overseen by an IT special education needs co-ordinator who was responsible for in-service training and for assessing and administering the loan of IT equipment. There was also an examinations concessions group who drew up a set of procedures to ensure that children with special needs got the best possible concessions during public examinations.

Lewis (1995) described the setting up of a specialist unit for dyslexic children in a comprehensive school. The school had 40 places for students with statements of educational needs of a dyslexic or specific learning difficulty nature. He talked about the conflicting demands of the national curriculum and the need for these pupils to have individualised structured teaching sessions within the school day and explained how this was achieved within these constraints. He emphasised the importance of all the teachers in the school being informed and responsible for children with specific learning difficulties and argued that the approach taken by the school had benefited many other children in the school. He also talked about the need to discuss with each pupil the nature of their support and the goals that they want to achieve.

Dyson and Skidmore (1994) carried out a survey of 27 Scottish secondary schools and 14 English secondary schools which were nominated as having developed good practice in relation to specific learning difficulties. As they point out, this survey relied on self-reporting by schools so it can tell us only what schools believed they were doing. Dyson and Skidmore report that, although there was great variability in how schools organised their support, some strong underlying factors were in evidence. These included the targeting of support for children in individualised packages which they term as 'eclectic, pragmatic, responsive and customised'. They found that all such schools had a clear conceptualisation of specific learning difficulties embedded in a strong whole-school special needs policy. Within this framework four major aims or areas of support were identified:

1   direct help with specific difficulties to improve basic skills;
2   improving curriculum access;
3   encouraging coping strategies and independent learning;
4   building up confidence or self-esteem.

There were also examples in both London and Scotland of local authorities that set up contracts with local dyslexia associations to provide their expertise and structured teaching methods to the education system.

Dyslexia-friendly schools

A logical outcome of a more social interactionist view of dyslexia is the need to adapt the wider school environment and reduce barriers to learning as well as providing more traditional forms of support. As the examples above demonstrate, there were individual schools which were successfully doing this, but the principles on which they were operating were not widely known or appreciated across local authorities or regions. MacKay (2001) used the term 'dyslexia friendly' to describe the provision he had developed for dyslexic children at a comprehensive school in Wales, which resulted in such children leaving school with good GCSE results. Swansea, like many local authorities in the late 1990s, was concerned by the rising number of statements of SEN it was having to issue for spld/dyslexia and the vocal dissatisfaction of parents. Parents were appealing to the SEN tribunal if their request for a statement was turned down and professionals were also frustrated by the lack of appropriate provision. Using MacKay's work as a starting point it spent 4 years developing a comprehensive authority-wide dyslexia-friendly school plan. This involved extensive consultation with parents, teachers, other professionals and the BDA. As a result the LA plan put in place or supported the development of:

• dyslexia awareness training for all teachers
• a specialist dyslexia teacher in nearly every school to advise other teachers
• close partnership with parents and children
• a resource bank of dyslexia-friendly materials in each school
• a whole school policy for supporting dyslexic children.

In evaluating the outcomes of this approach Springett (2002) reported that there was a reduction in SEN statements from 14 per cent to 2 per cent for dyslexia/spld and no appeals to the SEN tribunal board in relation to dyslexia in the last 2 years. In addition the local dyslexia voluntary organisation reported a halving in phone calls from parents wanting help. This suggested that where good dyslexia support is in place parents are much more likely to be satisfied that their children's needs can be met without recourse to a statement of SEN. An important part of this approach was a funding mechanism that allowed for pro-active support to be put in place before children 'failed' or were failed by the system.

The British Dyslexia Association with funding from the DfES (now DCSF) used this model to develop a resource pack entitled *Achieving Dyslexia Friendly Schools*. This has been very popular with schools and local authorities (Pavey 2007) and has prompted a number of local authorities and schools to adopt a dyslexia-friendly approach. 'Dyslexia friendly' is a beguiling term and there are concerns or questions about precisely what it means and what a school should be doing to live up to this term. To address this issue the BDA has developed a stringent quality mark protocol for local authorities to follow, which specifies certain standards that must be met. O'Brien (2005) reports on the experiences of Liverpool local authority, which was the first to be awarded dyslexia-friendly status under the BDA scheme. Again a fall in statements and increase in parental satisfaction was reported. Despite these initial successes there are still concerns about the future development of this approach. For example, when teaching staff move on will there be sufficient resourcing for new staff to receive training? Pavey (2007) also questions whether all the money saved by reduced statementing will be fed back into schools to provide an adequate level of support. Roland and Galloway (2004) found that new initiatives had to become embedded into the day-to-day practice of the school if they were to have a lasting impact. In research into schools that were developing dyslexia-friendly practice in one local authority (Riddick 2006, 2009, Coffield *et al.* 2008) it was found that although dyslexic children expressed a number of positives there were still areas of concern. Out of 43 dyslexic children 54 per cent said they received lots of red marks in their exercise books, 35 per cent said they were asked to read out loud in class even if they didn't want to, and 32 per cent did not have time to finish written work in class. Only 37 per cent thought their ideas were as good as everybody else's in the class and only 28 per cent thought their work was as good as everybody else's in the class. This raises questions about what might be happening in schools that have not signed up to this approach. It also raises questions about the relationship between the practices of individual teachers and the general policies and practices of their school. In the case of marking, for example, some schools have whole-school marking policies which advocate marking separately for content and presentation (spelling and grammar) and picking up on only a certain proportion of basic or key spelling errors for children with literacy difficulties. What percentage of teachers in a school need to be seen to be carrying out such dyslexia-friendly practices for it to achieve dyslexia-friendly school status and should the focus be on dyslexia-friendly teachers as well as schools? Teachers can quite rightly point out that a tick list of 'dyslexia-friendly activities' does not necessarily do justice to the complexity of classroom dynamics where a teacher's existing relationship with a child and the sensitivity and context in which an action is carried out and its appropriateness all play an important part in how 'dyslexia friendly' the child is likely to perceive it to be.

The role of voluntary organisations

The role of voluntary organisations has been important in many countries in raising the profile of dyslexia and/or specific learning difficulties and campaigning for better support and understanding in education establishments. In the past in particular such organisations were often viewed with suspicion or hostility by educationalists whereas in some countries they are now seen as a resource to be worked with. The New Zealand government announced (2007 Ministry of Education) that it was working collaboratively with the Dyslexia Foundation and SPELD (Specific Learning Difficulties) to better meet the needs of dyslexic children in school. In the UK the SEN Code of Practice (DfES 2001) stipulates that educationalists should work with voluntary organisations to support parents and their children. The Code points out that such organisations have valuable expertise that schools can draw upon and that schools should pass information on to parents about appropriate voluntary organisations. In England and Wales there have been close links between the Education Department and the British Dyslexia Association, which led to the joint publication of a popular and influential Dyslexia Friendly School Pack (BDA/DfES 2005). More recently the government (DCSF 2007) has given funding to the British Dyslexia Association to develop and expand its dyslexia helpline and to Dyslexia Action to evaluate a 3-year specialist dyslexia tuition scheme running in 10 areas of England. In Scotland an audit of early years provision for dyslexia and spld was commissioned by the Scottish Executive (Reid *et al*. 2005), and Dyslexia Scotland as a charity receives core funding from the government. In 2007 every school in Scotland received a copy of the DVD *Dyslexia at Transition* accompanied by a road show for teachers as part of their professional development. This was funded by the Scottish Executive and included input from Dyslexia Scotland. Both the British Dyslexia Association and Dyslexia Scotland emphasise that an important part of their role is to influence education policy and practice and where necessary campaign for change. The British Dyslexia Association (2009) says it is the voice of dyslexic people and sees itself as having an important role in reflecting and representing the views of dyslexic individuals, and their families, to education policy makers and professionals. In England and Wales, Dyslexia Action in contrast to this focuses on specialist dyslexia tuition for children and adults and dyslexia training for teachers. Voluntary organisations can thus fulfil a variety of roles and can differ in their outlook and aims. This raises debate about whether the best way for voluntary organisations to effect change is through close cooperation and working relations with official bodies or through a more independent and critical stance. In reality the wide range of voluntary organisations and discussion forums even within the area of dyslexia and specific learning difficulties means that different voluntary organisations can fulfil different roles.

Summary

1   There are diverse models of good practice for supporting children with dyslexia/specific learning difficulties in the mainstream school.
2   All teachers need to be trained to be aware of the signs of dyslexia/specific learning difficulties.

3   The best combination is where there is good whole school policy combined with a high level of individual teacher awareness.

4   A dyslexia-friendly school approach provides a useful basis on which local authorities and individual schools can formulate their own plans based on their specific circumstances.

Chapter 3

Researching the social and emotional consequences of dyslexia

It was traumatic for him, incredibly traumatic, every morning I had to pull him up screaming 'I don't want to go to school' and then I had to pull him all the way down to the school.

(Mother of 6-year-old boy later identified as dyslexic)

As mentioned in the introduction there is still relatively little research on the social and emotional consequences of living with dyslexia but there has been a notable increase in the last decade. Interested clinicians and educationalists have consistently pointed to the devastating effects that dyslexia or specific learning disabilities can have on some children's lives. Concern can be traced from Orton's early clinical work through both the Bullock (1975) and Warnock (DES 1978) Reports to the recent House of Commons Report (HCESC 2006) on special educational needs. This noted that failure to identify and give appropriate teaching to dyslexic children can lead to significant long-term economic and social difficulties. The large-scale PACFOLD (2007) study came to similar conclusions for children and adults identified as learning disabled in Canada. It should however be stressed that some individuals with dyslexia or LD can be highly successful in the long run and it is important not to assume that dyslexia inevitably leads to poor outcomes.

It appears that, whatever the debate about terminology and identification, at a global level there is agreement that such difficulties can have a detrimental effect on the lives of some children and their families. Despite this agreement this is a difficult and complex area to research. To start with, both dyslexia and social and emotional difficulties have to be clearly defined and identified before the relationship between them can be examined. To date much of the research has looked at children with reading disabilities or more generally at children with learning disabilities. This research has generally used a group comparison design so that, for example, the self-esteem of a group of reading-delayed and non-reading-delayed children would be compared. The problem with this approach is that individual differences between children can be masked and it doesn't relate the individual's specific experiences to their level of self-esteem. We might expect for example that a dyslexic child who has been well supported at home and at school would be more likely to have a reasonable level of esteem than a child who has not been supported well at either home or school. Another difficulty in researching this area, is that dyslexia is a developmental disorder which changes in its manifestations over time. It may be that social and emotional experiences change or fluctuate considerably over time and that circumstances, cumulative experiences and maturation all affect the likely outcome at a given point in time. If for example a study looked at 10-year-old dyslexics who had learnt to read and were well supported in the classroom and compared their self-esteem with that of their classmates no significant difference might be found. If this were the case this would be an interesting and valid finding in its own right. The danger would be in overgeneralising this finding and saying that dyslexic children don't have lower self-esteem than other children or even that 10-year-old dyslexic children don't have lower self-esteem than other children. These same children at 7 years of age, before they were identified as dyslexic and offered support, may have had very low self-esteem compared with their classmates. So, as with all cross-sectional research, the age and stage at which a child is studied are of key importance. Yet another difficulty is in selecting the right measures to tap into any difficulties or differences that dyslexic children display compared with their peers. A study by Porter and Rourke (1985) found that 10 per cent of a sample of 100 learning-disabled children had somatic problems such as migraines or stomach upsets despite scoring normally on an inventory of social and emotional functioning. These kinds of difficulties may account for some of the mixed findings to emerge from this area. Porter and Rourke found for example that 50 per cent of the children in their sample did not show social or emotional difficulties and in a study by Speece *et al.* (1985) one-third of the learning disabled children showed no social or emotional difficulties. The problem with these studies is that they are not specific to children with dyslexia, but they do underline the point that it is important not to assume that all children with dyslexia will automatically have social or emotional difficulties.

Because of the difficulties involved in following the ups and downs of children's lives and understanding the complexities of them, interest has more recently focused on different more qualitative methods of research such as ethnography, case studies, interviews and grounded theory. Although case studies and interviews are scarcely new to the scene, the more recent focus on trying to see things from the individual's perspective has probably informed and influenced how they are likely to be carried out. Quantitative and qualitative methods are sometimes seen as being in opposition to each other, whereas Mittler (1985) in reviewing research methods in special education states that 'it would be dangerously misleading to polarize or stereotype these methods as lying at opposite ends of a continuum'. He goes on to point out that these methods are often used in combination by researchers and that a study might, for example, start with a broad quantitative survey and then move into detailed qualitative case studies of individuals. In the past 20 years or so an important body of evidence on the social and emotional concomitants of dyslexia has come from personal accounts and life histories. Probably the best-known personal account in Britain is recounted by Susan Hampshire the actress in her book entitled *Susan's Story* (1990). As well as detailed individual accounts, several collections of interviews with parents of dyslexic children, and adults with dyslexia have been published (Osmond 1993, Van der Stoel 1990, Melck 1986). Although these books have included some comments by dyslexic children, the views of parents have predominated. Kavanaugh (1978) in pioneering work in the US published a book entitled *Listen to Us!* that was based entirely on the views of dyslexic children, which were first aired during discussions between them. Much of this early work has been produced by lay people often with first-hand experience of dyslexia. The aim has been 'to tell it how it is' and not to answer theoretical questions or provide highly systematic accounts. But in their own right they have provided an important level of description about how individuals live with dyslexia and they have raised numerous questions for further research. In particular it can be argued that they challenged some of the more dogmatic ideology surrounding dyslexia and provided compelling accounts of how prejudice and ignorance can combine to provide poor and in some cases atrocious educational practice. This has lead on to a series of more systematic interview studies of both children and adults with dyslexia. One of the first, by Edwards (1994), provides detailed personal case studies on eight boys attending a residential school for children with dyslexia. Despite the enormous diversity of these various accounts, consistent themes, issues and experiences can be identified; these will be discussed in more detail later in the chapter and will also be linked to findings from the study described in this book. On a more positive note interviews and case studies combined with evaluations of dyslexia-friendly approaches also give a clearer indication of the circumstances under which children can flourish. Because of the limited amount of research on the social and emotional consequences of dyslexia a number of overlapping areas of research relevant to this issue will be briefly reviewed.

Self-esteem/self-concept

Although the terms 'self-esteem', 'self-concept' and 'self-image' are sometimes used interchangeably they do have different but interrelated meanings. Self-concept is defined as an umbrella term that encompasses an individual's evaluation of themself at a cognitive (thinking), affective (feelings) and behavioural level. Self-esteem is taken as a measure of how far an individual's perceived self (self-image) matches up to their ideal self. Burns (1982) in an extensive review of the literature relating to self-concept and education argued that there are clear links between an individual's self-concept and school performance. He suggests that where an individual has poor academic performance and low motivation in school this is often linked to a poor self-concept. Lawrence (2006) and Elbaum and Vaughn (2003) make similar claims for the link between poor school performance and low self-esteem. Drawing on the work of Rogers (1951) many writers have suggested that in order to develop a positive self-concept an individual needs a sense of acceptance, competence and worth. It is postulated that these are learnt through social interaction first within the family, then school and the wider environment. This is seen as an interactional process with the child influencing the environment and the environment influencing the child. Both Burns and Lawrence in their overviews of the area stress that, although families have an important role in the fostering of good self-concept or self-esteem, teachers also have a vital role in this process. Lawrence states that 'whenever the teacher enters into a relationship with a student a process is set into motion which results either in the enhancement of self-esteem or in the reduction of self-esteem.' Lawrence goes on to suggest that many good teachers intuitively enhance the self-esteem of their pupils, but even so they might benefit from more explicit knowledge of the factors that help to enhance self-esteem.

One of the problems in reviewing the literature on self-concept and self-esteem in relation to academic performance is that it is unclear whether poor self-esteem leads to poor performance or poor performance leads to poor self-esteem. A third possibility is that some kind of interactional process takes place. Lawrence (2006) in reviewing research in this area favours an interactional explanation and argues that on this basis it is important to work on a child's self-esteem and skills in tandem. Marsh with various collaborators (Marsh and Craven 2006) has carried out a series of large-scale statistical studies from which he concludes that there is a two-way interaction, with achievement affecting academic self-concept and academic self-concept affecting achievement. Most researchers agree (Marsh 2005, Battle 2002, Coopersmith 1967) that self-esteem and self-concept are developmental in nature and move from a global, relatively undifferentiated state in young children to a more complex hierarchical state with a number of clearly differentiated components feeding into global self-esteem as a child grows older. There is still much debate on the precise nature of any hierarchical model and the developmental history underpinning it. Marsh (2005) has carried out extensive research in this area and gives a simplified outline of how such a model might look (Figure 3.1).

What is also uncertain is the degree of individual differences in the way that the self-concept is structured and operates. It may be that some individuals operate more heavily on the basis of a global self-concept whereas others operate more heavily on the basis of differentiated aspects of self-concept. Self-esteem is relative to those qualities or achievements that an individual values and perceives they have done well at. Outside of school and to some degree as adults we can invest time and energy in things we value and are good at and avoid those things we are less good at. At school or college literacy is central to the learning process and is difficult to escape so it is not surprising that it poses a threat to the self-esteem of individuals with dyslexia. In an extensive review of research on self-esteem Elmer (2001) concludes there is evidence that individuals with very high self-esteem differ somewhat from individuals with average or lower self-esteem. They appear less responsive to negative feedback and are able to discount or ignore it, whereas individuals with more modest self-esteem are more sensitive to feedback and their self-esteem is more readily lowered by negative feedback. Because of these individual differences in how people respond to various kinds of feedback, psychological processes that might mediate this such as attribution style and self-efficacy have been investigated and are discussed in more detail later in this chapter. Elmer

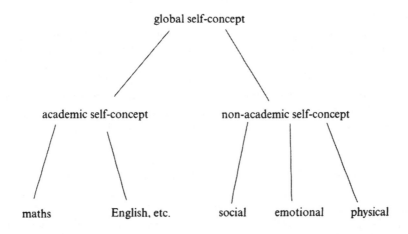

Figure 3.1 A simplified hierarchical model of self-concept or self-esteem, based on Marsh (1992).

(2001) reports that in addition to the powerful influence of parents on self-esteem there is evidence for a genetic component to self-esteem or at least for the psychological processes underlying self-esteem, which may predispose individuals to respond to feedback in different ways. He also acknowledges that 'self-esteem can be damaged by repeated, unambiguous and public failures and rejections' (p. 60). Battle (2002) claims that once an individual's level of self-esteem is well established it becomes difficult to alter and remains relatively stable over time. This is not to say that self-esteem can't change over time but that the general pattern appears to be one in which self-esteem fluctuates around an average for a given individual. The reason for concern over children with low self-esteem is that it can negatively influence their motivation and goal setting, and persistent very low self-esteem is associated with a greater risk of high anxiety and depression.

Measuring self-esteem or self-concept

Studies that attempt to measure self-esteem run into a number of methodological difficulties. The first is in selecting a valid and reliable means of assessing self-esteem: this is usually done by means of a self-esteem inventory, which relies on the subject responding to a set of specific questions. This raises questions about how honestly and accurately the subject responds to the questions. More recent well designed self-esteem inventories try to get round this problem: the *Culture-Free Self-Esteem Inventories* (Battle 2002) for example include a defensiveness scale. Given that we know that a number of variables such as the gender, colour and role of the tester can affect children's performance differentially on various tests of ability, it might also be the case that the role of the self-esteem tester and the context in which the test is carried out might affect the children's responses differentially. It has been suggested that some children with learning disabilities might defend themselves by denial and that this might in turn influence how they respond to a self-esteem inventory. Self-esteem inventories vary in accordance with the model of self-esteem that they are based on. The major difference is between those that simply give a global self-esteem score (Coopersmith 1967, Lawrence 2006) and those that in addition to a global score divide self-esteem or self concept up into a number of contributing areas (Battle 2002, Marsh *et al.* 1991) such as academic, physical and social self-esteem. Children's self-esteem scores may therefore vary depending on the sensitivity and appropriateness of the instrument used. Another difficulty in assessing self-esteem is that little is known about the way in which day-to-day events may influence children's self-perceptions. A study by Callison (1974) found that children's self-concept could be altered by a single incidence of feedback. In this study he first gave 8-year-old children half of the Piers-Harris Self-Concept Scale followed by a maths test. Half of the group of 28 were told that they had performed badly on the test and half were told that they had performed well. They were then given the second half of the self-concept scale to complete. It was found that children who had been given negative feedback scored significantly lower in their self-concept scores on the second part of the test. This suggests that events immediately prior to a self-esteem or self-concept inventory or scale could significantly influence the results. Despite these methodological difficulties Elmer (2001) concludes from his review that there has been considerable improvement in the measurement of self-esteem and relatively quick and reliable ways of assessing self-esteem are now available.

Indicators of high and low self-esteem and the role of self-efficacy and attribution style

Whatever the debate about assessing self-esteem there is general agreement that a number of behaviours are characteristic of children with high self-esteem and a number of other behaviours are characteristic of children with low self-esteem. Children with high self-esteem are said to display more confidence in their own ability and to be more willing to volunteer answers and try out new learning situations, whereas children with low self-esteem show little confidence in their own ability, give up easily and are often fearful of or avoid new learning situations. A crucial difference appears to be that, whereas children with high self-esteem generally expect to succeed, children with low self-esteem generally expect to fail. Butkowsky and Willows (1980), in a study comparing children with reading difficulties with children of average or good reading ability, found many of these characteristics. The poor readers in their study had lower expectations of success not only on a reading task but also on a drawing task. They responded more negatively to failure and were more likely to give up, thus increasing the likelihood of future failure. They also differed in their attribution style from good readers. Poor readers tended to 'blame themselves' by attributing failure to their own incompetence and success to environmental factors such as luck, whereas good readers attributed success to their own ability. Again the question can be raised as to whether attribution style is a cause or an effect of poor reading or both. This style of thinking fits well with Seligman's notion of learned helplessness. Seligman (2006) claims that individuals who have been put in a negative situation from which they cannot escape and over which they feel that they have no control will become apathetic and demoralised. More importantly, when these individuals are put in a more positive situation they persist in their apathetic behaviour and thus display learned helplessness. In a similar vein Bannister and Fransella (1971) in extending Kelly's (1955) work on personal construct theory argue that in order to change an individual's behaviour you need to change their personal constructs (self-beliefs). Although some empirical evidence has been presented to support this point of view, behaviourists can equally present evidence that changing behaviour can lead to a change in self-concept. More recent theorising (Beck *et al.* 1979, Beck 2005) attempts to reconcile these positions by arguing for a cognitive behavioural approach that recognises the interrelated nature of cognition (thinking) and behaviour. This gets back to Lawrence's point that in the absence of more convincing evidence it is safest to assume that we need to work on both children's self-beliefs and their learning skills. Lawrence (1971, 1973, 1985, 2006) found that an individual counselling approach focused on children's self-beliefs was consistently more successful than a traditional remedial reading approach alone in improving the performance of poor readers. Lawrence found that counsellors did not need to be highly trained professionals and that anyone with a warm sympathetic approach could with limited training fulfil the role. At a common sense level, working on individual skills in combination with personal support would seem the best option. Other studies suggest that this support doesn't need to be in the form of formal counselling sessions and that what is required is an understanding and interested adult who gives the child support and encouragement and helps them develop more positive self-beliefs (Lackaye and Margalit 2006, Raskind *et al.* 2002). This issue will be further explored in Chapter 10, where children's and adults' views on the teachers they find most helpful will be examined.

Self-esteem in children with dyslexia or specific learning difficulties

A longitudinal study (Gjessing and Karlsen 1989) of 3,000 children in Norway distinguished a sub-group of children with specific learning difficulties from the cohort. It was found in this study that dyslexic children in general had a poor self-concept which was reflected in their lack of self-confidence and poor peer relationships. Several earlier studies (e.g. Rosenthal 1973, Thomson and Hartley 1980), have found that dyslexic children have low self-esteem compared with non-dyslexic children. Thomson (1990) used the Battle (1981) *Culture-Free Self-Esteem Inventories* to test the self-esteem of three groups of children with dyslexia. The first group were tested when they were first interviewed for a place at a specialist school for dyslexia, the second group had already attended the school for 6 months and the third group had attended the school for 18 months. Thomson found there was a significant increase in self-esteem over this period of time, which he attributed to the benefits of specialist schooling. The results from this study would have been stronger if the same group of children had been followed and tested at each of these time intervals but, despite this, several interesting points emerged from the study when the four sub-scales for general, social, academic and parental self-esteem were compared. On the first test children's lowest area of self-esteem was for social (32 per cent) followed by academic (45 per cent) and their highest was parental (87 per cent). By the third test their social esteem was 84 per cent and their academic was 77 per cent and their parental remained at 87 per cent. This would suggest that the major source of low self-esteem for these children was the mainstream school environment and especially children's sense of failure in comparison to their peers. Studies by Chapman *et al.* (1984) and Fairhurst and Pumfrey (1992) have found that reading-disabled children score lower on their perception of academic ability compared with non-reading-disabled children. Chapman *et al.* found that children's perception of ability was closely related to success in school and was relatively independent of intelligence as measured by the WISC-R, a standard IQ test. They propose that, although it can be argued that children are being realistic about their level of ability in terms of school performance, these kinds of beliefs may set up a self-fulfilling prophecy of expecting to fail. Whereas Chapman *et al.* were looking at 9-year-olds, Fairhurst and Pumfrey were looking at third-year pupils in three secondary schools. They found that, in addition to the lower self-concepts as learners, the poor readers had a significantly higher rate of absence than the competent readers. They suggest that this high rate of absenteeism combined with their low self-concept and poor performance in school can all combine in a negative downward spiral for some of these children. Another factor that they found contributing to this overall picture was that the poor readers also scored lower on a sub-scale designed to look at their perceptions of their role in the classroom; this showed that they felt less valued and less important than the better readers. Casey, Levy, Brown and Brooks-Gunn (1992) studied a group of middle-class pre-adolescent children with reading disabilities. They found that these children had low self-esteem and were more anxious and less happy with school than a control group of non-reading disabled children. All these studies were conducted some time ago when school policies and practices were somewhat different and there was less awareness and recognition of dyslexia/splds. Nevertheless these studies along with several more were important in providing clear evidence to back up clinical impressions that children with dyslexia were at greater risk of experiencing low self-esteem than other children.

More recent studies on dyslexia and self-esteem

It could be supposed that with changes in policy and practice we should expect children with dyslexia/specific learning difficulties to be having more positive experiences of mainstream school. It is hard to make direct comparisons because most of the past and present studies are relatively small-scale and children were selected and assessed in different ways. Nonetheless by looking at more recent studies we can at least gain an indication of how children are faring now. Humphrey (2002) compared the self-esteem of 63 dyslexic children in mainstream classes or specialist dyslexia units with that of non-dyslexic children in mainstream school. He found that dyslexic children as a group had lower self-esteem than non-dyslexic children and the dyslexic children in mainstream school had significantly lower self-esteem than the dyslexic children in specialist units. Humphrey also noted that half the children, especially before they were identified as dyslexic, reported they had been humiliated or criticised by teachers because of their poor literacy skills. Burden (2005) reported that on the Myself as a Learner Scale (MALS) children with splds in mainstream school received a mean score of 60.8 whereas the mean for non-dyslexic children was 71. He also reported that when dyslexic children switched from mainstream school to a specialist dyslexia school in year 8 their mean MALS score was 57.9 whereas children in year 9 had a mean of 66.5 and children in year 10 had a mean of 68.5. This suggests as in Thomson's work that the mainstream school can be a more difficult setting for some dyslexic children and that their self-esteem or academic self-confidence may improve when they move to a more 'dyslexia-friendly' setting. One difficulty for mainstream schools is that dyslexic children are usually comparing themselves with non-dyslexic children in terms of their literacy and academic performance whereas in special settings they can make more favourable comparisons with children with similar difficulties (Frederickson and Jacobs 2001). Based on a series of studies Marsh and Hau (2003) report that comparison with their peers is the most critical factor in how most children rate their academic self-esteem. Whereas some studies report that dyslexic children or students as a group have lower general self-esteem (Undheim 2008, Palombo 2001, Riddick *et al.* 1999) others report that only academic self-esteem or self-concept is lower than that of non-dyslexic children (Zeleke 2004). Again this probably depends on the measure being used, how the sample of children or young people is selected, their age, personality and educational circumstances.

What causes low self-esteem or academic self-concept?

Although there is agreement that low self-esteem or low academic self-concept is experienced by a number of children and adults with dyslexia the precise reasons for this are still unclear. As already indicated at a common sense level it seems obvious that if literacy is central to education then individuals who have literacy difficulties are likely to struggle within the education system. The issue is about exactly what factors mediate this process and lead to individuals experiencing low self-esteem or low academic self-concept. Is it largely through dyslexic children making negative comparisons with other children, or through negative feedback they receive from teachers, parents or peers, or from frustration at not being able to access the curriculum, or a combination of these or other factors? The problem with cross-sectional studies is that they only give us a snapshot of the child's self-concept at a given point in time; they say nothing directly about how the child came to acquire their particular self-concept or what sort of developmental history it might have followed. This is a more difficult area to research as a number of complex and interacting variables are likely to be involved. These include the child's temperament, cognitive abilities, personal beliefs and social and educational experiences. Despite these complexities a number of researchers (Lawrence 2006, Rix *et al.* 2006, Singer 2005, Gurney 1988, Burns 1982) believe there is clear evidence that children's self-concepts as learners are strongly influenced by their teachers. In the interviews to be reported in this book parents were firmly of the opinion that in primary school their child's self-esteem was directly linked to the particular teacher they had that year. A number of recent studies have combined measures of self-esteem or ratings of well being with in-depth interviews or questionnaires to try and gain an understanding of the factors that lead to individuals experiencing high or low self-esteem. One source of information has been interviews with adults with dyslexia or LDs about their past experiences. These have the disadvantage of being retrospective and we know that autobiographical memory is not always reliable but on the other hand individuals are able to give a holistic and developmental account of their education. Relatively successful adults stress the importance of backing from their parents as a child and having at least one person in the education system who 'believed' in them. Over a number of studies individuals with dyslexia or poor literacy skills score higher on self-esteem once they have left full-time education although their self-esteem still tends to be lower than their non-dyslexic peers. This again suggests that school or further education can be a challenging environment for dyslexic individuals. Ingesson (2007) interviewed 75 teenagers and young adults about their experiences of school and beyond. At the time of interview 47 were still in education and 28 had left education. As part of the interview participants were asked to rate how they felt in school at different ages and how well they thought they had succeeded. Over 50 per cent of interviewees rated their well being as low in elementary school (7–10 years), and middle school (11–13 years) but then it improved throughout schooling with the majority ranking it as good in secondary school (14–16 years) and over 70 per cent ranking it as good or very good by upper secondary (17–19 years). As students grew older they were more likely to think they were succeeding well but 80 per cent felt that dyslexia had influenced school and school achievement quite a lot or very much. The question is what has brought about this improvement in well being for some of them: is secondary school a more benign environment for them or have they become better at compartmentalising their self-esteem and concentrating on the areas they are good at? Ingesson thinks both these factors have probably contributed. In Sweden students can choose a vocational curriculum in upper secondary school and take courses such as sport or floristry, which were commented on very positively by the dyslexic students. Only 13 per cent of the dyslexic students chose purely theoretical courses and only 13 per cent chose to go to college in comparison with 43 per cent of the overall student body. It should be noted that no comparisons were made with the well being of non-dyslexic students and no standardised measure of self-esteem was used. Other large-scale studies of all children's self-esteem show that it tends to rise and fall in relation to key transitions throughout children's school careers (Marsh 2005). It also leaves open the question of whether some students' choice of largely vocational courses is seen as a positive coping strategy or as a negative strategy that limits their long-term aspirations.

Armstrong and Humphrey (2009) noted in their interview study with college students that some appeared to re-invest their self-esteem in alternative areas such as music and suggested that this can be seen as a psychologically healthy strategy.

In our (Riddick *et al.* 1999) study with 16 dyslexic university students matched with non-dyslexic students we found on the Culture Free Self-Esteem Inventory dyslexic students scored significantly lower in self-esteem and on the State–Trait Anxiety Inventory some also scored high on anxiety. On a five-point rating scale the dyslexic students rated themselves as feeling significantly more anxious at school and less competent in their written work. At university they rated themselves as less competent in their written work and in their academic achievements. At both school and university they thought their written work was not a true reflection of their level of ability. Perhaps not surprisingly, in semi-structured interviews with the same dyslexic students, reports of their past and present experiences were closely aligned to their self-esteem and anxiety scores. Andy, one of the two dyslexics students who scored lowest in self-esteem and highest in anxiety, spoke several times in his interview about his low self-esteem and how he still had very negative recollections about his time at school. He started his interview by saying 'school was a nightmare from day one'. Patrick, the other student with very low self-esteem and high anxiety, said 'confidence, what confidence? I haven't got any confidence.' Both Andy and Patrick recalled humiliations at both primary and secondary school, neither was supported by his family, and neither received any appropriate literacy intervention. Patrick was identified as dyslexic only at the end of his school career and Andy was identified as an adult. In comparison only one of the dyslexic students scored in the high or very high category for self-esteem whereas 10 of the 16 non-dyslexic students did so. This student had strong support from his parents, who moved him very quickly from his first, unsupportive, primary school to a supportive one and his dyslexia was identified early on. He has mainly positive recollections of school where he was always outstandingly good at maths and was now taking a maths degree. These variations in experience have been reported across a number of interview studies (Armstrong and Humphrey 2009, MacDonald 2007, Raskind *et al.* 2002). Other studies have looked at the contribution of specific factors, such as social class, age of identification, overall ability and degree of literacy difficulties, to how children and students fare. Combining information from both these approaches suggests that it can be helpful to think in terms of risk and protective factors for general well being and progress at school for dyslexic children (Table 3.1).

In reality there is overlap and interaction between many of these suggested factors, with some such as early identification or intervention probably playing a pivotal role. Children who are identified and given the right intensive reading support and social support early on may develop better literacy and coping skills so they are less likely to compare themselves unfavourably with their peers or attract negative feedback from their teachers. Elbaum and Vaughn (2003) reviewed much of the research on interventions to improve self-concept or self-esteem in children with LDs. They noted that, for younger children, improving their academic skills and achievements appeared to be the best way to raise their self-esteem or improve their self-concept whereas with some older children it may be important to work also on their perception of themselves as learners. The focus now is in looking more closely at how specific factors such as academic achievement impact on children's coping strategies and approach to their work. Lackaye and Margalit (2006) reported that fifth-grade children with

Table 3.1 Protective factors and risk factors

Protective factors	Risk factors
Early identification	Late identification
Effective early reading intervention	Lack of effective early reading intervention
Parental support	Lack of parental support
Positive primary school experiences	Negative primary school experiences
Positive secondary school experiences	Negative secondary school experiences
Less severe literacy difficulties	More severe literacy difficulties
Good academic achievement	Poor academic achievement
Special skill or talent	No special skill or talent
Supportive non dyslexic friends	Socially isolated or bullied
Friends or role models with similar difficulties	No friends or role models with similar difficulties
Teacher or adult who 'believes' in the child	No special adult benefactor
Leading to or interacting with the following	
High self-esteem	Low self-esteem
High self-efficacy	Low self-efficacy
Positive coping strategies	Negative coping strategies
Positive attribution style	Negative attribution style
Low anxiety	High anxiety

learning disabilities when compared with non-learning-disabled children were lower on achievement, academic self-efficacy, effort investment, positive mood and hope and were higher on negative mood and loneliness. Self-efficacy is a prediction of how well someone thinks they will do on a specific task. Bandura (1997) reports that if you take two children with the same level of ability (based on previous performance) and ask them to perform a task the child higher in self-efficacy is likely to achieve better results. The reason for this according to Bandura is that high self-efficacy leads to greater effort and persistence whereas low self-efficacy has the opposite effect. The problem is that if dyslexic children have low self-efficacy for various literacy tasks they are likely in the long run to invest less energy in them and give up trying as hard as their peers. This in turn will exacerbate the difficulties they already have and put them even further behind their peers. Raskind *et al.* (2002) in a 20-year follow up of students with learning disabilities report that factors related to how children and adults dealt with difficulties related to their dyslexia were better predictors of long-term success and well being than factors such as academic achievement, socio-economic status and IQ. They called these positive factors 'success attributes' and listed among them (Raskind *et al.* 2002, p. 202):

- self-awareness
- pro-activity
- perseverance
- goal-setting
- the presence and use of effective support systems
- emotional stability.

They noted that the 'successful' adults often commented on mentoring from significant others and the support and encouragement they received from parents and teachers during their school years. This also lead to them reporting that they had been effective at asking for appropriate support and accepting support when it was offered. On the basis of this evidence Raskind *et al.* (2002) like Lawrence (2006) argue that an approach just based on improving literacy skills may not be sufficient and that some children need to be helped to develop these 'success attributes'.

Attributions

Attributions are the reasons we give for either our own behaviour or that of others. If a child reads out a passage from a book in a stumbling and faltering style they could say that the reason for this is that they were not given a chance to practise it beforehand by the teacher, that it was an exceptionally difficult passage to read, or that they are a very poor reader. The first two explanations are external ones – in other words attributions are made to either what the teacher did or the difficulty of the passage – whereas in the third case the child makes a negative internal attribution to their own inability, in other words blaming themselves. An attribution to their own poor ability to read as well as being internal is also likely to be an unchangeable one in that the child wouldn't expect to do any better on another occasion. If they had said they had read badly on this one occasion because they were tired this would be a changeable internal attribution that suggests that if they were not tired they could do better. As indicated previously the problem is that repeated perceived failure at a task such as reading may predispose a child to a negative attribution style. There is also the issue of how specific or general the attribution is. If a child says 'I'm no good at reading out loud but I'm good at understanding what stories are about and I'm good at making stories up', this would indicate that their attribution is a fairly specific one; whereas another child might give a more global attribution such as 'I'm no good at anything to do with reading or writing' or worse still a very global attribution such as 'I'm stupid and no good at school work'. What is concerning is when children are making negative, uncontrollable, unchangeable and global attributions to their own lack of ability or skill. Seligman (2006) suggest that when failures are usually attributed to internal, stable, and global causes that are seen as uncontrollable this can be characterised as a pessimistic explanatory style whereas when failures are attributed to external specific and unstable (i.e. changeable) causes that are controllable this is a more optimistic style. Eisner (1995) posits that if a child has repeated experience of uncontrollable events this may lead to negative attribution style whereas repeated experience of controllable events will lead to a more positive attribution style. There is interest at present in attribution retraining, whereby children are taught to attribute any achievements to their own effort and ability and to feel that they have control over their own learning and that change is possible (Riddick *et al.* 2002, Humphrey and Mullins 2002, Burden 2008). It seems important that children are helped to see their difficulties as quite specific ones, which with effort can be worked upon or managed, and also to identify what they are good at. Ben, a child followed from the age of 7 years, was delighted when as a demoralised 7-year-old it was suggested to him that it was English that was a 'stupid' language rather than him being stupid for having difficulty learning it. Gross (1993) advocates that because of the tendency of children with learning difficulties to 'blame' themselves for failure and to attribute success to 'luck' it is important that negative feedback be aimed only at specific external and changeable aspects of their performance (for example, 'I think you were so involved in writing this really exciting story that you forgot your capital letters today') and that when giving positive praise for performance this be linked to general attributes of the child ('you've done really well to remember capital letters, it shows what a hard worker you are and how much you are helping yourself to improve').

Gibb *et al.* (2006) on the basis of reviewing a number of studies suggest that attribution style is relatively flexible when children are younger and appears to become more fixed from around the age of 12 years. They also note that there are a number of studies showing a relationship between parents' attributional feedback to children for negative events and children's attribution style. In the study reported in this book mothers described instances when in trying to cheer their children up and make them feel more positive about their school work they would offer them more positive attributions for their difficulties. In a study with older teenagers (Riddick *et al.* 2002) and in this study children also gave examples of when parents or teachers had offered them more positive attributions. These were part of everyday social interaction and neither teachers nor parents would have explicitly called this attribution retraining. At present we have little information on what role this type of informal attribution training plays in how dyslexic children perceive themselves as learners. Singer (2008) noted in her study that dyslexic children reported that they often repeated silently to themselves positive statements made to them by their parents when they were facing negative learning experiences at school.

What is also unclear is how far negative attributions are produced by dyslexia-unfriendly learning environments and how far they can be prevented by making environments more dyslexia friendly. At one level it is difficult to stop a child from making any negative comparisons to other children but the way a class is structured may minimise or amplify this process. A dyslexic child in a class where they are asked to read out loud and have their spelling test score regularly revealed as part of ordinary class practice is likely to make more negative comparisons than a child in a class who is not asked to do these things. In detailed observational research on ability grouping in primary school classrooms Ireson and Hallam (2001) noted that some teachers drew far less attention to ability grouping within the classroom than other teachers did and this impacted on the way children perceived themselves. It could be argued that, as well as changing children's attributions, teachers' and schools' attributions and practices sometimes need to change. When teachers are puzzled, concerned or frustrated by a child's poor literacy performance they can sometimes mistakenly attribute this to laziness or general lack of ability and act in accordance with their beliefs. Teachers need support and appropriate training to give them insight and understanding into why a child is behaving in a certain way so they can develop constructive explanations which allow them to put positive strategies in place.

The long-term consequences of negative attributions, and low self-esteem at school

One particularly important question that arises is what the long-term effects of low self-esteem or negative attributions might be. Kosmos and Kidd (1991) carried out a study on the personality characteristics of adult dyslexics. They found that dyslexic women scored high on the 'pleasing others' scale and dyslexic men showed a lack of self-confidence, a tendency to self-defeating thoughts and questioning of their own ability to reach goals. These findings, it could be argued, fit with a poor self-concept or low self-esteem. Even if these results are replicated it still doesn't demonstrate that poor self-concept in adulthood is a result of earlier schooling, as it could be an outcome of difficulties that the adults are still facing, especially in the work situation. Susan Hampshire, the actor, recounts what happened when she was asked at the height of her fame and success to read a story on children's television. She had spent four days trying to learn this story word for word as she knew she would not be able to read it directly from the book whilst on camera. Despite her strong reservations because of her dyslexia her protests were waved aside and she started to be filmed reading from the book with the following consequences:

> I was now not only sweating, blind, uncoordinated and laughing inanely, but started to shake as well . . . In the pit of my stomach lay the pain of frustration and humiliation.

But methodologically these kinds of experiences are difficult to disentangle in terms of causation and Susan Hampshire herself relates these feelings in part to her childhood:

> Once inside the studio, the feeling of emptiness in my head that I had as a child returned. I looked at the book and I couldn't see it. The more I panicked the less I could see.

A danger of case studies is that, as with astrology, just the bits that fit the story might be picked out. But, as argued in Chapter 1, if they are used judiciously in conjunction with more empirical research they can add life and insight to bare figures. In the Kosmos and Kidd study, for example, it was claimed that dyslexic women scored higher than non-dyslexic women on the 'pleasing others' scale. More research would be needed to verify this but it does fit with Susan Hampshire's claim that as a child and to a lesser degree as an adult she desperately wanted to please others. The following three quotations on this issue are all from her autobiography:

> I desperately wanted to be liked and I assumed that no one could like someone as stupid as me.

> I wanted to please.

> If you are inventive, loving, always smiling and laughing, people will forget that you are stupid.

Preventing low self-esteem and raising low self-esteem in dyslexic children

As was demonstrated in Chapter 1, there is increasing evidence that the cognitive deficits underlying dyslexia are long term for more severely affected individuals and that spelling and writing are equally if not more difficult areas for them to master. This being the case, studies that look at the self-concept or self-esteem of dyslexics over an extended time period when they are struggling with these skills would add to our understanding of the relationship between self-concept and academic performance.

More general inclusive practices and dyslexia-friendly approaches can be seen as pro-active strategies which alongside appropriate individual learning support increase the chance of children developing a positive attribution style, high self-efficacy and a healthy level of self-esteem. This seems to be part of what is happening when dyslexic children are moved from a less supportive to a more supportive specialist dyslexia school environment with improvements in their self-esteem noted (Burden 2008, Thomson 1990). There is some evidence for this in mainstream schools as well. Ben, a child followed from 7 years of age (Riddick *et al.* 2002) had his self-esteem assessed on the Culture Free Self-Esteem Inventory (Battle 1992) at 7 years of age and again at 17 years. At 7 years of age his severe dyslexia was not acknowledged by his primary school and no appropriate support was offered. He had moved into a class with a teacher who was very critical of his work and had become distressed and anxious. Although he had a small group of friends he had poor motor skills so was often on the fringe of play-ground games. When observed in class by the educational psychologist he appeared to spend a lot of time off task and seemed very demoralised. After assessment he had several years of structured reading and later study skills intervention with positive support from a special needs teacher and his parents. He moved to a secondary school with a positive attitude to dyslexia. Here he was given a range of appropriate support and received particular encouragement from the English teacher, which increased his motivation and led to an improvement in his work. He started to feel a valued member of the school community and did outstandingly well in maths and science. At 17 years of age he commented spontaneously that his self-esteem was now much higher than it had been in the past (Table 3.2).

In this case as in Thomson's study there is a high score for parental self-esteem; in other words children feel valued and well regarded by their parents. Nugent (2008) and Singer (2005) also report that most dyslexic children feel their parents play a positive and supportive role and hold them in high esteem. These groups of children may not be representative of all children with dyslexia; they appear to have particularly concerned and well informed parents who have been pro-active in having them identified as dyslexic and/or in obtaining them appropriate support. Although in the minority, in studies like these, there are cases where dyslexic children or adults report that their parents are critical of their poor literacy development and school performance (Riddick *et al.* 1997, Singer 2005). We tentatively concluded in our study (Riddick *et al.* 1997) that parents with less experience of education and less understanding of dyslexia were more likely to adopt this stance. As with teachers this often seemed to be born out of

Table 3.2 Scores for Ben on the Culture Free Self-Esteem Inventory Form A (Battle 1992)

Self-esteem	Age 7	Age 17
General	Very low	High
Social	Low	High
Academic	Very Low	High
Parental	High	High

genuine concern and frustration at a child's poor academic performance and a lack of understanding of the reasons underlying this.

Although there is a large literature on parenting styles and the development of self-esteem in children within the context of the home environment, there is almost no research on how parents respond to the kind of low self-concept or esteem that appears to be related to learning difficulties at school. In the study to be described in this book, concern over low self-esteem and how to improve it was a major preoccupation of the majority of mothers in the study. This will be discussed in detail in Chapter 8 of this book.

Behavioural and emotional difficulties

There is a general consensus from a mixed body of research that, along with low self-esteem, some children with reading disabilities are more likely to have behavioural or emotional difficulties (PACFOLD 2007, Sanson 2006), although it should be emphasised that this does not apply to all dyslexic children. Evidence would suggest that overlap exists between these areas and that many of the methodological problems encountered in researching self-esteem are also evident in researching behavioural and emotional difficulties. Again much of the research has focused on children with a range of learning disabilities and not on children with dyslexia or specific reading difficulties. Differences in the criteria for identification, the sensitivity and appropriateness of the measuring instruments and the sampling strategy used probably account for the variability found in estimates of the prevalence of behavioural and emotional difficulties in children with reading difficulties. Some of the available data has come from samples of children referred for special educational or clinical intervention and the reliability of prevalence estimates based on these samples is open to question. Maughan (1994) provides a useful review of much of the research in this area in terms of both methodology and data, and the comments on methodology are still relevant today. She suggests that the most reliable estimates of prevalence rates generally come from epidemiological (whole population) studies although these are still open to problems of measurement and definition. The large-scale Isle of Wight epidemiological study found that a quarter of 10-year-old children with specific reading delay also displayed antisocial behaviour (Rutter, Tizard and Whitmore 1970). This immediately raised the question of whether poor reading led to antisocial behaviour or antisocial behaviour led to poor reading or if some common underlying factor such as social deprivation or cognitive deficits was related to both sets of difficulties. They found that the reading-delayed children with antisocial behaviour were similar in many respects to the reading-delayed children without behavioural difficulties and bore less resemblance to the children who just displayed antisocial behaviour. This was taken as evidence that behavioural difficulties were generally secondary to reading difficulties. This kind of study says little about the processes that lead from reading to behavioural difficulties so more recent studies of a prospective longitudinal design have been used to look at the development over time of behavioural and emotional difficulties as well as providing further evidence on prevalence rates. These studies have followed children from before they enter school or on entry to school over a number of years (Jorm et al. 1986, McGee et al. 1988, Pianta and Caldwell 1990). Overall these studies have found an increasing correlation between reading difficulties and behavioural problems over the primary school period. They also found that in the early and middle primary school years these difficulties mainly took the form of inattentiveness and restlessness and that overt behavioural difficulties in the form of conduct disorders were less frequent at this age although they increased somewhat by late primary. These findings fit well with accounts by dyslexic children and their parents of their experiences at school:

> I want to be like invisible, I just cut myself off.
>
> (Riddick 1995b)

> Eventually I'd sort of turn off and dream my way through the day. Actually that's quite easy to do if you're undisturbed for long enough. You get almost catatonic. I don't think that it helped that I was always very well behaved, very quiet. So no one took any notice.
>
> (Osmond 1993)

> So I just used to sit there and sort of dream and look out of the window . . . Nothing was interesting to me. I became withdrawn and bored and sort of put my mind on hold. I felt very isolated and alone.
>
> (Osmond 1993)

> She told me he sometimes deliberately broke the point of his pencil 10 times a day.
>
> (Van der Stoel 1990)

> I was for ever being told off and was the laughing stock of the class. Turns at reading aloud were a disaster. Well then I really threw in the towel! I'm quite a spitfire and my self control went completely.
>
> (Van der Stoel 1990)

In the Bruck (1985) inner-London study, which looked at a clinical sample of learning-disabled children from socially disadvantaged backgrounds, it was found that 85 per cent were rated as having poor adjustment during the school years when compared with a control group of non-learning-disabled children. Spreen's 1987 study reported similar findings. In both cases it was found that adjustment problems had significantly decreased by adulthood, suggesting that they were closely related to children's experiences in school. Heiervang *et al.* (2001) compared the behaviour of 25 dyslexic children aged 10–12 years with a matched control group of non-dyslexic children on the Child Behaviour Checklist (CBCL), Teacher Self Report (TRF) and Youth Self-Report (YSR). The dyslexic group had significantly higher scores on the CBCL and the TRF and the authors concluded that dyslexic children displayed a range of behaviour problems that could not be ascribed to their social background or upbringing. Coupled with previous studies this suggests that if the needs of dyslexic children have not been met by 10–12 years of age their increasing frustration and/or demoralisation leads to them playing up or withdrawing in response to a seemingly hostile learning environment.

Another finding from the longitudinal studies is that some reading-disabled children show behavioural difficulties before they enter formal schooling (Sanson 2006). Whether these behavioural difficulties are a concomitant of the pre-reading linguistic difficulties that a proportion of reading delayed children have or they are due to other factors such as adverse social environment is as yet not clear. At present there is considerable interest and debate over the co-occurrence of learning disabilities with behaviour problems and particularly ADHD (Cutting and Denckla 2003). What is apparent is that the linkage between reading and behavioural difficulties is a complex one, which will probably reveal multiple causation and interactional effects. Nonetheless the evidence in general, corroborated by personal accounts, suggests that some primary-age children will present with overt behaviour problems but that more are likely to present as well behaved, quiet and compliant although they have detached themselves from much of the learning process. It is these unengaged children, many would claim, who are easier to overlook especially in large or demanding classes.

Hales (1994) suggests that in the past the social and emotional consequences of dyslexia have been underestimated and that research that has treated dyslexics as 'broken learning machines' has given us only a partial understanding of what dyslexia entails. Hales administered a personality questionnaire (16 PF; Cattell *et al.* 1970) to a group of 300 people with dyslexia aged from 6 years to over 18 years with the majority being of school age.

He cautions that it would be naive to expect there to be a specific dyslexic personality but he argues that this research can give us some indications of how individuals with dyslexia develop over time. He found that early school age children had scores which indicated that they were tense and frustrated, in the middle school years scores indicated low motivation and high anxiety, and at secondary school the scores indicated a desire to keep in the background. Hales also found that during the middle school years there was a noticeable drop in confidence and optimism, especially among girls, which mirrors more recent findings (Ingesson 2007). One of the most striking findings overall was the inverse relationship between anxiety and IQ, with low-IQ children from middle school years onwards tending to have higher levels of anxiety. This counters the myth that is sometimes subscribed to that 'intelligent' children suffer more and underlines the importance of not having assumptions about how particular groups of children will respond to dyslexia. Hales speculates that more intelligent children may be more sympathetically treated by the world or they may be able to develop better coping strategies. Further research is needed to corroborate these findings but they do show that we need to know more about how children with dyslexia develop over time.

The effect of emotion and mood on thinking

Given the low self-esteem and high anxiety in literacy tasks and arithmetic that is often reported for individuals with dyslexia, it is surprising that cognitive psychologists researching in this area haven't looked at this issue more closely. Research by Dutke and Stoebber (2001), for example, found that high test anxiety impaired performance and Darke (1988) and Owens (2008) reported that working memory was particularly affected by anxiety. As poor working memory is already considered to be a key part of the processing difficulties that dyslexic children encounter it seems likely that anxiety will further impair their performance. Yasutake and Bryan (1995) give a useful review of some of the research in this area and conclude that positive affect (emotion) can enhance children's performance on tasks such as learning new vocabulary and doing maths and that negative affect can detract from their performance. They claim that for learning-disabled children (the US term closest to specific learning difficulties) the benefits of positive affect are particularly large and suggest that simple strategies to increase positive affect could be used in the classroom. In two studies by Bryan and Bryan (1991) it was claimed that simply getting children to close their eyes and think of something 'wonderful' for 45 seconds improved their performance on 50 maths sums compared with children who were asked to count to 50. It may well be that some teachers already use similar strategies in the classroom. One particularly good and positive teacher of grade 2 children explained how she attempted to make spelling tests less stressful by trying to convince all the children in her class that they really enjoyed them!

Looking in detail at life histories, case studies and interviews

The great strength of these approaches is that they can give a holistic and long-term account of an individual's life. A criticism can be that they emphasise a within-person perspective, but examination of these accounts reveals that much of the focus is on how individuals see environmental factors impinging on them. Cognitive deficits/differences are usually raised only in relation to various environmental demands such as learning to read and spell. Miles (2006) has warned against the danger of confusing primary and secondary difficulties. If a child with a primary cognitive impairment has difficulty learning to read and in response to this goes on to develop behavioural difficulties, it is important that the behavioural difficulties be not then seen as the primary cause of the child's reading difficulties, although by now they may well be a strong contributory factor. On the uncluttered world of the page this might seem an insultingly obvious point but in the messier world of the classroom such issues can become more confused. One mother in the study to be described recounted a clear example of this. She was a primary school teacher herself and was aware that her son was having immense difficulty learning to read and write, although at that point he had not been identified as dyslexic. At 7 years of age he had a new teacher who was not sympathetic to his problems, he became very distressed and his behaviour at school deteriorated:

> It got to the stage where I heard myself saying as my little boy cried himself to sleep at night, 'It's not long now' (to the end of term).

He started wetting the bed, and came home shaking if he had a spelling test to revise for the following day. His bad behaviour at school was frequently reported to his mother:

> The problem was by then you couldn't see the wood for the trees because the behaviour problems had become paramount.

Harry's mother suggested to the teacher that Harry's behaviour might partly be a response to a learning difficulty of some kind and was told:

Rubbish, he's just very immature, when he learns to behave properly and knuckles down to the work he'll be OK.

The following year when Harry was 8 years old he had a teacher who was more sympathetic in her outlook. She realised in conjunction with Harry's mother that something underlay the bad behaviour that he was displaying in class. By half term she had identified him as dyslexic and appropriate support was set in place. From this point Harry's behaviour started to improve again.

Although a life history approach cannot be used in an empirical sense to 'prove' cause and effect it can suggest what might be happening and guide teachers and parents in checking out their suspicions or hunches. It can be argued that a life history approach is a useful adjunct to a curriculum-based approach that focuses on the learning difficulties that a child is having at a specific point in time. Children bring to a learning situation their past experiences, emotions and expectations, and by understanding these it is easier to get a wider picture of what might be happening. The problem for many teachers is that they don't automatically have access to a child's life history and what they do know may be second-hand and filtered through the school's perceptions of the child's past experiences. Harry, for example, had an August birthday and therefore was a little immature for his year group. In addition some of the cognitive deficits underlying dyslexia such as problems with sequencing led to difficulties with tasks such as tying up shoelaces, which added to the picture of a somewhat immature child. The problem was that this was then used exclusively to account for his disruptive behaviour whereas a fuller picture, which showed that he was reasonably well behaved in pre-school and grade 1 and responded well to supportive and encouraging teaching, would have suggested that immaturity alone was not a sufficient explanation for his behaviour. In addition his mother's reports of his specific difficulty with reading tasks and the distress that they were causing him would suggest that this area needed investigating.

Life history inevitably involves bias and self-selection of what is presented and this can cause problems of validity and belief for both teachers and parents. This is made more difficult because they are observing children in totally different environments to which children may respond in different ways. Many of the parents in the study reported in this book and in other case studies said that their dyslexic child became quiet and withdrawn when they entered school. But this was often not noticed by the school because they had not seen the child before school or in the home environment so from the school's point of view the child's behaviour was normal and not a cause for concern. Again many parents reported that their child was showing distress at home as a direct consequence of going to school but it was difficult for the school to take this on board as the child was not showing this distress to a noticeable degree at school. The old adage 'seeing is believing' seems to apply and can perhaps explain some of the difficulty parents and especially teachers have in believing one another. The following is a typical account given by many parents on the difference in their child at school and at home:

He became a withdrawn, frightened, timid child at school. But once he was at home he was completely different. He'd be full of confidence and happy once he was outside, playing with his motorbike.

(Osmond 1993)

Edwards (1994) documents in detail the lives of eight teenage boys attending a boarding school for children with dyslexia. In a sense it can be argued that these boys ended up in boarding school because they were extreme cases in terms of their reactions to mainstream school, with all eight displaying behaviour problems and seven of the eight truanting. Edwards points out that she originally chose these boys as examples of 'successful dyslexics' who had developed well in their special school and was shocked herself when she started interviewing them to find the degree of pain and humiliation these boys still felt over their past experiences. They all felt they had been neglected, humiliated and teased in their mainstream schools and five of them felt they had been treated unfairly or punitively by teachers. In all eight cases this had led to lack of confidence, self-doubt and sensitivity to criticism and in five cases boys reported that at the worst points in their school career they had felt extremely isolated and despairing, often wanting to hide or die. These same themes of distress and humiliation run through the interviews reported by Osmond and Van der Stoel and these sorts of experiences were not uncommon in the study to be described in this book. Although the degree and the range of such difficulties can be debated it is clear that how dyslexic children and their families cope with dyslexia is closely related to how such children are treated in school.

Summary

1   Both quantitative and qualitative methods have a role to play in researching the social and emotional consequences of dyslexia.
2   For most dyslexic children reading, writing and spelling are their primary problems but these can lead to secondary problems such as inattentiveness, low motivation, restlessness or disruptive behaviour.
3   Reading-disabled children do as a group have lower self-esteem than non-reading-disabled children.
4   Teachers have a strong influence on a child's self-concept as a learner.
5   Systematic strategies can be employed to improve a child's self-esteem and self-concept as a learner.
6   Dyslexic children need specific help for their literacy difficulties allied to general help for their social and emotional well being.

Chapter 4

Introducing the study

Phenomenology as a research approach attempts to study human experience as it is lived.
(Layder 1993)

As has already been pointed out in this book there appears to be less systematic research on the social and emotional consequences of dyslexia despite the indications from personal accounts that some children and adults with dyslexia do experience such difficulties. One reason for this may be that social and emotional difficulties are more difficult to quantify and much might depend on the sensitivity of the measures used. Another reason which applies to many areas of special needs is that the majority of research is carried out by academics and educationalists. It can be argued that inevitably their own role and perspective influences the kinds of questions they choose to ask and the kind of research they carry out. From the perspective of school and cognitive psychology it is the difficulty in learning to read, write and spell that is probably most striking. In contrast children and parents are not generally in a position to carry out or inform academic research so issues of particular concern to them may not be adequately researched. Oliver (1981) criticised much academic research on disability on these grounds and argued for the voices of disabled people to be heard so they could set their own agenda in terms of the research that needed to be carried out. Disability studies has made a powerful contribution to how disabilities/differences are conceptualised and has challenged mainstream culture to make changes which reduce the barriers for disabled people and respond to their particular needs (Shakespeare 2006, Barnes and Mercer 2007). This ideology has in turn had some influence on the culture of education and the development of inclusive practices (Barton 2007). In recent research children with a diverse range of disabilities and special needs and their families have been consulted (Lewis *et al.* 2007, Woolfon *et al.* 2007) about their experiences of learning. This research based on an inclusive ideology has been helpful in mapping out the commonalities between children with differing and overlapping SENs and informing the principles of inclusive practice. On the other hand, because it has reported on the perspectives of very mixed groups of children without distinguishing between them, the aspects of need that tend to be related to a specific difficulty such as dyslexia, autism or deafness are not well delineated. Radical critics would also argue that, however sensitively done, the researchers are still setting the agenda and deciding the kinds of questions that should be asked. In response to this sort of criticism case studies have been gathered in which individuals have been allowed to speak for themselves and no set questions have been imposed upon them (Campling 1981). With increased use of information technology individuals with dyslexia have made their voices heard through internet discussion groups and blogs and it could be argued that this has democratised the process. Despite these developments there are concerns that the views of a vocal minority might dominate the landscape and may not represent the wide range of views of individuals with dyslexia. The issue of whose voice gets heard and how to moderate this process is one that applies to all attempts to encapsulate or represent the 'voice' of a specific group of individuals. Informal case studies such as those on dyslexia by Osmond (1993) and Van der Stoel (1990), although valuable, did not employ a systematic sampling policy and were thus open to the criticism that the views of an unrepresentative sample were being heard. In the case of dyslexia in the past it was often suggested that the views of middle-class parents and their children predominated although recent studies (Ingesson 2007, MacDonald 2006, Singer 2005, Pollak 2005) including the one in this book have been careful to draw on more representative samples or to redress the balance by focusing on 'non-traditional' students or students from poorer socio-economic backgrounds. Similarly the welter of evidence from clinical case studies, parents' letters and so on on the social and emotional consequences of dyslexia is all open to the charge of unrepresentativeness. Another difficulty is that, because some local authorities do not recognise dyslexia, it is only by parents taking the initiative to have their children assessed outside the formal educational system that their children are identified. But again critics would claim that such parents are 'pushy, neurotic and overambitious' and their views are not representative of parents as a whole. The problem has been that, in quite rightly criticising the lack of representativeness, some critics have dismissed the evidence completely rather than seeing it as a starting point for more systematic research. As Riddell, Brown and Duffield (1994) found in their Scottish-based survey of special needs, obtaining a representative sample of children with dyslexia was easier said than done. They found that because many local authorities were critical of the term 'dyslexia', children had not been identified on this basis and it was therefore difficult to obtain a representative sample of such children. Only in a case where a local authority has a clear and comprehensive policy for identifying and supporting children with dyslexia is it possible to obtain a representative sample of children. The purpose of the present study was to investigate the currently more commonplace situation of children who are identified and supported either partly or entirely outside the local authority system.

Although many opinions are offered by professionals (Riddick 1995a) as to why parents choose to call their children dyslexic, there appears to be little research to back up their suppositions. One of the major aims of the present study was thus *to look closely at the process by which children are identified and labelled as having dyslexia*. Another related aim was *to gain a clear understanding of how living with dyslexia appears from the individual perspectives of children and their parents*. And a final aim was *to explore the possible social and emotional consequences of having dyslexia*.

The main study involved interviewing 22 children and separately interviewing their mothers, leading to a total of 44 interviews. In both cases a standardised semi-structured interview schedule was used. Madge and Fassam (1982) used a similar methodology to learn about the lives of physically disabled children and made the following comment on their use of a direct interview technique: 'First of all we found that valuable information on the attitudes, experiences and needs of physically disabled children can be gained from asking direct questions.'

Both Greenspan (1981) and Hodges (1993) consider that structured interviews can be used as a way of assessing the well being of children and adolescents. Greenspan argues that parents and children's reports should not be looked upon as interchangeable and that ideally separate information should be obtained from both sources. Greenspan also asserts that children and adolescents can reliably self-report and that the accuracy of this has been verified by checking children's accounts with information from someone who knows the child well. Lewis *et al.* (2007) report on the value and validity of listening to children's views as part of a series of studies they carried out for the Disability Rights Commission. They also raise the important question of who listens to or attends to the views that children express. In recruiting children for the study it was made clear that this was their choice and that they were free to say no or to withdraw from the study if they had second thoughts. Children were also informed that their views would be published and several commented that they were keen for their views to be known and this was a major motivation for them taking part.

In the main study children ranged in age from 8 to 14 years. They all had a discrepancy of at least 2 years between their reading and/or spelling age and their chronological age or scored below the fifth percentile on the Wide Range Achievement Test (WRAT) reading and/or spelling test. All the children were assessed either by local authority educational psychologists or by chartered clinical psychologists. They all attended either the Newcastle or the Durham branch of the Dyslexia Institute (now known as Dyslexia Action) for 1 or 2 hours of specialist tuition a week, usually out of school time. All the children attended mainstream school for their full-time education. Ten were at primary school, one was at middle school and 11 were at lower secondary school. Children attended 20 different schools located in six different Local Education Authorities. The children were all white and of British origin, which reflected the intake of the Dyslexia Institute and the predominantly white population of the north east. The high ratio of boys to girls again reflected the intake of the Dyslexia Institute and the ratio that is usually reported for individuals with dyslexia. Of the 22 families 12 were classified as middle class and 10 were classified as working class. Three of the families were headed by a single-parent mother and the children had no contact with their fathers. Children ranged in IQ on the Wechsler Intelligence Scale for Children from 92 to 128 with a mean of 110.

This sample was chosen to be as representative as possible of the children attending the Dyslexia Institute and was not intentionally biased in favour of any particular sub-group. Twenty-two of the 23 families approached for the main part of the study agreed to take part. One mother refused, because although she was keen to be interviewed herself she felt that her son had been so distressed in the past by the difficulties he had associated with his dyslexia that he disliked talking about the subject and it was never directly discussed at home. As well as the three fatherless families, several fathers worked away from home for long periods of time (for example, in the navy or on oil rigs) and several more worked away from home for shorter periods of time (for example, on business). It was also the case that it was almost entirely mothers in this sample who brought their children to the Dyslexia Institute for sessions and they stated that their husbands, although generally concerned, had little day-to-day involvement in the issues surrounding their child's dyslexia. For these reasons mothers alone were interviewed although fathers were not specifically excluded, and their views were discussed during the interviews.

The information in Table 4.1 is basic information that was collected on all the children. Detailed psychological reports itemising children's cognitive difficulties in more detail were available, but lack of space and confidentiality mean that only occasional points from these are included. The WISC-R (Wechsler Intelligence Scale for Children – Revised) is a popular assessment tool because as well as giving an overall IQ score it also gives separate Verbal and Performance IQ scores. These two areas in turn are made up of a number of sub-tests.

Table 4.1 Basic information on the main study sample of children with dyslexia at the time of their interview

Child	M/F	Age on interview	Age on assessment	Reading age	Spelling age	IQ WISC	School	Affected relative
DG	M	12.6	11.10	6.10	8	113	J	?
JK	M	9.11	10.7	WRAT 12%	WRAT 1%	92	J	YES
SH	M	8.5	7.7	5.9	5.7	105	J	YES
SW	F	13.9	13.5	10.0	WRAT 4%	100	S	?
RS	M	11.8	11.1	8.3	8.3	106	S	YES
HW	M	8.6	8.3	WRAT 1%	WRAT 7%	123	J	YES
AR	M	10.6	7.6	6.0	>5	128	J	YES
DSt	M	13.3	9.11	8.5	7.11	123	S	YES
DSl	M	11.11	9.9	6.6	6.5	95	J	YES
GS	M	11.3	10.6	9.2	8.4	120	J	YES
LS	M	13.11	12.5	10.0	8.9	avg*	S	YES
EB	M	13.2	11.10	6.9	>5	avg*	S	YES
EC	F	11.8	11.1	8.3	8.3	106	J	YES
MK	M	10.6	8.0	6.0	5.11	avg*	J	YES
MC	M	9.11	8.2	<5	5.10	92	J	YES
RT	M	11.5	10.6	8.11	8.6	avg*	S	NO
JA	M	13.1	10.0	7.0	7.0	119	S	NO
SH	M	11.9	9.9	7.9	7.0	106	S	YES
KP	M	12.4	10.5	7.9	–	126	S	YES
MF	F	11.9	11.1	6.8	8.2	107	S	YES
LA	F	12..0	11.2	9.1	9.0	105	S	YES
SS	M	14.3	11.2	8.9	7.8	113	S	YES

Notes
* Some psychologists preferred to give the band an IQ score fell into rather than a specific figure.
? under *Affected relative* refers to two cases where there had been no contact with the child's father or family so this information was not known.

Peer (1994) claims that what is striking on tests such as the WISC, the Binet and the BAS (British Ability Scales) is that children with dyslexia often show an uneven or 'spiky' profile. With the WISC each sub-test is given a scaled score out of 20, with 10 being an average score. A variety of profiles are found, with the ACID profile being considered one of the more typical. In the ACID profile poor arithmetical, digit span, coding and information skills are found. These are attributed to the child's poor working memory and poor visuo-motor skills. High scores in other areas such as comprehension, similarities and block design suggest good abstract reasoning. RT, a child not included in the main sample, achieved the scores given with the sub-tests when tested at 7 years 2 days on the WISC-R (Table 4.2). Interestingly he commented spontaneously that he had remembered the numbers in the digit span test by saying them in twos to himself – a strategy which is known to improve digit span performance! His mother also noted that at 5 years he still couldn't count to 10 and at 7 he still didn't know his telephone number or his two times table, which had been taught at school. This raises the question of whether RT used a compensatory strategy to improve his performance on the digit span test. It also illustrates the importance of pooling information from a number of sources and not making decisions on the basis of single test scores, which can be influenced by a wide range of factors. The question of different profiles is still an area of some debate but the general point is that uneven profiles like RT's do indicate marked areas of strength and weakness which may lead to puzzling school performance. Siegel points out that an equal number of non-dyslexic children have uneven scores on the WISC, which suggests that we should not overinterpret such differences and that tests that look more closely at processing skills and specific literacy tasks may be of more value (Reid and Wearmouth 2009).

The interview schedule

Children, parents and teachers were talked to on an informal basis to ascertain major issues before the interview schedules were devised. Both specialist teachers and parents were consulted about the suitability of the content and arrangement of questions for the children's schedule. Greenspan (1981) on the basis of 10 years' research claims that children can be interviewed about personal and emotive topics without any negative effects as long as the interviews are well conducted and take place within a supportive environment. The schedules were then piloted on five mother–child pairs before being used in the main part of the study. As one of the purposes of the study was to

Table 4.2 Sub-tests of the WISC-R

Verbal		Performance	
Information	14	Picture completion	13
Comprehension	19	Picture arrangement	13
Arithmetic	10	Block design	17
Similarities	19	Object assembly	15
Vocabulary	13	Coding	10
Digit span	16	Mazes	17

look at both the differences and the similarities in the perspectives of children and mothers, questions were designed with this in mind. So, for example, both children and their mothers were asked a number of identical questions such as how would they explain dyslexia to someone else. In addition both children and mothers were asked questions that were specific to their role and perspective. Mothers, for example, were asked how they had first heard about dyslexia and what sort of personal support they tried to offer their children, whereas children were asked questions about whether they thought other children noticed their difficulties and, if so, if they tried to explain them. A mixture of open-ended, fixed alternative, factual and scaled questions were asked. The purpose was to obtain qualitative data, backed up by some simple descriptive and quantitative information. So, for example, mothers were asked, 'In general how do you feel at the moment about (child's name) having dyslexia?' They were also asked fixed alternative questions such as 'What influence, if any, do you think being dyslexic has had on (child's name)?'

'None/some/a lot.' Probes were also added so that qualitative information could also be obtained from questions like these, but these were rarely needed as most respondents spontaneously explained their choice of category. By having a mixture of questions simple cross-checking of information was possible. Miles and Huberman (1994) suggest that simple forms of counting are a useful way of checking that qualitative data is being represented and interpreted as accurately as possible. Validity was also checked by triangulation between teachers', parents' and children's responses and by comparing information with that available from reports and documents. Mothers were asked a total of 36 questions, covering early development, identification, support at home and at school, specialist support, effects on the child and family, and expectations for the future. Children were asked 28 major questions covering home life, difficulties related to dyslexia, support at home, school and Dyslexia Institute, views on dyslexia and how they thought other children viewed their problems. (See Appendix for the full parent's and child's interview schedule.) Whenever data is presented giving the number or proportion of children or mothers who reported a certain thing this is always from this main study. Most of the quotes used to illustrate these figures are also from this main study. Both children and parents were given the choice of being interviewed either at the Dyslexia Institute or at home.

Parents gave their permission for access to educational and psychological reports and assessments. Because these were of a confidential nature they have not been directly quoted from but have been used to provide background information. The names of all the children and parents have been changed to protect their identity. Several mothers said that they were quite happy to be named and to stand by the views they had expressed but it was thought best to have an overall policy of anonymity for all those who participated. For similar reasons schools, local authorities and teachers have not been named and where necessary names have been changed.

All five teachers at the Dyslexia Institute the children attended were interviewed and some of their views are reported where they are relevant to general issues about 'living with dyslexia'. Five children in their mid-teens and their mothers were interviewed in a later study. The same basic interview schedule was used but an additional section on subjects such as exams and technology was added. These five young people had also attended the Dyslexia Institute and had been identified and assessed in a similar manner to the main study. In total data from 59 semi-structured interviews is included (see Table 4.3).

Table 4.3 Interviewees

Semi-structured interviews	
Children (aged 8 to 16 years)	24
Mothers	24
Specialist teachers	5

A small amount of information from informal interviews with class teachers and educational psychologists has been included when it has been of particular relevance to a specific child or issue. In a university-based study students with dyslexia were interviewed and assessed on a number of measures including self-esteem, anxiety, writing performance and educational performance (Riddick *et al.* 1997, 1999). Occasional points of relevance have been included. Similarly qualitative information from students and adults during assessment for dyslexia has been included. Data on another child, RT, who has been followed for a number of years and for this reason was not included in the main study, is also occasionally given. The original interview schedule was replicated with families currently attending Dyslexia Action and two families just receiving support for dyslexia in the mainstream school. There were no marked differences in their overall responses and experiences from those reported in the original interviews so these have not been reported in detail although occasional relevant experiences are included.

Although a semi-structured interview schedule was used the number of open questions combined with the chronological arrangement of them led to a strong narrative thread emerging from many of them. A drawback of question-by-question analysis or thematic analysis is that the overall coherence or power of these 'stories' may be lost. In order to represent some of these stories the case studies in Chapter 12 present shortened versions of full interviews. Smith and Sparkes (2008) suggest that a variety of approaches to analysing narrative in the field of disability should be employed to give as full an understanding as possible of the complexities of people's lives.

Chapter 5

Early indicators

I just knew something was wrong but I didn't know what it was.
(Mother of 5-year-old boy with dyslexia)

Given the controversy over dyslexia and the many informal explanations given by professionals of why parents call their children dyslexic (Riddick 1995a) an important part of the study was to look in detail at how and why parents came to identify their children as dyslexic. As with many disabilities that do not have easily identifiable physical markers it appears that the process by which parents do this is often a gradual one that takes place over a period of time. In order to try and follow this process a roughly chronological perspective was followed in asking questions (see Appendix for the full parental questionnaire) and in presenting the information a roughly chronological framework has been used. In order to give a coherent explanation to some questions mothers would shift between the past, present and future and in presenting the evidence maintaining this has sometimes been necessary. Where possible the information has also been placed within the context of other research on identifying both dyslexia and special needs in general.

Relatives with dyslexia

As a prelude to asking about early indicators, parents were asked if any close family members had dyslexia or similar problems. As has already been discussed in Chapter 1 there is strong evidence that a predisposition to phonological difficulties and subsequent dyslexia is inherited in something like 70–80 per cent of cases (Gilger and Wilkins 2008, De Fries 1991). This is an active area of research, so these figures are best viewed as provisional and open to future revision, but the principle of high heritability does raise some important questions about its significance in identifying dyslexia. If, for example, a parent has been identified as dyslexic does this mean that the family are more likely to identify any of their children who have similar problems at an early age? In a similar vein does this information on heritability alert professionals to the increased risk of reading and spelling disorders that some children run?

Finally, what is the personal significance for children with dyslexia of having an adult relative, and especially a parent, who is dyslexic? This last issue will be examined in more detail in Chapter 11 on personal support. In response to the general question

Table 5.1 A close relative with dyslexia or similar problem (*n* = 22)

Yes	18
No	2
Not known	2[a]

a Two mothers were single parents who had had no contact with their child's biological father or family since the child's birth.

about family members with dyslexia or similar problems the following information was given.

In six cases a father and in five cases a mother of a dyslexic child were claimed to be dyslexic or to have had similar difficulties. Thus 50 per cent of children were being brought up in families where one parent was thought to have had similar problems as a child. In some cases several members of a family were identified as having reading and spelling difficulties. Uncles, aunts, cousins and siblings of the dyslexic child were all mentioned several times. This evidence is not being offered in a strictly empirical sense, as most of it is inferential, but it does offer some insight into the way that lay people characterise and identify difficulties. In 17 of the 18 cases the adult was identified as possibly dyslexic only after the related child was formally identified as dyslexic. In two cases mothers had been formally assessed after their children were identified and in both cases they were confirmed as dyslexic. In the rest of the cases more informal evidence was offered. Where mothers thought that their husbands had had similar difficulties they would often recount that their husband had hated school, had not learnt to read until late and was still an appalling speller:

> His dad can't spell and he had a lot of problems in school. He hated school from day one, you know, and he can understand how he really feels. Sarah, his sister, had extra reading in junior school and her spelling is still very poor.

> My younger brother had severe spelling and writing difficulties at Harry's age [8 years] and became a truant.

> His dad really. His spelling is dreadful. He didn't get any exams at school.

> I think my brother had a problem. But obviously it was never detected. He had difficulty with reading, but basically it's his spelling. It's atrocious.

> My husband has terrible spelling. He was ten before he learnt to read. He hated school and he left the moment he could.

Two wives mentioned that their husbands had changed jobs specifically because of their literacy difficulties and another wife said she did her husband's paperwork because of his literacy difficulties. In some cases the husband's difficulties were openly discussed and acknowledged at home but in other cases, although wives had strong suspicions, their husbands did not openly acknowledge their problems. Mothers with dyslexia spoke quite openly about their own difficulties and recalled specific examples of the kinds of difficulties they encountered in school:

> I had great problems from that (copying off the board) at school. I can remember everybody else going out to play and I was still sitting there copying it down and I think that's something they don't realise.

Mrs Harding also recalled similar difficulties with copying off the board:

> Oh it was horrific. I'd get the wrong line down, then I'd score it out.

She recounted her own difficulties in writing letters to her husband in the forces and her determination to improve her spelling and writing. At school she had acted the class clown and tried to cover up her difficulties with reading and writing as much as possible:

> I bluffed my way through school cos you couldn't dare admit you couldn't do it. I'd love to get myself assessed. It's not because you've got nothing upstairs. If I've got a form to fill in I always take it home and do it. But I find I'm getting a bit better. I build on what I've got.

So for half the families in this sample, although the term 'dyslexia' had not been used in the past, at least one parent had experienced similar difficulties and in all these cases spelling was still considered to be a problem. In many cases mothers spoke of dyslexia in a way that implied that they saw it as on a continuum. Mrs Street, who had a dyslexic son and had been identified as dyslexic herself, also commented on her daughter's difficulties:

> My daughter has difficulty with spelling. I'd say she's slightly dyslexic.

> Her middle sister has slight reading and spelling problems but the other two are OK.

> Well, I'm a weak speller and Emily, that's his younger sister, has weak spelling compared to her other abilities.

Mothers thus appeared to distinguish between siblings who had no problems, siblings with slight problems and siblings with severe problems. There was also some concern over whether younger siblings were going to have the same difficulties, especially if they appeared to be following a similar developmental pattern. In considering identification it would therefore seem important to recognise that in a substantial proportion of families this takes place not on a 'blank canvas' but against a background of experience of similar difficulties. None of the parents knew about the heritability of such difficulties before their child was identified as dyslexic so this experience was not explicitly used by families to help identify their child as dyslexic.

Early speech delay and difficulties

Orton (1937) claimed that speech delay and stuttering were more common than usual in a sample of dyslexic individuals examined by him. The Isle of Wight study (Rutter *et al.* 1976) found that speech milestones were more commonly delayed in children with specific reading delay. Snowling and Stackhouse (2006) present evidence to support the claim that dyslexia should be viewed as a type of speech and language disorder. They both consider that, whereas some dyslexic children present with obvious and specific language difficulties in their earlier years, for others the difficulties are more subtle and difficult to identify. At present the degree of overlap between children with specific language impairment and children with reading and spelling problems is not clear. Stackhouse (1991) says:

> It would be wrong to suggest that all children with reading and spelling problems have a speech and language disorder and it would be equally wrong to give the impression that all children with speech and language problems will also have a specific learning difficulty.

She goes on to suggest that the children who are most at risk of having reading and spelling problems are either those with developmental vocal dyspraxia (difficulty in saying words despite no obvious physical impairment) or those with phonological disorders who have difficulties contrasting sounds in order to distinguish between spoken words. This was of relevance to the present study because 7 of the 22 mothers said that their child had some form of early language difficulty.

Mothers were asked two major questions about early identification. One question centred on when they first became aware there was a problem and what the nature of the problem was, the other on their child's development prior to their being aware there was a problem. So the second question (2a) specifically asked:

> Looking back were there any earlier signs that (child's name) might have difficulties?

This question was basically asking mothers if with the benefit of hindsight they could identify any earlier difficulties that they thought had a bearing on the specific reading difficulties that they all identified as the first real problem that their child encountered at school.

As can be seen from Table 5.2 a simple head count was made of the different difficulties mentioned by mothers. Most of these mothers were being asked to recall their child's development from several years previously and it therefore seems likely that these figures might be an underestimate rather than an overestimate. Alternatively it could be the case that people unconsciously add information that fits a certain picture. But evidence such as early reports, and the fact that four of the seven children were claimed to have early language delay and did in fact receive speech and language therapy, would suggest some degree of accuracy in mothers' recall:

> Well first of all he didn't start talking until he was two and a half, and then he went to speech therapy for six years. Because he had problems with his pronunciation and his fluency.

> He was very late talking. He must have been two and three quarters before he was putting a sentence together.

Table 5.2 Mothers' recall of early developmental problems which with hindsight they think relate to dyslexia

Developmental problem	n =22
Difficulties learning days of week/months of year	13
Clumsy	9
Late learning to ride a bike or swim	8
Difficulties learning nursery rhymes	7
Difficulties learning the alphabet	7
Late talker	7
Poor at remembering instructions	4

> She wasn't talking at two, apart from a few simple words like 'mum' and 'dad'. We put it down to all the ear infections she'd had.

> He only had a few single words by two and his speech was never very clear, so then he had speech therapy.

This evidence is not being presented as strict empirical evidence but simply to suggest that parents can identify a range of impairments before they formally recognise that their child is having difficulty learning to read and write. Fawcett and Nicolson (2008), whilst acknowledging the importance of the relationship between phonological deficits and dyslexia, argue that we might be premature in simply identifying one specific deficit and that this in turn may be the outcome of more general processing deficits that affect a number of skills, or may be only one of a number of deficits. They go on to suggest that a more 'ethological' approach, which looks at the kind of difficulties that children display on a day-to-day basis, is an important adjunct to more empirical research. 'Those who have round the clock experience of living with dyslexic children often form a very different view of their skills than do researchers who see them only for a brief testing period.'

They also point out that, in Augur's (1985) summary of the kinds of difficulties mentioned by parents as well as language difficulties, motor difficulties were common. In the present study it can be seen that, although language difficulties are the most frequently mentioned, a significant number of children are also thought to have had motor difficulties in their early years:

> He was clumsy, very clumsy. He used to fall off chairs and things. We used to laugh about it, but looking back at it, it was probably symptomatic somehow. It was just one of those things, he was a clumsy child, couldn't learn to ride a bike and things like that . . . Couldn't clap in time or remember his nursery rhymes.

Whereas some children were described as having a whole range of difficulties in other cases mothers were quite emphatic about the kinds of difficulties their child did not have:

He couldn't learn the alphabet, couldn't learn days of the week, his tables he still doesn't know [age 12] and just very poor short-term memory, but he's always been very well co-ordinated.

He had a good memory for some things, but nursery rhymes and things like that he couldn't do.

It took a long time for him to learn to ride a bike. He spoke pretty quickly, every-thing like that. The main thing I found with David, if you asked him to do some-thing, to go and fetch something, he'd come back and say, 'What did you want?' I could never train him to do that . . . He would get mixed up with the days of the week and say, 'Thursday, Wednesday,' but he was able to tell the time very quickly.

He was laid back in everything. He was late walking, late talking. He'd choose the shortest way to say anything.

Apart from those children who had severe language difficulties, parents didn't appear to view their children's pre-school impairments as a major problem or an indi-cator of future difficulty. Within the context of the family it appears that most of these impairments were easily accommodated and were not in themselves generally a cause for serious concern. Two mothers, for example, in recalling that their children had never learnt nursery rhymes said that at the time they had simply attributed this to their children not being interested in nursery rhymes. In general these early impairments were accommodated by parents in terms of individual differences in development both in terms of age and range. Only two mothers out of the 22 thought that even with hindsight there were no pre-reading indicators that their child might have a problem:

Really he didn't have any problems, he was fine. It was really the actual reading he got so frustrated on.

Again this evidence is not being offered in a strictly empirical sense because moth-ers will vary in their recall of difficulties and also in what is perceived as a difficulty. Even with easily quantifiable behaviours such as the number of times a baby wakes up at night (Scott and Richards 1988) mothers vary in their perception of whether this is a problem or not. What is important is that, as well as being in line with other parental accounts and the more empirical evidence, it suggests that mothers can with hindsight identify a range of early impairments but they did not treat these at the time as serious long-term indicators of future problems. In the cases of the children who were described as having the more severe and widespread impairments mothers saw them as immature and hoped they would catch up. Parents whose children had speech delay felt that, far from alerting them that their child might have future difficulties with literacy, this tended to confuse the issue and hold up their realisation. So speech delay or problems were often seen as an explanation by mothers for their children's slow progress in learning to read and write. Mrs Thompson described this process clearly:

And it was while he was attending speech therapy. I was becoming aware that there were problems with what he was doing at school. But of course he was in the

Junior school when I started doing something about it, and really it was because he had speech problems I had put a lot of it down to his speech problems, and I thought if he matures and his speech gets better, he'll grow out of it.

It was not suggested to any of these mothers by either clinical or educational professionals that their child might be at increased risk of having a specific reading or writing difficulty. As these children were identified no sooner than the other children in the sample, it appears that their speech difficulty was not alerting professionals to the increased risk of a reading difficulty.

Mothers whose children had other kinds of early difficulties, most commonly intermittent hearing problems, also said that this tended to delay their realisation that their child had a long-term reading and writing problem and not just a temporary delay caused by the difficulty. Mrs Slatter, for example, fell into this group. Her son Dean had been diagnosed as having a hearing problem at the age of 6 years and had also missed quite a lot of schooling during the first 2 years because of two operations. Mrs Slatter also felt that others used this as an explanation for Dean's literacy problems:

A lot of people reckon it's the operations he had in a short space of time.

It may well be that these factors contributed to Dean's difficulties, but his mother felt that the problem was that these were used as a total explanation and it was assumed that Dean would catch up, without the need for any specific help.

Many of the mothers in this sample stressed that their child was basically happy and well adjusted before they went to school. None of the mothers in this sample thought that their child was particularly difficult or anxious before they went to school, nor did any of the mothers describe themselves as particularly anxious about how their child would cope with school. A few of the mothers whose children had the most extensive difficulties seemed to have some inkling that all might not be well but the majority were surprised by the difficulties their children encountered in school. An issue relating to identification that several mothers brought up was the birth order of their child. In this study there were 10 first-born children, 11 second-born and one third-born. Several mothers of first-born children felt that this held up their realisation that there was a problem because there was nothing to compare their child with:

But the trouble is when it is your first child, there's nothing to judge it against.

Whereas mothers of second- or later-born children were aware of the differences, many stressed that they held back or avoided making negative comparisons if they could on the grounds that each child was different and they didn't want to prejudice their later child's development by having a negative view of them:

I was very aware I had a daughter first. I didn't want to compare him . . . not to put pressure on him because she had done it.

Despite this, mothers of second- or later-born children did feel that the differences they could see did help to alert them to the difficulties that their younger child was having:

He didn't recognise words in books that his older brothers had.

At two, three and four he didn't do any of the things that Emma [older sister] did.

In summary, it appears that mothers generally felt quite strongly that their child was basically as intelligent as other children. None of these mothers were suggesting that their child was exceptionally intelligent; they were simply saying that their child was as intelligent as other children and that lack of intelligence did not seem to be a viable explanation in their view for their child's subsequent difficulty in learning to read and write. The majority of mothers recognised at the time or with hindsight that their child had certain specific difficulties or impairments but they felt that there was sufficient evidence to believe that their child was fundamentally as intelligent as other children.

When were problems first spotted, and by whom?

Mothers were asked how old their child was when they first became aware that their child might have problems. They were also asked if they or someone else was the first person to spot the problem and what kind of problems their child displayed. As has been suggested before, recognising that your child has a problem is often a gradual process. Children ranged in age from 4 to 7 years when their mothers first thought there was a problem. The average age was 5.25, although this included one child whose aunt was head of a teacher training college and had two dyslexic sons of her own, so he was identified particularly early through this connection. If this child is excluded, the average age for first suspecting there was a problem was around 5.5 years. One mother thought that her 4-year-old son was going to have problems because he didn't display any of the pre-reading skills that his two older brothers had displayed. Apart from these two cases the other 20 mothers all felt that their awareness that there was a problem was closely tied to their child's formal education and particularly the introduction of pre-reading or reading activities at school. Even so most of these mothers said there was a gradual building up of suspicion, with them trying where possible to give their child the benefit of the doubt. One mother said, for example, that her suspicions gradually built up over a 2-year period when her child was from 4 to 6 years old, but that she had made excuses for him not beginning to learn to read because he had an August birthday and she had therefore put his lack of progress down to immaturity:

> I just knew he didn't fit into any normal category. He had a lot of the characteristics of a slow learner, but he certainly wasn't a slow learner. He broke every Frank Smith[1] rule in the book, he couldn't remember from one day to the next, and in the end I did what a lot of other mothers of dyslexic children have done, I threw the reading book across the room.

These difficulties were accompanied by her son showing severe distress at home and considerable behaviour problems at school. This mother was an experienced primary school teacher, but she was mystified by her son's difficulties:

> I kept saying to my husband, 'I wish someone could tell me what is wrong with this child.'

Several mothers said that initially, although they knew something was wrong, they couldn't put their finger on what it was:

I just knew something was wrong, but I didn't know what it was.

I mean as soon as he started school I knew something was wrong because from being a bright little boy he started getting quieter and quieter and I knew there was something wrong at school. And I would go in and say, 'How's Josh doing', and it was just a bit slow, you know. He's young for his age and so on. And I just couldn't get through to anyone that he'd changed, that he'd got a problem, that he wasn't dim.

In response to the question about what kind of indicator first alerted them to their child's difficulties, 80 per cent of mothers said it was their child failing to learn to read and the remaining 20 per cent said it was the fact that their child was failing to keep up or was making slow or no progress:

She had been at school two years and she could only string about four words together and even then she had difficulty . . . she couldn't read at all, basically.

I noticed he would never read, they bring this book home and he never wanted to read it. I mentioned it at school. The teacher said, 'Oh, he's very bright, it'll come.' That sort of put it off.

Well he didn't seem to have any problem before he went to school, it was when he got to school he had these problems. Definitely by the second year I knew there was a problem. He obviously looked under so much pressure, his body language and that, he looked pale and agitated and he couldn't tell what it was. I could tell he wasn't learning to read and things very quickly, but then again I didn't want to be too pushy. Because I knew too many people who were always going up, and you think, 'Hold on, he'll do it, he'll learn' and then he didn't.

She became withdrawn and quiet at school; at home she was babyish and clinging, she seemed miserable a lot of the time. She brought her troubles home with her. She dreaded going to school.

Another mother whose son had to be dragged screaming to the infants every day commented,

I thought there was no hope when he was in the infants.

What emerged was that for many mothers their concern was largely contingent upon their child's response to not learning to read. Out of the 22 mothers, 17 said that their children became stressed and unhappy during their first few years in school because of the problems they were having with their academic work. Mothers saw this as a problem that arose specifically from the demands and expectations of school and not one that emerged from their own expectations. Others, such as educationalists, may argue with the validity of parents' views, but there was no evidence at a qualitative level that these parents were any different in their range of views and expectations from other parents. It was also the case that 18 of these parents had other non-dyslexic children who were progressing through school without any dispute or difficulty. One mother, for example, said that she fully accepted that her older non-dyslexic son was not at all academic and she had taken his relatively poor performance at school quite philosophically. Only two mothers in this sample reported that disruptive behaviour at school was an early indicator of their child's problems. The majority of mothers reported that their children became quiet and withdrawn at school and expressed much of their unhappiness at home. Many mothers reported an increase in temper tantrums, nervous habits such as stuttering, insomnia and bed wetting and increased crying and reluctance to go to school:

> He used to burst into tears for the least little thing, and he used to have these temper tantrums in sheer frustration. In fact he often said, 'Do I have to go to school?'

This was not a particularly extreme example and Mrs Roberts and her son Adam were seen by others as calm sensible people and Adam behaved well in school. Despite this, Mrs Roberts said she had difficulty when she broached the subject of Adam's problems with his teacher:

> Well, she said I was being a bit neurotic, and it was a question of he wouldn't do any reading and he wouldn't do any writing, and I said, 'Do you not think the word is "can't"?' and she says, 'No, I don't!'

What seemed to be happening was one of two things: either children displayed different behaviour at school and at home and this therefore gave parents and teachers different perspectives, or children displayed troubled behaviour at school, which was interpreted differently by teachers and parents. In both cases it can be argued that the validity of parents' views was being denied or disputed.

The specialist teachers at the Dyslexia Institute were also interviewed about their perception of parents, among other issues. They had all previously been classroom teachers in mainstream schools, and felt that since working in a situation where they had a lot more individual contact with parents they had become much more likely to believe in the validity of what parents told them. One teacher, for example, said that her father had also been a teacher and that she felt she was brought up in a teaching culture where blaming parents was the norm.

Learning to read

These concerns of mothers were heavily reinforced by their experiences of helping to teach their children to read. Of the 22 schools 19 had a school reading scheme which involved children bringing home books to read to their parents. The most common word used to describe this experience by mothers was 'traumatic':

> Over the years it was terrible, it was traumatic. They just don't want to read books.

Mrs Thompson similarly mentioned that the main difficulty was in getting her son to even start reading a book:

> And if there was a problem, it was just to get Ryan to read a book. You see, you try all the different approaches, the calm laid back approach, the forceful approach, you try everything and nothing works.

Mrs Andrews when asked about teaching her son to read simply said:

> I tried, and tried and tried and tried.

Mrs Falkner experienced similar problems with her daughter Mandy:

> Oh, hated it. Mention reading a book and there were tears and all sorts. And I mean, even though the teachers kept saying 'you must get her to read', I'd say 'you try and get her to read, because she's not interested.'

Mrs Hansen's rueful comment on the school's paired reading scheme (in which an adult and a child read out the words together) was:

> I've read lots of books he hasn't.

Other mothers found that their children became overdependent on the pictures that accompany the words:

> He didn't even use to bother to look at the words. He knew he hadn't got a hope in hell of getting them right. He just used to look at the picture and work out the best thing to say. He was quite good at that! He often didn't say anything like the number of words on the page and he didn't even use to start words with the right letter. That went on for years.

All these mothers had other children who had learnt to read quite easily using these methods so it seems highly unlikely that failure could be attributed to the particular approach taken by mothers. Several mothers mentioned the frustration of finding that their child frequently couldn't remember a simple word that they had read only a line or two before or that they persistently muddled up words such as 'was' and 'saw' and often omitted simple words like 'and' and 'the' or constantly failed to put endings such as '-ed' and '-ing' on words. Although many early readers make these kinds of errors it was the frequency and persistence with which errors were made that mothers noticed combined with their child's obvious dislike of reading:

> It took her about three years to learn to recognise the word 'said'. I thought she was never going to do it!

Osmond (1993) in his interviews came across similar experiences:

He'd bring reading work home from school and we'd try and read it with him. But it was an impossible exercise. One word he'd read correctly on one line, but it would be wrong on the next. They'd be simple words like 'and' and 'the'. It was such misery for him, absolute misery. There was no joy in it, no success for him and as a result it was a kind of nightmare.

Mothers thus found themselves in the difficult position of being expected by the school to listen to their child read when their child was extremely reluctant to do so and found it a very difficult task to do. Many of the mothers asked the school for specific advice on how to help their children, but only 2 of the 22 mothers said they were given any advice over and above the general advice given to all parents on listening to their children read.

There is not sufficient room in this book to go into the considerable debate over the teaching of reading and the attendant role of reading schemes. Critics of reading schemes such as Smith (2004, 2006) have emphasised the importance of 'real books' in the teaching of reading. Turner (1990) has countered by criticising the overdependence on a real books approach and claims that this has led to a decline in reading standards. National reports reviewing the teaching of reading in the UK (Rose 2006), Australia (Rowe 2005) and the US (IRA 2002) all stress the importance of the systematic teaching of phonological skills albeit skilfully related to wider reading skills and the broader curriculum. Bryant (1994) suggests that children need both a real books and a phonetics approach and that the two approaches are best seen as complementary to each other rather than in opposition to each other. The theoretical underpinning for these two approaches comes from the wider debate over whether children are best taught to read using a top-down or bottom-up approach. The top-down approach has been heavily influenced by psycholinguists such as Frank Smith (2006) and emphasises the importance of learning to read through reading for meaning with the use of 'real' books. The bottom-up approach argues that complex skills such as reading need to be broken down into their component sub-skills and that children need to progress from the simple to the complex with the use, for example, of graduated reading schemes and the systematic teaching of phonics (Pressley 2006, Shankweiler and Fowler 2004). Pressley (2006), like Bryant, argues that both approaches are necessary and that the needs of individual children are probably best met by differing combinations of these two approaches. Ireson (1995) in a survey of 121 primary school teachers reports that nearly all of them claimed to use a combined approach to teaching reading. Whether a real books or a structured reading programme approach or a mixture of the two is employed, difficulties can arise at the early stages, at which some critics claim there is insufficient linkage between early reading skills such as phonics and the task of being expected to read a simple book. Some reading schemes pay more attention to phonics than others but the experiences of many of these children suggests that they had insufficient skills to progress through the reading scheme at the expected rate and that many of them were left floundering. Rose (2006) in his report on the teaching of reading in the UK emphasised the importance of 'quality first teaching' (p. 17): in other words the need to include highly systematic and skilled teaching of phonics within a reading programme that promotes interest, motivation and the application of skills. He argues that high-standard first-wave teaching of reading for all children should reduce the number of children who struggle and need to go onto second- and third-wave teaching.

He acknowledges that children with what he terms 'specific neurological difficulties' may well need specialist third-wave teaching.

Key factors from early identification

Before drawing some general points from the study sample, some provisos need to be added. Although the results may be representative of parents who identify their children as dyslexic, they may not be applicable to the same degree to all children with such difficulties:

1   These parents may be more conscientious and alert to difficulties than other parents.
2   They may be better informed about the nature of such difficulties.
3   A higher proportion may have similar difficulties themselves.
4   Children may have been more likely to attend schools with an approach to reading that exacerbated their particular difficulties.

Within the constraints of these provisos there did appear to be evidence that many of these children had a number of early indicators that they were at increased risk of reading delay or dyslexia. Although all these indicators were observable by parents they became aware of the significance of them only once they were familiar with the concept of dyslexia. The most obvious of these were:

1   relative(s) with a similar problem
2   early speech delay or difficulty with no obvious physical cause
3   difficulty with verbal sequencing, e.g. alphabet, days of the week
4   being clumsy or slow to learn to ride a bike, swim, tie up shoelaces etc.
5   difficulty learning nursery rhymes
6   poor short-term memory, e.g. poor at remembering new names, messages etc.
7   little interest in identifying letters or words for fun
8   disliking and/or being very poor at reading books sent home from school.

There was no evidence at a qualitative level that parents were unrealistic or over-ambitious about their children's early development; if anything they appeared to tolerate quite significant delays in certain aspects of their children's development before expressing concern. In a study carried out in the US (Chen and Uttal 1988) mothers of first-grade children said they would be concerned only if their child's performance were close to one standard deviation below the average. Research carried out in the Grampian region of Scotland (Booth 1988) found that 85 per cent of parents whose children had specific learning difficulties were accurate in their perceptions of their children's learning difficulties. Pumfrey and Reason (1991) also found that parents were generally quite realistic in their expectations of how their children would progress. In other areas of special needs such as hearing impairment, parents have been found to be highly reliable in their judgement that their child has a hearing problem (Webster and Ellwood 1985). Webster and Ellwood suggest that 'a parent's worries should always be taken seriously and as often as not are found to be justified'. Although it can be argued that hearing impairment is a different type of special need from dyslexia, parallels can be found in the difficulties that some parents have in getting their child's problem recognised. Particularly in the past some parents of hearing-impaired children were told that they were overanxious and imagining difficulties or that the child would grow out of their difficulties. Even with a relatively easily identifiable condition such as hearing loss, it is only in the last 20 years that there has been a shift towards seeing parents as reliable detectors of difficulties.

Given the present interest in developing early screening tests for dyslexia it would seem both desirable and feasible that information from parents be used either to supplement screening or to alert professionals to children at increased risk of such difficulties. Such information would need to be treated with caution and common sense, but it could alert teachers to some high-risk children and suggest children they would want to keep a close eye on or talk to parents in more detail about. Screening always raises problems of false positives and negatives and when based on parents' observations alone issues of reliability are also raised. But despite these drawbacks it seems important that some systematic approach to collecting information on early indicators of difficulty be implemented before children begin to fail, or at very least if a child is showing difficulty with reading or pre-reading skills, and that a teacher know what questions to ask parents about the child's development and knows the significance of the replies that they give.

Summary

1 Many families already have some experience of dyslexia or similar problems, although in the majority of cases it has not been formally recognised in adults.
2 Mothers can with hindsight identify a number of possible early indicators of dyslexia.
3 The majority of mothers are realistic in their perception of their child's overall development and general level of intelligence.
4 Some children with speech and language difficulties have a higher risk of dyslexia.
5 All the children in this sample were considered well adjusted and 'normal' by their mothers before entering school.
6 A large majority of mothers in this sample 'knew' that something was wrong during their child's time in infant school.
7 The majority of mothers in this sample found that their children encountered considerable problems with the school reading scheme.

Note

1 Smith is a psycholinguist who has a strong influence on many teachers' approach to reading.

Chapter 6

Identifying dyslexia

I danced down the street. At last we knew what was wrong.

(Mother of girl with dyslexia)

By the time the children in this sample had been through infant school all the mothers, bar one, felt that something was definitely wrong. The next series of questions looked at the process, from their point of view, by which their child was identified as having dyslexia or specific learning difficulties. Questions were asked about who first suggested that the child was dyslexic or had a specific learning difficulty and what the response to this suggestion was. Mothers were also asked how they came to find out about dyslexia and how they felt when their child was identified as having dyslexia or a specific learning difficulty. The following responses were given to the question 'Who was it that first suggested that the child might be dyslexic?'

Mother	15
Friend	1
Teacher	5
Professional relative	1

In just over two-thirds of cases a lay person initially suggested the child was dyslexic and in under a third of cases a professional initially suggested that the child was dyslexic. Of the 17 mothers who asked the school if their child might be dyslexic, in 11 cases they claimed that the school was dismissive, in five cases the school was seen as non-committal and in one case the school was in agreement. This information tells us only about mothers' perception of the situation. It may be that in some cases schools had their own formulation of the problem but there was not effective communication between school and home on the nature of the problem. Whatever the case may be, half the mothers in this sample felt that initially the school was dismissive of their suggestion. Many of these mothers backed up their claim by giving specific examples or quotes of comments made to them by teachers. Mrs Roberts described what happened when she started expressing her concern over how unhappy her son appeared to be at school. She herself wasn't sure what was wrong at this stage but simply wanted the school to look into it:

Well she said I was neurotic. I didn't get any joy out of them so then I went to my sister-in-law [head of teacher training college]. She assessed him and said he was dyslexic and that he hadn't done a thing in the two years he'd been at school. So I decided to send him to the Dyslexia Institute. Of course all this didn't go down very well with the school. I was told, 'If you want to waste your money, it's up to you.'

Mrs Slatter was also concerned about her son's lack of progress and his unhappiness at school:

I thought something was up. I was told I was an overprotective mother and Dean was just a slow learner and there was nothing wrong. And I, being foolish, left it and the next year we went to parents' day and looked at his work and there was absolutely no progress. Again I voiced my opinion and again I was told I was being silly. And I thought, 'No, I don't think I am,' and so I went about it myself and I got in touch with the Dyslexia place through the telephone. I thought, 'In for a penny, in for a pound. We'll try this.' My husband agreed that there was something there; he was just stopped solid for two years and the trouble was, with him being intelligent, he knew there was something wrong and he couldn't understand what was wrong with himself. You don't want to stir up the water but you have to.

Mrs Slatter felt that she encountered a negative attitude to dyslexia at both the school and the local authority level:

The head wouldn't acknowledge it at all, he said there was a two-year waiting list for an LA [local authority] assessment. The trouble is, you get more help in some areas than others. I think he [head of LA] was totally against dyslexia, he didn't believe in it.

Mrs Carter similarly felt that the school was dismissive of her concerns:

But the only thing was every time I mentioned dyslexia it was like a taboo word.

The experiences recounted by these mothers were typical of those recounted by the two-thirds of mothers who initially suggested to professionals that their child was dyslexic.

The process of identification

For many families identification is a gradual process that goes on over a period of time. The process of identification that is described also follows closely the processes described by Booth (1978) that families with children with developmental delay experienced. In Booth's study he identified four main stages that families went through in getting their child identified. These stages were:

1   the growth of suspicion
2   seeking professional advice
3   suspending judgement
4   the growth of conviction.

In both studies parents began, usually over a period of time, to suspect that something was wrong. In the second stage parents then sought professional advice. In the majority of cases either parents were reassured that there wasn't really a problem, and were typically told that the child would catch up, or they were told that they needed to readjust their expectations and accept that their child was a bit slow but again it was suggested that there wasn't any serious problem. Parents then went away temporarily reassured, or at least, in deference to the professionals, prepared to give the child the benefit of the doubt. But the child's subsequent lack of progress and in the case of most of the dyslexic children their evident unhappiness convinced their parents that something was wrong. Once parents reached this stage of conviction they were determined not to be fobbed off by professionals and were prepared to seek alternative advice, if necessary, until they received a satisfactory explanation for their child's difficulties. Although the dyslexic children's problems were very mild in comparison to the severe problems of some of the developmentally delayed children, the same difficulties in getting some professionals to take parents' concerns seriously appeared to be in evidence. In both cases the absence of physical markers and the reliance on behavioural observations made it important for early identification that there was a good relationship between parents and professionals and that professionals took parents' concerns seriously.

Parents as clients or partners

Wolfendale (1997) argues that traditionally parents have been treated as clients and it is only recently that there has begun to be a move towards treating them as partners. Wolfendale lists a number of characteristics of both the client and the partner concept.

Client concept

- Parents are dependent on professional opinion.
- Parents are passive recipients of services.
- Parents are in need of redirection.
- Parents are peripheral to decision making.
- Parents are perceived as 'inadequate' or 'deficient'.

Partner concept

- Parents are active and central in decision making and in its implementation.
- Parents are perceived as having equal strength and equivalent expertise.
- Parents are able to contribute as well as receive services.
- Parents share responsibility.

Although both positive and negative experiences were recounted by mothers, the majority of experiences fitted with the parent as client concept. This may help explain the long delay experienced by most families between suspecting there was a problem and getting it identified to their satisfaction. The average period of time for this was 4 years and led to the median age for children to be assessed and identified as dyslexic at 10 years.

Differing views among professionals

Many families found that there were differing views among teachers as to the nature and extent of their child's difficulties. Mrs Thompson had noticed that her son was becoming very distressed about school work. She herself had come across various articles about dyslexia and found that he fitted most of the points. She felt that her initial tentative approaches to the school were not productive:

> I didn't get far at all with them. In the early stages it was a case of the usual, 'Oh, he'll catch up, some of them are slow,' and so on.

But when her son was seven he had a different teacher who agreed that there was a problem:

> His teacher said, 'I don't know what it is, but there's definitely some block there with Ryan, why he can't learn to read and write like the other children, because he's bright enough and there's no reason why he shouldn't.'

For over half the mothers in this sample, conflicting opinions among professionals were reported as part of their experience of trying to get their child's difficulties identified and supported. This conflict could be at the level of the school with different teachers having different views or it could involve outside professionals such as educational psychologists:

> Well, I asked the head if he was dyslexic and she said, 'No, I don't think he is,' and his teacher said he's not. Then the educational psychologist saw him. She'd taken a course in dyslexia and she thought he was. She told us off the record to get specialist help for him.

> The school were pretty noncommittal. 'It'll come, she'll be all right,' and so on. Eventually when she was nearly 10 they did refer her to the educational psychologist. She was very supportive; her own daughter was dyslexic. She suggested unofficially that we sent her to the Dyslexia Institute.

> I was confused by all the dispute among the professionals. His second teacher referred him to the educational psychologist. He assessed him and said it would all come together and there wasn't anything to worry about. Then his next teacher said there definitely was a problem and that he needed help. They're the experts, I felt betrayed.

Several mothers said that they were told by various professionals including class teachers, special needs teachers, head teachers and educational psychologists 'off the record' that their child was dyslexic and would benefit from specialist help outside the school. In many of these cases the person in question either mentioned that they had a dyslexic child or had received specialist training in dyslexia. It perhaps says something about the general climate of the school or the local authority that professionals felt the need to stress that these recommendations were being made off the record. Macbeth

(1989) found that, when teachers gave opinions to parents on choosing schools, the advice was usually given unofficially. Macbeth suggests that this is because teachers are reluctant to comment on their fellow professionals and states that 'The closing of ranks by teachers poses an important professional problem.' As far back as 1978, Robinson commented that the current political climate and lack of support left professionals who wanted to practice in a different way, 'in a very exposed position':

> His teacher thought something was wrong, she suggested we try the Dyslexia Institute. She said she was sticking her neck out in suggesting it.

Even when a child had been identified as dyslexic by a bona fide professional and this had been accepted by the school at a general level, this didn't guarantee that individual teachers would agree with this:

> And his teacher did say to me once, 'I don't think that Mark is dyslexic.' And I said, 'Well, with all due respect, do you know anything about dyslexia?' And she said, 'no.' I says, 'Well, how are you qualified to turn round and say to me he isn't if you know nothing about it?' I said, 'I could bring you in plenty of literature if you'd like to read it,' but she declined to do so.

This comment, along with most of the comments quoted so far in this chapter, was made by a working-class mother. These comments illustrate the wide variation in parents' views and approaches and warn against the danger of having simplistic and stereotyped views of what parents from a particular social class think. Blaxter and Paterson (1982) suggest that clear and consistent social class differences in child rearing are present only at the extremes of the classification system. Ribbens (1994) argues that it is oversimplistic to divide parents into working class and middle class because this misrepresents the complexity of the data and tends to ignore aspects of the data that show no class differences in child rearing. It also means that the considerable variations within class are often overlooked. This is not to deny that it is highly likely that children from socially or economically deprived backgrounds are more likely to be overlooked or to have their difficulties attributed to other causes. But it does suggest that it is important not to hold stereotyped assumptions about how parents from a particular background will behave. Several of the most assertive and articulate mothers in this study were from a working-class background, whereas there were several unforceful middle-class mothers who felt they had little power to influence the school. It may well be that overall there are more assertive middle-class parents but it is important not to assume that all or even the majority of middle-class parents fit this stereotype.

In the seven cases in which someone other than the parents first suggested the child was dyslexic, mothers were asked what their initial reaction to this suggestion was. In all cases parents were basically in agreement with the suggestion. In some cases they had already wondered themselves if the child was dyslexic but hadn't liked to voice these opinions to professionals. In other cases they knew nothing about dyslexia and reserved judgement until they had checked out for themselves what the label meant:

> I must be one of the few people who hadn't heard about it. I hadn't even come across it, so I hadn't thought about it before. It wasn't until he was getting special

help at school that one of the teachers said sort of very diplomatically, it wasn't officially, had I heard about dyslexia. Perhaps it could be the case. I wanted to know if it was possibly the case. At least you've got an avenue to follow.

The following comment was made by a mother who was herself a primary school teacher:

I can honestly say I never knew a lot about it which is why I didn't think of it. I just knew he didn't fit into any normal category.

Sources of information on dyslexia

Given that in 15 cases mothers said that they were the first one to suggest that their child was dyslexic this raises the question of where they got their knowledge of dyslexia from. In the cases in which someone else first suggested the child was dyslexic there was still the question of where mothers got the bulk of their information about dyslexia from. In response to the question 'Where had they initially learnt about dyslexia from?' the following replies were given. Some mothers mentioned more than one source of initial information and some couldn't remember precisely where they'd first heard about dyslexia, although this uncertainty was confined to which aspect of the media they'd first seen it mentioned in.

Magazines (9), papers or books	13
Television or radio	5
Dyslexia Institute publicity or information	4
Teacher	1
Friend	1

Although these figures are best taken as a rough approximation, they do show quite clearly that the media is the major source of information. A common pattern was for a mother to first read an article or hear a programme about dyslexia and to think that the outline of dyslexia that was given fitted well with the difficulties that her child was experiencing. As mothers became more convinced that their child might be dyslexic they actively sought further information and, for example, borrowed books from the library or obtained pamphlets from specialist organisations. In the updated interviews further information was more likely to be sought via the internet. Many mothers commented that once they were aware of the possibility of their child being dyslexic they noticed increasing coverage of dyslexia in the media:

Well his support teacher first suggested he might be dyslexic, then I read an article in the paper and then I read a couple of books. Just recently Ryan and I watched this QED programme about it together. He said, 'Oh yes, that's what I do.'

I can't remember. I really can't. I'd probably read a little bit, or saw a little bit, but it was only a tiny bit. I knew nothing about it whatsoever, it was only after that, that I made it my job to find out as much as I could . . . I don't know if it's a case that once you get started, it becomes easier to find more, but obviously over the past few years there has been more realisation about it. It's on the television and the paper did a big thing about it recently.

I saw something about it in a magazine and then there was this radio programme I think.

The more I read articles and so on the more I thought it described Darren so much, although he didn't have all the elements, he wasn't clumsy or slow to talk. After that I read some books from the library.

With the wider use of the internet more information is potentially available to parents and the majority now use it as an important source of information. The drawback is that they have to sort through a lot of conflicting information and it can be difficult to discriminate between more and less reliable information sources. Most parents are well aware of this issue and treat the internet with caution (Riddick 2008). A recently interviewed parent who suspected his son might be dyslexic said that he started by consulting a couple of professionals who he knew were knowledgeable about dyslexia rather than consulting the internet first. His reason for this was, because he was aware how conflicting information can be, he wanted some pointers from people he trusted on which online sources to consult and also to give him a perspective against which he could evaluate the information. Not all parents are in the position to do this and some have to make their own judgements about what to consult. Riddick (2008) found in an interview study of parents of children with autism that parents rated information given to them by professionals and reputable organisations (such as the National Autistic Society) as the most credible. Although many found the internet a useful source of information a minority felt that the amount of information available was overwhelming and avoided looking for additional information. Other parents felt compelled to find out as much as they could in order to support their child even if it sometimes worried or perplexed them. A difficulty for parents and sometimes even teachers is in deciding what counts as a 'reputable' source.

Mothers' reactions to the label 'dyslexia'

Mothers were asked how they felt when they were told or had it confirmed that their child was dyslexic. Twenty of the 22 mothers described themselves as 'relieved' when they were told that their child was dyslexic:

Oh god, such a relief! It was the first time he wasn't lazy, wasn't stupid. It wasn't his fault.

Really I was quite relieved to know, because it's an explanation. I think you're disappointed for them, aren't you, and a bit anxious about what it means.

Well, I was relieved in a way. I wasn't upset at all. Because I just thought, 'Well yes, now we've got something to work on.' Well, maybe he'd never get rid of the problem, but at least there's specialist help we can get.

Mothers stressed the importance of having an explanation, of their child no longer feeling stupid, and of practical plans for helping the child being possible once they were identified as dyslexic. One mother who had great difficulty in convincing the primary school that there was a problem, despite her son being three years behind on his reading and spelling, described herself as 'thrilled' when he was finally identified as dyslexic. Another mother, who had received conflicting advice from professionals throughout her daughter's primary school and had been told that she wasn't dyslexic, described herself as 'devastated' when at 12 years of age her daughter, at the instigation of her secondary school, was identified as dyslexic. She felt that she had been 'fobbed off' by professionals and blamed herself for believing them. Sixty per cent of the mothers blamed themselves to varying degrees for not having followed their own convictions. Mrs Graham, whose son was also assessed on the advice of his secondary school and found to be over 5 years behind in his reading, made the following remarks:

> I felt guilty I hadn't followed my own instincts in the first place. I feel really guilty about that. But you know, if you're talking to professionals, you expect them to know. I really wish I'd followed my own instincts.

So for over half the mothers relief was tinged with regret or guilt that they had not had their child identified sooner.

Children's reactions to the label 'dyslexia'

Children were also asked what they thought about being called dyslexic. In order to try and guard against children giving the answer they thought the researcher wanted to hear they were deliberately asked the negative leading question of 'Didn't they resent being called dyslexic because it made them feel different?' All the children denied this, and 21 of the 22 children were positive about the label 'dyslexia':

> I'm glad I'm called dyslexic rather than lazy.

> I'm not branded as thick now.

> I quite like it, I used to wonder why I couldn't keep up.

> It helps me understand.

> It's OK. It has helped.

> I'd rather know I've got dyslexia than think I was an idiot.

> It's quite helpful. It's better to get it sorted out.

> Now I know there's a lot of people with the same problem.

Several dominant themes could be identified from children's comments:

1   Not thinking they were 'thick' or 'stupid'.
2   That it had helped.
3   It had specifically helped them to understand why they had been having difficulties.
4   That there were children with the same difficulty.

Mothers' comments also backed up many of these themes:

It did help him because he said, 'I'm not stupid. I haven't really got a stupid brain.'

He needs a reason for everything. He thought that something was wrong with him.

He was pleased because he thought that he was thick, stupid and an idiot.

The only child to express negative feelings about the label 'dyslexia' was the young-est child in the sample who said, 'I mind a little bit because she [his mother] tells the whole world.' This raises an important distinction between the private and the public aspects of the label. Whereas as already shown all but one child found the label helpful at a personal level, 50 per cent of the children didn't find the label helpful at a public level (Riddick 1995a), mainly because of teasing by other children:

I find it helpful, but I'd rather others didn't know.

Although in this sample numbers are too small to be categorical, two factors did appear to relate to children's willingness to use their label in public. One factor was the general attitude of the school. The two schools in this study that were most open and supportive of the concept of dyslexia both had children attending who were willing to say they were dyslexic:

Oh everybody knows. I use it quite a lot in fact.

Whereas some of the schools that were most negative about the concept of dyslexia were the ones where children reported considerable teasing:

They used to call us [me] 'spacker'.

He used to call us names, 'dim', 'spacker', 'thick'. I used to get quite upset.

This information fits with other research from the special needs area (Swann 1985) that shows that the attitudes of the school and the individual teachers within the school to special needs children are important in determining the attitudes of the rest of the children. Sophie, in the extended case studies in Chapter 13, talks about the negative attitude of other children in her school to dyslexia and the problems that this causes her. The other factor appeared to be related to children's level of self-esteem or confi-dence combined with the verbal ability to stick up for themselves. The two boys who gave the two longest male interviews and both scored high on the Lawrence self-esteem inventory and were rated high in self-esteem by their mothers both said they were will-ing to talk about dyslexia in school. According to their own accounts and those of their mothers they were willing to fight their corner in a verbal sense and both mentioned independently that they had used the example of Einstein to defend themselves:

Oh Einstein dead thick, eh?

Why label?

It is sometimes suggested that middle-class parents opt for the label 'dyslexia' because they see it as a socially acceptable and advantageous label for their children to receive (Riddell *et al.* 1992, Reid 1994). In the current study over half the mothers thought that teachers and sometimes other parents thought that they were making 'excuses' for their child by calling them dyslexic. In fact several mothers said they didn't use the word 'dyslexia' at school for fear of antagonising the school and making things worse for their child. There were no discernible class differences, with equal numbers of working-class and middle-class mothers reporting these kinds of experiences:

I was made to feel over anxious and neurotic. Yes it made me feel very demoralised, I even ended up crying.

Oh, all the way along I was made to feel that I was making excuses.

And I was getting all those knowing smiles that say, 'You're the over-fretting, para-noid mother.'

The teachers in the primary school definitely thought I was making excuses.

I keep a low profile for fear of antagonising them.

These views suggest that, for half the parents at least, using the term 'dyslexia' had negative as well as positive aspects to it. These parents didn't feel that the term dyslexia was 'socially acceptable' within the context of their child's school; neither had the label 'dyslexia' given them access to additional or more appropriate resources within the school system. This would suggest that, for a significant proportion of parents, more complex or alternative explanations for choosing to call their children dyslexic should be sought. Many mothers mentioned their reluctance or embarrassment at having to make a 'fuss' and many did not want to be seen as a 'pushy' or 'neurotic' parent:

I'm not that sort of person. I hate to make a fuss.

Another mother, whose son was found to have a reading age of 6 years 9 months at the age of 11 years, described her experience:

I could tell he wasn't learning to read and things very quickly, but then again I didn't want to be too pushy. Because I knew too many people who were always going up, and you think, 'Hold on, he'll do it, he'll learn,' but then he didn't. Now I feel guilty.

It can be argued from the responses given by parents in this study that a label such as 'dyslexia' serves a number of purposes but a fundamental reason for parents choosing this label is its 'goodness of fit' in terms of describing and explaining their child's difficulties:

> The more I read articles and things the more I thought it's just describing Robert so much.

The majority of mothers went on to add that once there was a label or an explanation it also gave them a much clearer idea of what sort of help was needed:

> We knew what help he needed then.

> I was relieved, at least something could be done.

Allied to this some parents saw this as the first real recognition that their child had a problem and that this wasn't just a figment of their imagination:

> I kept saying to my husband, 'I wish someone would tell me what is wrong with this child that he can't do the normal things.'

Mrs Wood's son had been coming home from school very distressed and upset and was having behaviour problems at school. Suggestions to his previous teacher that he might have a learning disability had been dismissed. When he got a new teacher she quickly recognised that he had a problem:

> She called me in before half-term and said, 'If this little boy isn't dyslexic, I'll eat hay with the horses.' I walked out of school on cloud nine because finally someone had said there is a problem here.

Parents also felt it was important to be able to explain to their child what the problem was:

> Dean couldn't understand what was wrong with himself. He kept asking me, 'Am I thick?'

From the point of view of parents they wanted a label which accurately described and explained their child's difficulties and accounted for the puzzling discrepancies in their child's performance. In 50 per cent of cases, parents felt that at an informal level their child had been labelled as 'thick or slow' by the school and in 25 per cent of cases they felt they had been labelled as lazy. It can be argued that this an unhelpful way to view any child's difficulties, but what parents were specifically objecting to was the inaccuracy of these attributions as a total explanation for their child's difficulties. Mrs Andrews described her frustration with being told that her 7-year-old son couldn't read because he was 'slow'. At 8 years he was assessed by the educational psychologist and found to have an IQ of 120:

I'm very frustrated. We could have saved him a lot of heartache. The trouble is people think you're just pushy neurotic academic parents. I'd be the first to accept that my older son isn't academic, but he's not dyslexic either!

Mrs Faulkner also objected to her daughter's reading difficulties being put down to slowness:

The thing the teacher did say once, that irritates me now, was that she was very slow at school, slow to learn. And basically she's not slow to learn. It was the reading that she was slow to learn. And I think that was a lack of understanding.

Several mothers talked about their own caution in giving their child a label:

I don't think you should give them labels willy-nilly like. You have to weigh it up. But really it was no contest, the state he was in, so much harm had been done, it could only get better.

Several mothers were told by educationalists that they didn't believe in labelling children. Jordan and Powell (1992) comment that 'an educational dogma had developed which discredits the labelling of children.' It is important that the validity and usefulness of any particular label be kept under review and the purpose or purposes behind using it be clearly understood. It is also important that the people who have to live with a label have ownership of it and have a major say in what context and for what purpose the label is used. It can be argued that labels of disability can be used to describe or explain an individual's functioning at the biological, psychological and sociological levels. Most people with disabilities want labels that are socially positive and don't reinforce negative or inaccurate stereotypes of themselves. Hence the constant changing and renegotiating of labels that takes place. One fundamental change has been the move away from labels that describe the person in terms of their disability such as blind or mentally handicapped to terminology that puts the person first, such as 'she has a visual impairment' or 'he has a learning disability'. Despite this move there is still disagreement and controversy over labels and some people with visual impairments, for example, prefer to call themselves blind. Thomas (1982) comments on this, 'disability is not only a matter of medical and administrative definition, it is a personal one of how each person with an impairment defines him- or herself.' He also points out that different groups such as the public, professionals and disabled people themselves will have different perceptions of the nature and meaning of disability. In the present study many of the mothers were aware that teachers and especially educational psychologists preferred to use the term 'specific learning difficulties':

Basically they were in agreement, except they never called it dyslexia: they called it 'specific learning difficulties'.

Most mothers didn't object to this as long as there was clear agreement with the school on what the child's difficulties were and what should be done about them. Mothers and children preferred to use the term 'dyslexia' as opposed to 'specific learning difficulties'. It could be that this was a particularly biased sample as subjects were recruited through the Dyslexia Institute but in Pumfrey and Reason's (1991) wide-ranging survey and in Riddell *et al.* (1992) it was also found that parents preferred the term 'dyslexia' to 'specific learning difficulties'. If we look at these two terms in a wider social and psychological context this is perhaps not surprising. At present nearly all the lay litera-ture, personal accounts, information and specialist support services, and role models of adults are accessed through the term 'dyslexia'. In this study it was found that both parents and teachers were confused about what 'specific learning difficulties' meant and to what extent it was exchangeable with the term 'dyslexia'. From the perspective of educationalists 'specific learning difficulties' may seem a more equable and acceptable way of characterising children's difficulties but for children and their families it doesn't offer the same degree of personal understanding, personal identification and personal support. Blaxter (1976), in discussing disability, points out that there are inevitable tensions between clinical definitions, which can be 'individual, qualified and provi-sional', and administrative categories, which are required to be 'rigid, dichotomous and designed for large groups of people'. Pumfrey and Reason (1991) in their survey of educational psychologists noted that 87.4 per cent said that they found the term 'specific learning difficulties' useful in their work and that 30.4 per cent found the term 'dyslexia' useful. The majority of educational psychologists said that they were aware that parents preferred the term 'dyslexia' and although they avoided the term they did not object to parents using it. Although it is important not to get too bogged down in semantics it is important where different groups are using different terminol-ogy that there be clear communication between them. In some cases in this study, when there was not clear communication about the connection between the terms 'dyslexia' and 'specific learning difficulties', parents thought that educational psychologists were being dismissive of their child's problem and were denying that they were 'dyslexic':

> So this dreadful man came out and did tests with Josh. I don't know what they were; Josh wouldn't talk about them. And then he called me into school, sitting beside the headmistress, who didn't believe there was anything wrong with him except he was thick. And he said, 'Well, there's nothing wrong with your child. He's just a very bad speller. I've got a boy who's a bad speller as well, and there's nothing you can do about it.' So that was it really.

In both the large-scale inquiry by Pumfrey and Reason (1991) and the large-scale study in Scotland by Riddell, Duffield, Brown and Ogilvy (1992) it was found that parents were unhappy about the length of time it took for their children to be identi-fied and assessed. They were also unhappy about the lack of specialist support and the lack of training and understanding of dyslexia displayed by many classroom teachers. Booth (1988) reported a study carried out in the Grampian region of Scotland in which all the children referred to the schools' psychological service for suspected specific learning difficulties over 1 year were recorded. The average age for referral was 9 years 7 months. Psychologists thought on the basis of interviews with parents that 85 per cent of them were reasonably accurate in their understanding of their child's learning difficulties and 75 per cent were judged to be realistic in their expectations. The other suggestion put forward (Reid 1994, Riddell *et al.* 1992) why parents prefer the term 'dyslexia' to 'specific learning difficulties' is that this is a way of securing resources or provision. Given that many parents are aware that educational psychologists favour the term 'specific learning difficulties' it seems illogical to suggest that parents favour the term 'dyslexia' simply in order to access resources. In the present study all the parents felt they had 'failed' to obtain adequate support for their children at school and using the term 'dyslexia' had not for them been a successful way of accessing either school or local authority resources. It can be argued that many labels highlight likely needs and suggest the kind of provision or intervention appropriate to meet those needs. Most parents whose children are identified as having cerebral palsy, for example, might expect their children to receive physiotherapy. One wouldn't necessarily argue on this basis that parents seek a label of cerebral palsy simply in order to get physiotherapy for their children. This reasoning leaves out the important role of personal understanding and identification that a particular label can offer.

Summary

1 The majority of mothers initially found out about dyslexia through the media.
2 Identification was for most families a gradual process.
3 In two-thirds of cases mothers took the initiative in asking if their child might be dyslexic and in just under a third of cases a professional first suggested that the child might be dyslexic.
4 The majority of mothers who took the initiative in asking if their child was dyslexic felt that the school was dismissive of their suggestion.
5 Over half the parents experienced conflicting views among the professionals.
6 Ninety per cent of mothers described themselves as relieved when it was confirmed that their child was dyslexic.
7 Ninety-five per cent of children were positive about 'dyslexic' as a personal label for understanding their difficulties.

Chapter 7

Parents and teachers

The myth (of the bad parent) is pervasive and its power should not be underestimated for it can lead well meaning teachers to treat perfectly able parents with suspicion.

(Hannon 1995)

Before looking at the present study in more detail it is necessary to consider some of the general issues surrounding research on parents and teachers. The first point is that much of the research is rooted in the concerns of educationalists and inevitably involves institutional or school-based perspectives on a given question or issue. Ribbens and Kirkpatrick (2004) in commenting on research into families point out that most of it is concerned with publicly defined social policy issues or professionals' concerns and little of it is from the perspective of family members themselves. A similar situation is found when the extensive literature on special needs education or for that matter education in general is examined. More recently, influences from social research and the introduction of approaches such as 'grounded theory' have emphasised the importance of researching issues from the perspective of the individual involved. In grounded theory for example it is argued that the researcher should have as few preconceived questions as possible in order to allow the participants to define what the issues are from their perspective. Another influence has been the disability rights movement, which has emphasised the importance of disabled people speaking for themselves. An issue that arises in looking at children with special needs or disabilities is to what degree their voices are heard and to what degree their parents' voices are heard. The general tenet behind such approaches is that children and parents should be listened to and that their views should influence both research and practice.

Dyson and Skidmore (1994) carried out a survey on the provision for specific learning disabilities in secondary schools in Scotland. These schools were not picked to be a representative sample of all schools but were invited to participate because they had features of interest to the research team. Of 41 nominated schools, 27 schools spread across five regions responded. Schools were specifically asked in the survey questionnaire what sort of contact they had with the parents of children with specific learning disabilities. They were also asked how this contact differed from the contact they had with other parents of children with different forms of special needs. They summarise the response to parental contact in the following way:

For most schools parental involvement was entirely positive, and the need to be aware of potential conflict with parents was minimal.

The majority of schools said that their contact was no different or was much the same as the contact they had with other parents. This was the case even when parents had sought advice from outside the school. A few schools felt that parents of children with specific learning disabilities needed more specifically targeted contact but only two schools mentioned support specifically for parents. It is interesting to note that, in researching this issue, five different teacher interviews were constructed and used in case study schools. These included interviews with heads, subject specialists and learning support teachers but at no point were the views of the parents or children themselves sought on provision for specific learning disabilities or on the relationship between school and home. This was a well carried out piece of research but it does illustrate the point that much of what we know is from the teacher perspective.

Teacher stereotypes

Atkin, Bastiani and Goode (1988) carried out extensive studies on the relationships between parents and teachers and were involved at a practical level in carrying out in-service training in this area. They start by making the point that most work on home–school relations 'is viewed entirely from the professional perspective'. They also comment that over a period of time they were forced to ask uncomfortable questions about their own assumptions and became aware of deficiencies in their own evidence and perspective:

> In the first place we had become rather suspicious of many of the claims that prac-tising teachers were making about what parents were like. Increasingly, we began to consider that such claims were rooted in teacher lore and staffroom mythology, rather than in first hand experience and direct evidence, being strongest where actual contact was weak or limited.

In the present study the children's specialist support teachers at the Dyslexia Insti-tute were also interviewed. They had all been classroom teachers in mainstream schools before taking their specialist training and changing jobs. One of the questions they were asked was whether their inclination to believe what parents told them had increased or decreased as a result of having more personal contact with parents. The one teacher who had spent half her time on parent liaison when in mainstream school felt that she hadn't changed in that she had always had a lot of sympathy with what parents told her. The other three all felt that they had changed in their attitudes as a result of working more closely with parents and were now more ready to accept the things that parents told them. Riddick (1995a) has commented on the 'myths' surrounding dyslexia and in particular the myths about the parents of children with dyslexia. Like Atkin *et al.* (1988) she found that most of these appeared to be based on folklore and that almost no empirical evidence was offered to back up the assertions being made. There appeared to be a powerful myth of the overambitious, unrealistic middle-class parent who couldn't accept that they didn't have an academic child. Although it may be possible that the occasional parent may fit this description, it has been overgeneralised to produce a pervasive and glib stereotype which is helpful neither to parents nor to educationalists. Not all educationalists hold this type of stereotype but at an informal level it is still quite frequently used. Dewhirst (1995) carried out a series of interviews with teachers on the subject of dyslexia. The following is a brief extract from an interview she conducted with an experienced special needs support teacher. This teacher stressed that she thought it was important to keep up to date and that she had done so by attending in-service training courses:

INTERVIEWER: Have you done any specialist training in the area of dyslexia?

TEACHER: Oh God that! No, no I haven't (pulls a face). Why?

INTERVIEWER: Why did you pull a face when I asked you that?

TEACHER: Well . . . I mean, it's one of those things that has been conjured up by 'pushy parents' for their thick or lazy children; quite often both.

INTERVIEWER: What exactly do you know about dyslexia?

TEACHER: Well, basically they can't read or write. It's supposed to be about problems in communication isn't it? Generally it's children who are either too lazy or haven't got the brains and their parents can't hack it.

This teacher went on to expand that the problems were invariably caused by over-ambitious middle-class parents either putting too much pressure on their children or overprotecting them by using the label 'dyslexia' when in her terminology the children really needed 'a good kick up the backside'. A case of damned if you do or damned if you don't! Kunda and Oleson (1995) describe a range of evidence which suggests that people are good at finding ways of explaining how almost any attribute can be linked to any outcome and as in this example are quite capable of explaining how opposite attributes (too pushy/not pushy enough) can lead to the same outcome. They also claim that this process actually reinforces an individual's belief rather than diminishing it. Later in the interview the following question was asked:

INTERVIEWER: If you haven't any training in the field of dyslexia do you think really that you should be making judgements about it?

TEACHER: Yeah, it's a gut feeling you know, when you have been teaching as long as I have you get to know which kids have problems and which kids are pulling the wool over your eyes.

This raises the important point that those educationalists who are most hostile to or critical of the concept of dyslexia are the least likely to read about or take further training in a condition that they don't think exists. To be fair to teachers like this one, many of them received no training on dyslexia or specific learning difficulties during their initial training or received a critical account of it which either implicitly or explicitly put forward the myth of dyslexia as a figment of the imagination of ambitious, unrealistic middle-class parents. Many of the parents in this study were aware of this stereotype and as mentioned in Chapter 6 were anxious not to be seen as unrealistic, pushy parents. Newson and Newson (1987), drawing on their extensive longitudinal study of child rearing, found that parents were generally reluctant to criticise the school or the teachers directly even when their child was making poor progress. They suggest that fear of being seen as a 'difficult' or 'overprotective' parent is often at the root of this and that parents are frightened of making things worse for their children. Mrs Graham, a single parent on a low income, made the following comment:

> I resent them thinking that we're all wealthy neurotics.

Mrs Slatter had been told in the past by her son's class teacher that she was being overprotective and there wasn't any problem, despite the fact that he was making little progress and was becoming distressed and unhappy:

> To tell the truth I was frightened of her, that domineering teacher. I backed down, I thought, 'Ee well, maybe I'm wrong.'

Atkin *et al.* (1988) note that 'To this day we maintain a healthy scepticism of teacher stereotypes.' One of the difficulties with stereotypes is that they can be very resistant to change as they appear to be linked to powerful and fundamental belief systems. Stephan (1985) observes that 'stereotypes are notoriously difficult to change.' Even when sound empirical evidence is presented some individuals will keep their beliefs intact by ignoring or criticising the evidence or, where possible, treating the case as exceptional. Kunda and Oleson (1995) found that people attempted to explain away individuals who strongly challenged their stereotypes by claiming they were different in some way from the group as a whole. They conclude by saying: 'On the practical side, our findings have disturbing implications for the likelihood that people will change their stereotypes in the normal course of their daily lives, as they encounter individuals who disconfirm their stereotypes.'

Stephan (1985) also suggests that simply exposing people to individuals who disconfirm their stereotypes is no guarantee that they will revise their stereotype. It has long been suggested that one reason why people hang on to their stereotypes is because they serve important needs such as justifying their own position, authority or behaviour (Allport 1954). More recently it has been suggested that on top of this there may be a cognitive reason in that people tend to defend themselves against anything that challenges their expectations even when it doesn't seem to be related to specific needs. These kinds of findings allied to a lack or avoidance of training may help to explain how some teachers can still dismiss dyslexia by invoking the stereotype of the overanxious, overambitious parent. On a more positive note it has been found that one of the best ways to change stereotypes is to get people from different groups working together on some common goal or purpose. Hannavy (1993, 1995) reports on an early reading and writing programme for children who are struggling. This involves parent–teacher partnership and has been tried in a number of different catchment areas with different groups of parents from different socio-economic backgrounds with a high degree of success. She noted that one of the most positive outcomes of the study was that it enhanced parent–teacher relations and that teachers who at the beginning had been dubious about including parents so closely in their children's learning became enthusiastic advocates of such an approach.

Different conceptions of parent–teacher relationships

Bastiani (1987) gives a useful overview of the different ideologies which he suggests have underpinned parent–teacher relationships. He outlines four major ideologies: compensation, communication, accountability and participation. The compensatory ideology had its roots in the Plowden Report (1967), which stressed the importance of parents' attitudes to their children's education. In doing this it proposed that an important task was for the less supportive families to be made more like the supportive families. This in turn encouraged deficit or pathological models of families to be applied and led to the development of interventions based on the notions of compensation and positive discrimination. Despite the good intentions of this approach based on post-war aspirations of educational opportunity for all, critics have pointed out that the Plowden Report was naive in not giving sufficient weight to the powerful influences that political and social factors have in shaping the relationships between parents and teachers. Drawing on the groundwork of Plowden, by the 1970s the role of good communication between schools and parents was seen as vital in promoting good parent–teacher relationships. The strength of this communication ideology was that it focused on the practical organisational issues involved in ensuring that good communication took place between school and home. Although nearly all those involved in children's education would agree that good communication is an important starting point, critics have expressed concern that the danger is in assuming that what is communicated is unproblematic. They argue that in some cases some parents and teachers may view an issue from very different assumptions and perspectives and that clear communication without a more fundamental shift in attitude will not necessarily lead to agreement. Another issue concerns what is meant by good communication. Bridges (1987) points out that professionals sometimes have a paternalistic model of communication whereby they see themselves enlightening uninformed parents and don't conceive of themselves as also learning from parents.

With a political shift in the last 20 years to viewing parents and children as consumers and schools as part of the market-led economy has come an accompanying emphasis on accountability and responsiveness to consumer demands and choices. Under the accountability ideology there has been concern to elicit parents' views on home–school relations both as direct consumers of the service and as part of the wider external audience that schools are accountable to. Despite the reservations expressed by a significant proportion of educationalists and parents regarding treating schools as part of the market place, accountability has expanded our understanding of home–school relations. It can be argued that the ideology of accountability has encouraged research that focuses on the issues and experiences which are of particular concern to parents. The level at which the concerns of parents are delineated is dependent on the type of research employed. With market survey-type techniques, figures are presented which can lead to generalisations about groups of parents based on simple divisions such as class or culture. Bastiani (1987) comments that, with a move to more in-depth qualitative methods such as open interviews, we can move beyond these relatively crude types of generalisations and begin to appreciate the wide variations in views between parents assumed to be in the same category. In a similar vein the wide variation in views between teachers is of equal importance and needs to be taken into account in any comprehensive picture of parent–teacher relations.

Parents as partners

The ideology of participation or partnership between teachers and parents has emerged out of elements of the ideologies of compensation, communication and accountability. But what distinguishes it from the other ideologies is the notion of parents and teachers as equal partners with equal rights and responsibilities. Wolfendale (1995, 2002) has written extensively on this model and as illustrated in Chapter 6 has spelt out in detail the differences between viewing parents as clients and parents as partners. The difficulty with the partnership model is that it presupposes that organisational and social changes based upon adequate resources can be made in order for parents and teachers to spend sufficient time together to work in partnership. Wolfendale (2002) has acknowledged that with the present pressures on schools it is hard to see how such a model can flourish. She has also pointed out that, even when the organisational changes are made to facilitate this model, one cannot force individuals to adopt it, and that practices can be subverted. Barton (2007) argues that a fundamental problem is that the interests of the school and those of parents of children with special needs are not always the same.

In many countries partnership with parents has moved up the political and educational agenda and in England and Wales, for example, the second chapter of the SEN Code of Practice (DfES 2001) is entitled 'Working in Partnership with Parents'. Despite such policy initiatives more recent studies (Hodge and Runswick-Cole 2008, Rogers *et al*. 2006) conclude that some professionals still have a deficit model of parents and expect parents to comply with their views, and that in consequence some parents are still fearful of questioning professionals because they do not want to be seen as demanding or unreasonable. Partnership models have been documented as particularly successful for specific activities such as home–school reading schemes (Topping 2001) and these have been widely adopted by schools. The problem again is that in some cases these appear to have been adopted by schools without sufficient research and commitment to the partnership model, so that listening to children read at home becomes a task prescribed by the school rather than a partnership between school and home. In the present study 19 of the 22 mothers said that they had participated in a home–school reading scheme. As described in Chapter 5 this caused considerable difficulty in every case bar one. In a small number of cases mothers thought that their concerns were appreciated by the teacher and in some cases the teacher would suggest alternative strategies that could be tried:

> I had a lot of contact with the school and to be honest they were quite good. They would suggest, 'Try this sort of thing,' or lay off it for a while, or ask him to read a paragraph and you read him a paragraph. They tried different things.

But the majority of mothers felt that their concerns were not really acknowledged and were disappointed that despite asking for guidance they were given no additional support or advice on how to deal with the situation:

> I was on my own really, they didn't give me any advice at all.

It is easy to envisage that from the teacher's point of view many of them were struggling to hear all the children in their class read on a regular basis and that finding time to do more than this was difficult for them. This highlights another difficulty with parent–teacher relations: teachers and parents can have differing priorities, so that, whereas parents are concerned with the needs of their own child, the teacher is trying to meet the needs in an equable manner of all the children that she or he teaches. Families and schools are organised in very different ways and this can easily lead to differences in perception over the nature and severity of difficulties. Connell (1987) argues that many parents don't see teachers as workers who are influenced by a whole range of workplace factors such as the way the school is organised, but instead judge teachers more as a kind of honorary parent. Given that many parents meet a particular teacher only a few times in the atypical circumstances of a parents' evening it is perhaps not surprising that they are not aware of all the factors that impinge on a teacher's performance. Both teachers and parents are in the position of forming opinions of each other based on very limited and partial information (Todd 2007). It is perhaps not surprising in these circumstances that misperceptions and stereotypes can arise. Connel (1987) argues that the stereotypes formed by both teachers and parents have a point. In the case of parents he suggests that these arise out of an attempt to make sense of what is happening at school based on very limited information. In the case of teachers he suggests that stereotypes such as the unsupportive or uninterested home are often used to explain children's performance and behaviour and thus help the teacher to survive in the face of a difficult and demanding job. In a similar vein Carugati (1990) has suggested that some teachers defend themselves against 'failure' by denying responsibility for children who fail. It can be argued that teachers are less likely to use the stereotype of the uninterested parent to explain the failure of middle-class children in general, or particular working-class children where there is clear evidence that parents are interested and involved in their children's education. In this case the teacher has to reach for the alternative stereotype of the pushy and unrealistic parent to either explain or deny the child's difficulties.

Clients or partners?

As already mentioned, Wolfendale has argued that parents can either be viewed as clients or partners by educationalists. Over half the parents in this sample felt that they had been openly blamed by the school in some way for their child's difficulties (Table 7.1) and therefore felt that the school, in Wolfendale's terminology, saw them as clients in need of redirection or as deficient.

In all these cases mothers claimed that some kind of direct comment had been made to them by the school. It could be argued that in some cases this may not have been the message that the school intended to convey, but several mothers were emphatic that they were being quite clearly blamed. When it came to accusations of being overanxious or overprotective these were applied equally to working-class and middle-class mothers in this sample. The following is a typical account of this:

> I knew something was wrong, but I was told I was worrying about nothing, and that she was just a bit slow learning to read.

Mothers such as this one thus found themselves in a difficult situation. If they carried on expressing their concerns this was further confirmation to the school that they

Table 7.1 Parents' perceptions of criticisms levelled at them by the school

Reported blame by the school	Number
Overprotective/overanxious	6
Emotional problems	2
Not doing enough at home	1
Spoilt	1
Child abroad for a year	1
Child moved school	1

were 'fussing', overanxious mothers. As well as environmental explanations centred on the home, 75 per cent of parents felt that, at an informal level, inaccurate within-child explanations for their child's problems had been used by the school. Fifty per cent of mothers thought that their child had been informally labelled as slow or thick by the school and another 25 per cent thought that their child had been branded as lazy:

She kept saying that he was slow.

What they feel is that he has got the ability but he won't try.

There was some evidence in this study that schools' explanations were linked to cultural stereotypes. Two of the three single parents were told that their child's reading problems were linked to home-based emotional problems and the third was told she was overanxious. One of these mothers described how angry she was when it was suggested to her that it might be an emotional problem:

They thought it was an emotional problem because he was from a one parent family, which I disputed because he was a happy-go-lucky kid.

Another mother from a working-class background was also annoyed when it was suggested to her that she didn't do enough reading with her son:

I get the impression they were thinking the mother isn't helping. I find a lot of people think it's because the parents don't sit down and read.

She resented this suggestion because she had always read to her son and she didn't think this suggestion would be made to a middle-class parent. Again mothers found themselves in a difficult situation. They had to either accept the school's explanation that their child was slow or lazy, and in some cases both, or risk being seen as an unrealistic 'pushy' mother if they argued that this was not the case. Several mothers pointed out that they argued that their child was intelligent only because they felt that the school was implying that their child wasn't learning to read or spell simply because they were 'stupid'. These mothers also pointed out that they weren't arguing that their children were more intelligent or more special than other children but that they were on a par with other children and that the explanation offered for their child's difficulties didn't fit with their own observations of the child:

He's of average ability like most of the world, but it's obviously that much harder for him. What I want is for him to survive and be happy in school and feel that he's as intelligent as other children.

Well, the psychologist said he didn't expect to find her in the top set, but she didn't deserve to be in the bottom set either, which I thought hit the nail on the head.

Another mother of a child of average intelligence commented:

As long as he can achieve his potential, that's fine.

The mother of an above average boy also commented:

You don't want Einstein, you just want to see them keeping up.

It's easy to see how misperceptions can arise on the part of both parents and educationalists. Some schools may not intend to convey the message that a child is slow but if this is how it is perceived by the parents they may in turn feel forced to argue that the child is intelligent. This in turn may be perceived by the teacher as an unrealistic parent with overinflated views of their child's ability. What can be suggested is that where stereotypes already exist such as the 'pushy parent' or the 'uncaring school' there is far more danger of behaviour being perceived in terms of these stereotypes. In summary it appeared that there were two key factors that influenced the relationship between teachers and parents of dyslexic children. One was the general nature of parent–teacher relationships within a specific school and also the way that individual teachers within the school responded within this context. This factor, it can be argued, is not specific to children with dyslexia but affects the way that all parents in the school are related to. But what can be argued is that the effect of viewing parents as clients rather than partners will have greatest impact where there is the most discrepancy in views between the parents and school as to the nature of a child's difficulties. This is related to the second and more specific factor, which is the school's view of dyslexia or specific learning difficulties and attendant practices. Where the school is highly negative or sceptical of the concept of dyslexia there is increased likelihood of poor parent–teacher relationships. Inevitably, where a school or a teacher sees parents as clients and is thus sceptical of their views and is also sceptical of the concept of dyslexia, there is the most danger of disagreement between school and parents. In some cases good parent–teacher relationships were seen by mothers as important when a school had declared itself uneasy about the term 'dyslexia' being applied. In these cases mothers felt that schools were willing to acknowledge some of the concerns that they had and to be sympathetic towards the child even though they wouldn't use the term 'dyslexia' in school.

Summary

1   Most research on children's schooling is carried out from the perspective of educationalists and not from the perspective of children or parents.

2   Both teachers and parents can form inaccurate stereotypes of each other based on partial information.
3   Some teachers subscribe to the inaccurate but powerful myth that dyslexia is entirely in the eyes of overambitious, pushy, neurotic middle-class parents.
4   Half the parents in this sample felt they had been stereotyped and blamed in some way by the school for their child's difficulties.
5   Stereotypes can be difficult to change.
6   It is suggested that the model of parents as partners working closely with teachers on shared goals is one of the most likely ways to reduce stereotypes.

Chapter 8

Home life and support

He wanted to be dead. There was nothing for him. He wanted his tie so he could hang himself.

(Mother commenting on her dyslexic son)

This chapter looks in more detail at mothers' observations of children's emotional responses to living with dyslexia and goes on to consider the kind of practical and personal support that mothers gave to their children to try and help them deal with their difficulties. Mothers were first asked what influence if any having dyslexia had had on their child. The results in Table 8.1 were obtained.

Many mothers commented that the worst effects had been before their child was identified as dyslexic and offered support. Several mothers said that it had been traumatic in the early days of school:

He used to wet the bed. He wouldn't get up in the morning and he had to be dragged to school.

He obviously looked under so much pressure that he looked pale and agitated.

He became much more moody once he started school and he had nightmares.

She was like a different child once she started school. There were tears and tantrums, she used to beg me not to send her, it was hell really. I didn't know what to do for the best.

It can be argued that behaviours such as bed wetting and tantrums are common features of early childhood and are not necessarily related to a child being dyslexic. Mothers seemed aware of this point and many were careful to point out those aspects

Table 8.1 Mothers' perceptions of dyslexia's influence on their children

None	5%
Some	40%
A lot	55%

of their child's development which they didn't think were related to dyslexia. One mother, for example, said that her son had always had sleep problems but she didn't think that these were related to dyslexia because they didn't tie in with what was happening to him at school. Another mother whose son was a persistent bed wetter made a similar point. Most mothers seemed to claim that particular behaviours or emotional states were related to dyslexia only when they thought there was a relationship between the child's experience at school and the behaviour or emotion in question. It can still be argued that mothers' personal perceptions were biased in this matter and that only more empirical research can check out the validity of these claims. Although this may be true there was a strong ring of authenticity about the accounts that mothers gave and in some cases there was corroboration from other sources such as teachers or educational psychologists expressing concern over a child's low self-esteem. In addition the 81 per cent of mothers with other children also stressed the difference in their dyslexic children from their non-dyslexic children in terms of their emotional response to school:

> Really, it's never given his sister any problems. I wouldn't even say she likes school that much but it doesn't bother her, it's never made her miserable the way it has him.

In some cases mothers described reactions which went on over a period of time:

> Like in French, if he's not doing terribly well, he finds it difficult remembering his words because of his short-term memory, and he gets very cross. He's never going to be academic, that's not in him anyway. But he's got disheartened and upset because he wanted to get good results like the other children and he wasn't. Then he stammers, and it's an emotional stammer. It comes and goes. But really it's more there than the times it's not.

Several mothers mentioned incidences which tied in closely with what was happening at school, such as a child getting very upset before a spelling test or coming home in a state because they'd been asked to read aloud in class (see Sophie and her mother in the extended case studies, Chapter 13). One mother recalled a period of a few weeks when her 6-year-old son was getting increasingly distressed. He was chewing all his jumper sleeves right up to the elbow so that they could no longer be repaired. In addition she kept finding him asleep on the stairs after he'd been put to bed at night. He generally appeared upset and distressed and his child minder, who had known him since a baby, was equally puzzled by the tantrums and distress he was displaying after school. At this point he had not been identified as dyslexic. His mother had no idea what was wrong but wondered if he was being bullied at school. She spoke to his class teacher after school one day. The teacher told his mother that she had concluded that her son was intelligent but that despite his good behaviour he wasn't trying hard enough to learn to read and write and she had therefore decided to put him under a period of concerted pressure. Discussion with her son revealed that this pressure was making him very unhappy and as soon as term ended his distressed behaviour disappeared. In another case a mother found that her son would feel sick and stop eating at the beginning of each school term and that it was only in the holidays that his eating really returned to normal. This was related quite specifically by her to his dread of returning to school and having to face tasks he couldn't do. In cases like this, where specific behaviours could be tied to specific events, mothers were fairly clear about what was happening. Where mothers were considering the possibility of more pervasive long-term effects they were more cautious in their statements and took time and care to answer the question. A single mother, whose son was a teenager, mused on the difficulty of sorting out the various causes for her son's behaviour:

> The problem is to fit in what's the adolescent part, what's the dyslexic bit and what's the bit that there isn't anybody else to take it out on. It's difficult trying to sort those out. He stopped going to school. He missed school for eight and a half days. In the end he was put on report. So I take him to the door every day, otherwise he's never there on time. That's the bit that I can't get through to people. People think dyslexia is about reading and writing. It's the whole organisational and motivational thing. If I stood over Luke and told him what to put on he'd get there in time.

This mother felt that the negative experiences her son had had at primary school, where he had been constantly called lazy, had had a strong and pervasive affect on his outlook:

> What I find difficult to get through to certain teachers is that he's had so many negatives that the positives aren't enough. The problem is they need to improve his self-esteem or he won't even try. If he thinks he's going to fail then he won't try in the beginning.

Many mothers spontaneously mentioned lack of self-esteem or confidence in discussing their child's reactions to having dyslexia:

> It was her self-esteem that really suffered.

> Because he couldn't read and write his self-esteem was dead low when he was younger.

In addition to this mothers were asked to estimate their child's present level of self-esteem on a five-point rating scale from very low to very high (Table 8.2). Without comparing these results with matched non-dyslexic controls it is difficult to know if these results are any different from the norm. But what was interesting was that half the mothers spontaneously mentioned that their child's self-esteem used to be much lower in the past. As can be seen from the figures this was most striking among the mothers who now rated their children as having above average self-esteem, but some mothers who rated their children average and even below average also claimed that their children had lower self-esteem in the past. Whereas some mothers used the term 'self-esteem' other mothers used the term 'confidence'. Whichever term was used mothers described a similar pattern with children losing confidence or self-esteem once they started school and especially if they had a particularly 'negative' teacher:

Table 8.2 Mother's estimate of child's self-esteem

Very low	2
Fairly low	6 (2 much lower in the past)
Average	7 (4 much lower in the past)
Fairly high	6 (5 much lower in the past)
Very high	0

> And over the years he changed from being a bright little normal child to losing confidence in himself, and I think he's just beginning to get it back after all those years ruined really.

> Well I would say he would be average . . . In the past I would have put it as very, very low. Because it was his self-esteem that really plummeted when he was at school and he couldn't do what the rest of the children did. His value of himself was nil really . . . and he wouldn't try and do anything because he thought he was going to fail.

Some mothers distinguished between their child's academic or school-based self-esteem and their self-esteem outside school:

> Fairly low coming into average but that's when we're talking about school. Otherwise higher because he can do lots of things.

In other cases mothers felt that their child's feeling of failure was so pervasive that it had started to colour all areas of their life:

> Oh, he couldn't do anything according to Mark. Even football that he loved, it was, 'I can't play football, I'm useless.'

> But another thing was he didn't have any friends at school. He was probably afraid that they would find out that he was slow or they would laugh at him or something and of course that made him feel dreadful as well.

This boy's mother went on to point out that since her son had been identified and supported and his confidence had improved he had made several friends, so it does seem plausible that his earlier lack of friends was related to his lack of confidence. Several mothers commented on their children becoming very withdrawn and quiet as they lost their self-esteem and some wondered if their children were depressed. One mother described how her happy, well motivated 8-year-old son who had always had lots of interests changed when he had a teacher who was very negative and critical of him:

> He cried at the slightest thing. He didn't want to see his friends and he couldn't think of anything he wanted to do.

Three mothers mentioned that on one occasion or more their child had said they wanted to kill themself as a direct consequence of the problems they were encountering because of their dyslexia:

> He wanted to be dead. There was nothing for him. He wanted his tie so he could hang himself.

> He got himself so wound up that night he said he wanted to kill himself and I thought, 'I can't believe this, what the heck is happening here?'

Van der Stoel (1990) in her interviews with Dutch parents of dyslexic children recorded similar incidences of depression and distress:

> Recently he's been depressed. I simply don't know what to do next.

> He was really bordering on the suicidal.

An examination of Osmond's (1993) interviews with parents, adults and children with dyslexia reveals strikingly similar themes of distress and loss of confidence:

> It took three years for Geoffrey to regain his self-confidence. He was so used to trying and failing at school that he had just given up.

> Immediately she began at primary school there was a familiar pattern of stress, frustration, panic and temper tantrums.

As has already been noted in Chapter 3 many educationalists and researchers have acknowledged the serious emotional consequences that dyslexia can have for some children, especially when it is unrecognised and unsupported. It should be emphasised that this is not specific to dyslexic children and that many children with a wide range of special needs are at risk of low self-esteem and personal distress. What it does suggest is that more research is needed to look at what factors are likely to lead to loss of self-esteem and distress in dyslexic children. Both personal reports and evidence from researchers (Fawcett and Nicolson 2004, Singleton 2002) strongly suggest that a major factor is lack of identification and support, particularly when this leads to teachers having an inaccurate or negative view of the child. What we don't know at present is how this might interact with other factors such as the severity and nature of the child's difficulties, the educational context in which they are trying to cope and their particular personality. We also need more systematic ways of following up the descriptions that parents give us. Parents will obviously vary in the language that they use and the way that they judge the severity of their child's problems. Objective measures of self-esteem, anxiety and behaviour are needed as well as objective assessments of the child's cognitive functioning and educational attainments. Such results need to be compared with those of non-dyslexic children before anything more precise can be said about the particular impact of dyslexia. What is also important is that these factors should be looked at on a longitudinal basis as the personal accounts clearly indicate that esteem and personal well being are closely related to the changing circumstances that children encounter. Given the number of complex variables involved it is perhaps not surprising that what also emerges is the reported degree of variability in children's responses, with some children showing considerable distress whereas others show relatively little distress according to their mothers. In the following example, Mrs Falkner, who was the only mother in the main interview sample who said that having dyslexia had had no effect on her daughter, felt that, although her daughter was not identified as dyslexic until she was 10, her school had been relatively supportive especially of her personal well being so that dyslexia had caused her little personal distress:

> I mean, she didn't seem to worry about it. I think she was too young to realise there was a problem. Give her another couple of years and she would have realised there was a problem . . . She takes it in her stride very well.

Interestingly this girl had one of the larger discrepancies in the sample between her reading age (6.8) and chronological age (11.1) when first identified as dyslexic, which would suggest that severity alone is not a reliable predictor of personal distress. As well as the supportive environment of the school another protective factor for her may have been that her best friend was also dyslexic and they were both identified around the same time:

> Believe it or not, her best friend at school was dyslexic as well, and they found out at virtually the same time, that they were both dyslexic. Which was a help for her.

Two mothers who both rated their sons as above average in self-esteem thought that having dyslexia had had both positive and negative influences on their development:

> In some ways it's hindered him, because he doesn't fulfil his potential, but in some respects it's made him more aware of other people's problems, so in some ways it's been good for him.

> I think it has given him a lot of character and push, he seems to want to strive to improve. I think it's made him more positive since he's found out, he's not so airy fairy about it now, he does realise it's going to be twice the struggle.

Both these boys reported that they had had quite difficult times at school in the past and both felt angry about being thought lazy and stupid by their former schools. This raises the question of how different families choose to view a specific impairment and how the personal qualities of both parents and children influence this process. Did the high self-esteem of these two boys influence their mothers' views or did their mothers' ability to see positive as well as negative aspects to dyslexia help their sons to maintain high self-esteem? In addition, what role do other skills and competencies play in this process? Both these boys were highly articulate (in fact they gave the two longest male interviews in the main sample) and both had a wide circle of friends. By their own accounts and those of their mothers they were both open about their dyslexia and were quite prepared to stick up for themselves at a verbal level:

> I don't think he lets anybody do him down.

Two mothers mentioned that success at a particular activity (captain of the school football team and winning horse rider) had considerably enhanced their children's self-esteem and helped to counter the negative effects of dyslexia. Scott, Scherman and Phillips (1992) reported a study in which they had tried to find out what distinguished 'successful' from 'unsuccessful' adult dyslexics. In this study they claim that the key factors were a supportive family background, early identification, and encouragement of talents and hobbies and a search for self-worth. In the current study mothers showed a high level of concern over their children's self-esteem and 80 per cent of them rated improvement in self-esteem as the most important outcome of their child's specialist support at the Dyslexia Institute:

> He's more self confident, and I'm sure that's had a lot to do with coming here.

> Well, it helped his self-esteem firstly.

Again it could be argued that mothers were misguided in their perceptions but their views were corroborated by the children and by specialist and in some cases class-room teachers. What is not clear is what aspect of identification and support led to the reported improvement in self-esteem. Does simply knowing you are dyslexic lead to improvement in self-esteem, or is the specific improvement in skills or the personal relationship with an adult who believes in you and encourages you of equal or more importance? It may well be that a combination of these factors in varying degrees are of importance depending on a child's particular circumstances, age, personality etc. The issue of how schools offer support and set about enhancing self-esteem will be looked at more closely in Chapter 9. In this chapter mothers' attempts to give practical and personal support to their children will be looked at in more detail.

Personal support

Mothers were asked what kind of personal support as opposed to practical support they offered their children. This fell into two main categories that often went hand in hand. One was countering the negative thoughts that their children had and the other was boosting their children's self-esteem or confidence by offering encouragement and dwelling on the positives. It could be argued that part of what mothers were doing was helping children to make more positive attributions about themselves. Mrs Knight, for example, said that her son often spoke of having a stupid brain; she would counter this by telling him:

> You're not stupid. It's just a problem that you have with one part of your brain which is not working properly that gives you difficulty with reading and writing and nothing else. You're good at sport and you've got lots of friends.

Mrs Roberts also offered her son reassurance when he said he was stupid:

> You're not stupid. You have to believe in yourself.

Mrs Kerslake described her son as saying 'I'm useless. I can't do anything.' In response, 'I'd always say, "Have a go at things. It doesn't matter if you can't do it. Just be positive. If you enjoy it, well, maybe you can do it."'

Mrs Thompson made the following comments:

> I just says, 'There'll always be things that other children can do that you can't do, but there again there'll be things you can do that they can't,' because he's pretty good at skating and things like that, you know.

Mrs Hanson described the strategies she used when her son came home upset about his homework:

> Cuddle him, 'We'll do it together. I know you can do it.' Tell him how good he is, but don't pressurise him.

Mrs Wood said that her response varied according to the situation:

> Sometimes I ignore it or I try to seem relaxed about it. Sort of try to defuse the situation, like make a joke of learning his spellings. His sister joins in, she marches up and down pretending to be his teacher and we all have a laugh about it.

Five mothers specifically mentioned stressing the positives, another five boosting self-esteem, four not being stupid and three offering encouragement. It can be argued that mothers were responding to negative images that children had received largely from outside the home.

Mothers therefore seemed very aware of the combined issues of how to give their children personal support and how to maintain or improve their self-esteem. Whereas with some children it was relatively easy to find things they were good at, for at least a third of the children this was much more difficult to do especially during their early years at school. Those children who, because of their specific cognitive impairments, were clumsy or poorly co-ordinated and had poor verbal fluency appeared to be at particular risk of low self-esteem. One mother pointed out that her daughter, when 7 years old, despite having a well above average IQ, could not read, ride a bike, swim, skip with a rope, tie shoelaces, put clothes on the right way round, tell her left from her right, recite the days of the week in order or hold a fluent conversation, neither was she particularly musical or artistic. For children such as this their 'failure' at learning to read, write and spell was compounded by their difficulties in mastering a number of other socially expected skills. Another mother whose son had experienced a similar range of difficulties pointed out that he had to spend so much time acquiring these basic skills that it hadn't left much time or energy for acquiring any special skills. Another mother whose son had an IQ in the superior range said that he would often come home from primary school and plaintively say, 'I wish I was good at something.'

His mother went on to comment:

> He was teased a lot by the other kids and often called thick and stupid. I don't think that should happen to any child, but the crazy thing was he was probably

brighter than most of them. The thing he's really good at is thinking, but that doesn't cut much ice, it doesn't give you any kudos with your friends.

Another mother commented that during the early school years:

His total value of himself was nil really.

Yet another mother said:

I think what hurt the most with Malcolm was last year [aged 10] he was even thinking about what he was going to do when he leaves school. He was coming home and saying things like, 'I think I'll be a lollipop man because you'll not have to do much written work.' And I thought, 'You know, you shouldn't even be having to worry.' You know really, your school days should be happy and even if you ask him, you know, because his brother is saying he will be staying on and doing his 'GCSEs', and Malcolm is saying, 'Well, I'm leaving school when I'm sixteen.' You know he still can't see what the future might hold . . . that he might be able to go on and do examinations and things like that.

From these accounts it appears that for a significant proportion of dyslexic children the early years at school can be particularly demoralising and lead to a considerable loss of self-esteem. The majority of mothers thought that being identified as dyslexic and appropriately supported was of key importance in improving their child's self-esteem. What is not clear from a sample such as this is what happens to children who are not recognised as having a specific learning problem by their parents. One of the mothers in the sample who was not recognised as dyslexic until she was an adult recounted her own experiences as a child:

Basically I think they [her parents] thought I was thick. They were always telling me how slow I was and how my younger brother would run circles round me when I was older. I must have been about six or seven when it was pointed out to me that he could write his name and address and say the alphabet. I hated him for it! Of course I thought I was stupid, it's stayed with me for the rest of my life really. That's why I'm determined the same thing won't happen to my daughter.

Practical support

Mothers were asked a series of questions about what practical support if any they offered their children in addition to help with their reading. The first question was 'What sort of practical support have you tried to offer (name of child) at home, or do you think it's best left to the experts?' The question was phrased in this way to try and ensure that mothers weren't made to feel that they were lacking if they weren't offering practical support and also to lessen the chance of their giving a socially desirable answer. It may also have been the case that some mothers might legitimately feel that they should leave it to the school. The following response to this question by Mrs Carter was a typical reply, in that many mothers had tried a whole variety of things:

Oh we've done pairs, like with cards. We've got all sorts of little games and things like they suggested. We've bought probably every book that's ever been suggested that might help. Like role playing books, we get through them, and all different sorts of things really, just to try and interest him. We've bought magazines about things he likes. But the thing was this year, I've taken him to the football . . . and I could have really cried because he sat down and started reading the football programme. And I thought, well that's the first time I've ever seen him sit down and read without being told to. We've bought the computer as well for Malcolm so we try . . . not that I've done a great deal with him, but sometimes if he gets his homework, we'll go on up and do a story on the computer. And because it's got the spell check and everything then he can print it out and take it into school. You know, I'll write that he's typed all the words himself, and things like that.

Mrs Carter was a working-class mother with three sons and a husband who worked away from home quite frequently. She by her own account had a lot of regular contact with school and spent a lot of time liaising with the teachers over Malcolm's difficulties. She didn't have paid employment outside the home and this meant that she could visit the school easily and also spend time giving her son practical support. What emerged in this sample was that it was those mothers who didn't work outside the home who generally had the most involvement with the school, and the most time to give practical support and campaign on their child's behalf. This included both working- and middle-class mothers in this sample and again underlines the importance of not having stereotypes about the degree of support and involvement by families from different class backgrounds. Peters *et al.* (2008) in their large-scale study of all parents reported similar findings with women not working outside the home or working part-time reporting higher involvement in their child's school life than mothers who were working full-time.

A simple count was made of the various activities mentioned by mothers (Table 8.3). Reading was included if it was over and above listening to reading as part of a home–school reading scheme. Many mothers like Mrs Carter mentioned trying a range of reading materials to try and engage their child's interest.

This is not a definitive list as many mothers may not have mentioned all the activities they had tried but it does serve to illustrate the wide range of activities included under practical support. Mothers were also asked how they had decided on what support to offer. Of the 22 mothers 19 said that they had basically had to decide for themselves as they had not been given any advice or guidance by the school. The remaining three

Table 8.3 Types of practical support offered by mother (*n* = 22 mothers)

Reading	11
Games	7
Homework	7
Workbooks	5
Phonetics	4
Storytapes	4

mothers said that they had been given some advice and support by the school. Many mothers said that they were disappointed at not being given any advice by the school especially when their children were younger and were struggling to learn to read and write. Many felt that in the earlier days in particular it had largely been a matter of trial and error, of using their common sense and seeing what did and didn't work:

> I think you have to try whatever you think. I went up a few times asking for help to both schools. I tried buying books, like the phonetic books and what not and we got to the stage where we worked through this particular book and I didn't know whether to go to the next book or whether we should learn them and I used to say, 'Look, I don't know what to be doing.' I'd be willing to do something but I don't know what.

> The school never gave me any advice. I was never really sure whether I should be correcting what he did, because I didn't want to make him feel that everything he did was wrong.

Several mothers mentioned this difficulty of not wanting to discourage their children by picking up on their mistakes all the time. Even within the context of practical support concern was expressed over how this could affect self-esteem or confidence:

> I tried to praise anything worth praising at all, just to try and encourage him. The thing we did most of all was to give Robert confidence above anything else, and he really seemed to gain that when he was about 9 or 10. He just became much more confident. He was a quiet, shy little boy at school before that.

Mothers were also asked if they came across any problems in trying to offer their children support. Their answers to this (Table 8.4) included both the support that they had instigated and the support that they were asked to give by the school in tasks such as reading and learning spellings and also the phonetic sound cards that the Dyslexia Institute asked them to do with the children.

Mrs Bell, whose son was now 13, talked about the problems she'd had over the years in trying to help her son:

> Er, well, it's died a death at the moment. But at the beginning I used to try and help him read his homework. I often offered to help with his homework, but he didn't want help. That's why he doesn't hand in very good stuff, he just wants the homework to be over with. We tried the paired reading scheme and he made it clear in subtle ways that he didn't want to do it and then it became such a slog . . . Well last year we went through a terrible stage where I was trying to get him to

Table 8.4 Problems experienced by parents in offering support

A lot of problems	19
Few problems	2
No problems	1

do the cards and that from the Institute. I'd ask him to go and get them and he'd disappear for an hour. So we didn't do them.

It's more difficult in the lighter weather because they want to be out playing. I sometimes feel a bit guilty, because I think, 'Eeh I should maybe be sitting down,' and then I think, 'Well, all his friends are out playing,' and you think it's a shame, isn't it? And then I think he would probably start and resent the fact, and then I think, 'Oh well, no, just leave it for a while.'

He doesn't like doing it. Well you can't do it without them knowing can you? When they're little you can, but when they get to Mark's age, it's, well, work isn't it? . . . and as I say, he doesn't like the fact that he has to do extra work. I mean I have tried to explain it to him as best I can. That it's for his own good.

Many would argue that these kinds of responses are no different from what may be found in many children of a similar age. What is different is that dyslexic children along with some other children with special needs require extra time and practice in order to access and progress through the curriculum:

The dilemma is whether home should be a safe haven, somewhere where she can relax and unwind or whether we should be helping her so she can cope better at school. I don't know what the answer is.

Many mothers were aware of this dilemma and expressed ambivalence and uncertainty about the kind of practical support they should give at home. This uncertainty appeared to be greatest when mothers didn't have specific advice on appropriate ways of helping their child. Mothers were happiest to carry out tasks when they could see the purpose of doing them and felt that they were geared at an appropriate level for their child's needs. The difficulties mentioned in Chapter 6 that arose with reading at home often appeared to be the outcome of a mismatch between the task and the child's level of skills. In a similar vein several mothers mentioned considerable difficulties with children having to learn spellings for spelling tests. Mothers thought that the spellings were usually too hard and that the priority was wrong in that there were a great many other simpler and more commonly used words that their child couldn't spell:

He was coming home with words like 'engine' when he still couldn't spell simple words like 'was', 'that', 'bus' and so on.

She gave them 20 hard spellings a week. He was worrying himself sick before the spelling test.

We used to spend hours learning the spellings. It was so hard for her. She insisted on doing them, cos she didn't want to be shown up in front of the other kids. She used to get in a terrible state about them. The worst thing was, it was a total waste of time because she'd forgotten them all by the next week.

Another important issue in relation to support was that families varied considerably in the amount of time and resources that they had available. Mothers who worked full time, had other younger children, were single parents or had husbands working away from home all commented on the constraints that this put on their time and energy:

Time, that's basically the main problem isn't it?

It's difficult in a sense because it's always me that has to do it you know.

Emma was the second of four children. Her mother had started working part-time so that they could pay for her two sessions a week of specialist tuition. In addition to taking and collecting Emma from her sessions she had to take her younger sister to speech therapy and help her younger son, who had a hearing problem:

She's missed out really. She's just had to get on with it. I do feel guilty about it, there just hasn't been the time.

Mrs Williams, a single parent who worked full-time and had a 13-year-old daughter, made the following comment:

When I come home from work knackered, the last thing I want to do is have a fight with Sian about her work.

In summary, a number of issues relating to support were discussed. Mothers were keen for guidance and advice on the sort of support they should give. They first looked to the school for advice. Where this was not available they used trial and error to try and find out what would work. With younger children in particular mothers said that they tried to capitalise on their interests and to use incidental opportunities to encourage reading and writing, for example:

I've been just lately trying to get him to write anything down. A couple of sentences is a real sweat. He did three or four lines totally on his own last night and I was ever so pleased, because it's the first thing he's ever done on his own in his whole life.

Once their child was identified as dyslexic some mothers turned to the specialist literature for advice and also to specialist organisations. Many mothers felt that the greatest pressure on them to give support had been before their children were recognised as dyslexic. Once children were being given specialist support mothers felt that this eased the burden on them and also they were given advice on specific structured activities. The nature of support changed with the age and needs of the child. With younger children support for reading and the use of games, tapes and flashcards were common whereas with older children the emphasis changed to help with homework, especially reading and checking things through, and the introduction of computers and spellcheckers. From the point of view of mothers the three biggest difficulties with support were:

1   not being clear what to do
2   not having sufficient time
3   not wanting to overburden their children.

Summary

1   Ninety-five per cent of mothers thought that having dyslexia had an influence on their child.
2   At least 75 per cent of children were reported to have gone through a period when they had displayed considerable distress of one sort or another.
3   The majority of mothers had been concerned by their children's low self-esteem and saw raising or maintaining self-esteem as one of their major tasks.
4   Mothers considered that one of the main benefits of their children's out of school tuition was that it raised their self-esteem.
5   Mothers found that as well as practical support they also had to give their children emotional support to help them cope with dyslexia.
6   Mothers would have liked more advice from schools on offering appropriate practical support.

Chapter 9

Views on school

We shouldn't approach dyslexics as broken learning machines.

(Hales 1994)

For both children and parents, a major part of the interview schedule focused on their experiences of schooling. Children were asked a series of 16 questions starting with what difficulties they thought they had at school both now and in the past, because of their dyslexia. They were then asked how they tried to cope with these difficulties and how they felt about them. They were also asked how other children and teachers reacted to their difficulties. Parents were asked a similar question about what difficulties they thought their child had at school both now and in the past because of their dyslexia. Both children and parents were asked what kind of things were generally found helpful and unhelpful in school and both were also asked to describe the best and the worst teacher that the child had encountered.

Perceived difficulties with work at school

Children's perceived difficulties may not accurately reflect their actual difficulties but, given the importance of self-esteem, self-efficacy and self-perception in the learning process, it can be argued that it is important to look at children's perceptions of their difficulties. In order to get as clear a picture as possible on how children perceived their difficulties they were simply asked: 'What sort of work do you have difficulty with in school because of your dyslexia?'

As has been noted before on the basis of clinical observation, some children appeared to find this an uncomfortable question to answer at an emotional level. Children appeared to have no difficulty in understanding the question at an intellectual level and in fact it could be argued that it was because children understood the question only too well that some of them found it uncomfortable to answer. At a general level children's perceptions of their difficulties fitted well with evidence from other sources such as reports by psychologists, classroom, special needs and Dyslexia Institute teachers.

Although there was some difference in the details and the way that difficulties were described at a general level there was also reasonable agreement between parents and children on the types of difficulties they had encountered. From Tables 9.1 and 9.2 it can be seen that both children and mothers claim that spelling and writing problems are the most frequent difficulties in relation to school work.

Table 9.1 Children's perceived problems with school work related to dyslexia

Perceived problem	Primary (n = 10)	Secondary (n = 12)	Total (n = 22)
Spelling	4	9	13
Writing about things	6	3	9
Slow work speed	2	7	9
Maths	3	3	6
Copying off board	3	3	6
Reading	1	4	5
Tests	1	3	4
English	3	1	4
Specific subjects (other than maths and English)	1	3	4
Dictation	0	3	3

Table 9.2 Mothers' perceptions of their children's problems with school work related to dyslexia

Perceived problem	Primary (n = 10)	Secondary (n = 12)	Total (n = 22)
Written work	7	10	17
Spelling	7	7	14
Maths	10	2	12
Reading	6	2	8
Slow work speed	2	6	2
Copying off board	1	1	2
Reluctant to work	0	2	2
Behaviour	1	1	2
Exams and tests	0	2	2[a]

Problems with maths or arithmetic

The high rating given to maths by mothers of primary school children may be because many of the children followed maths schemes that required a fair degree of reading accuracy. Several mothers felt that their child's progress in maths had been held up when they were younger because of their lack of reading ability. These mothers also felt that teachers were not always aware of the degree to which their children's maths was affected by their poor reading. In addition mothers and children mentioned problems with mental arithmetic and the learning of tables. Gillis Light and De Fries (1995) reviewed much of the evidence on what they term as the 'comorbidity of reading and mathematical disabilities'. They concluded from their review that the majority of studies indicate that between 50 per cent and nearly 100 per cent of children with reading disabilities also have difficulties with some aspects of mathematics. This raises the question of whether these difficulties are mainly due to common underlying cognitive deficits or to common environmental factors such as poor teaching or a negative attitude to learning. In order to try and answer this question Gillis Light and De Fries have drawn on data from the Colorado Reading Project, which was set up explicitly to look at the genetic and environmental contribution to reading disability. With additional funding this has been extended to include mathematics. In this extended study 148 identical twins and 111 fraternal twins were selected because one member of the pair was initially identified as having a specific reading disability. It was found that 68 per cent of the identical co-twins and 40 per cent of the non-identical co-twins also had a specific reading disability and that 49 per cent of the identical co-twins and 32 per cent of the non-identical co-twins also had a deficit in their mathematical performance. These findings are statistically significant and the researchers claim that this would suggest that common genetic factors contribute to the poor performance in reading and mathematics. Gillis Light and De Fries do not make it clear in their paper what aspects of mathematical performance are found to be lacking. They do mention that one of the tests used was the WISC-R arithmetic sub-test, which would suggest that they are talking about arithmetical performance. Another difficulty that they do acknowledge is that tests such as this involve word problems and it may therefore be children's poor reading ability that is hampering their performance. In order to try and control for this they tested a sub-sample of the children on the Wide Range Achievement Test for mathematical ability. This is a pencil and paper test that involves no word problems. Despite this it was found that children still performed badly, which would support the argument that specific underlying cognitive impairments affect both the reading and arithmetical performance of some children. However, there is also evidence that the reading and computational demands of arithmetic do significantly affect children's performance. Muth (1984) found that by artificially manipulating the reading and computational demands of arithmetical problems up to 50 per cent of the variance in performance could be attributed to these two factors. Many researchers and experienced professionals (Chinn and Ashcroft 2007, Geary 2003) have proposed that the deficits underlying reading and mathematical problems are in short-term auditory memory or in retrieval of information from long-term memory. Henderson and Miles (2001), as experienced teachers of dyslexic children, summarise the kind of day-to-day difficulties that children can have. They point out that, as well as the obvious difficulties in reading mathematical problems, some dyslexic children may have difficulty in remembering what operations are associated with what mathematical symbols. They may also have difficulty in knowing which direction they should move in when working out a sum and find it difficult to know where to place a decimal point. Reversals of numbers can sometimes cause problems, as in the case of a boy who would often reverse two-figure numbers so he would for example write 47 down as 74 as well as reversing the orientation of the 7. On top of all this is the well-known difficulty that many dyslexics have in learning multiplication tables (Chinn 2009) and their poor performance on the arithmetic and digit span sub-tests of the WISC. Darren, when tested at 9 years of age on the WISC-R, showed a profile that was typical of many of the children in the study in that his digit span and to a lesser extent his arithmetic were strikingly poor in comparison with his other verbal skills. Each sub-test is given a scaled score out of 20 with 10 being an average score. A child who got an average score of 10 on each sub-scale would end up with an IQ of 100. As can be seen from Table 9.3, Darren ended up with a verbal scale IQ of 130 despite the unevenness of his profile.

What is not clear from the literature at present is what the developmental history of

Table 9.3 Darren Street WISC-R Verbal IQ 130

Information	17
Similarities	16
Arithmetic	11
Vocabulary	15
Comprehension	15
Digit span	(5)

these difficulties might be and what proportion of dyslexic children encounter them. The relative lack of comment about mathematical problems in older dyslexic children might suggest that, as they resolve some of the earlier problems of reading, symbol identification, directionality and reversals combined with less emphasis on arithmetical skills, their difficulties decrease. The added use of calculators may also be helpful in diminishing problems. It is important that a distinction is made between arithmetic and mathematics as case studies would suggest that children can have a good conceptual grasp of mathematics despite poor arithmetical skills. An 11-year-old boy not in the main study talked about the problems that he had at school with maths. This boy had scored very highly on a mathematical reasoning test and above his age level in the SATs, despite being seen by his class teacher as only average because of his 'slowness' in doing maths:

> Sometimes they put loads of maths on the board with loads of tables. One morning Mrs T [class teacher] put about 20 sums up. I got really worried I didn't get it all copied down. Everybody else had finished and I was still writing them down. They were table sums all of them, and then I got all mixed up and I know bits of tables and they all get jumbled up . . . There are only 2 true types of sums. Like divisions are just a sort of take away and multiplications are a type of adding sum. I try to find new ways to do sums, else it gets boring.

Sian (13 years) when asked what she had difficulty with at school responded with:

> Maths, the reading bits, and mental arithmetic.

Clayton (1994) also endorses the importance of distinguishing between maths and numeracy or arithmetic. She raises the issue of how far we should expect dyslexic children with their poor short-term auditory memories to learn numeracy skills and at what point they should be allowed to use aids such as calculators and number squares. Mothers therefore seemed to be reflecting research findings in mentioning difficulties with specific areas of maths. They may have stressed these difficulties because they are a less expected and less publicised outcome of having dyslexia.

Writing, spelling and speed of work difficulties

Riddick (1995b) has commented on the relative prominence that children give to writing and spelling difficulties as opposed to reading difficulties. This may well be a function of the age of the children who were interviewed, as the average age of even the primary school children was 10 years. Many of them had improved considerably in their reading, possibly as a result of their specialist support, and several did mention that they had problems with reading in the past:

> I used to have problems reading, but now I read big books. Sometimes I get mixed up on things. A lot of hard words that I've forgot. I only have a little problem now.
>
> (Graham, 11 years)

> In the past reading, I was on a really low book, I used to resent it.
>
> (Emma, 12 years)

It may well be the case that, if 7-year-old dyslexic children were interviewed, reading would rank first or high in their list of difficulties. In fact the only primary child to mention reading difficulties in relation to school was the youngest child in the sample. This boy was 8 years of age when interviewed and had been receiving specialist support for only 3 months. When assessed 3 months previously he had scored on the first centile on the WRAT reading test and was still in the process of learning to read. He said he never read unless he had to because he found it too hard. Two of the secondary children who mentioned reading difficulties had discrepancies of over 5 years between their reading age and chronological age when initially assessed. Neither had been identified as dyslexic until quite late on and were still therefore working on their reading. The other two secondary-age children mentioned reading difficulties in relation to specific tasks and subject areas. One said that she had problems with reading in maths because of the need for complete accuracy and the other said that he had problems with subjects where a lot of reading was required because he couldn't read quickly enough. This highlighted the issue that concerns over speed and accuracy of work in a wide range of tasks (dictation, copying from the board, free writing, spelling, reading) tended to increase with age. Whether this is because of children's increasing awareness of their difficulties with age or because of the more stringent demands of the secondary school environment or some interaction between these two factors is not clear:

> Like copying off the board, I get frustrated cause it slows us [me] down. Like the teacher will be speeding ahead and my writing's slow.
>
> (David, 12 years)

> It's difficult to get things down fast enough.
>
> (Kathy, 12 years)

Some children also spoke of the dilemma of whether to go for speed or accuracy in their work as they were well aware of the trade-off between them:

> If a teacher dictates work I can't write fast and neatly.
>
> (Luke, 13 years)

At a more general level children spoke repeatedly about the constant pressure of 'keeping up' and the constant humiliation of always finishing last or getting the lowest mark in spelling tests:

> I usually finish my work last.
>
> (Graham, 11 years)

Some children spoke of their frustration at being told to hurry up or be more tidy in their work when they felt they were already doing the best that they could:

> Just saying like, 'Hurry yourself up,' and things like that when I cannot go any faster.
>
> (David, 12 years)

Other children spoke of their upset at being called lazy or careless for not spotting spelling or punctuation errors or words missed out:

> If I knew I'd spelt it wrong I wouldn't spell it the way I had to start with. It always looks all right to me
>
> (Mandy, 11 years)

Some children such as Ewan were upset when they were accused of not having done homework such as learning a list of spellings or part of their tables:

> Spellings and tables I always used to get them wrong. Then I used to get wronged [told off]. They said I didn't do them but I couldn't.
>
> (Ewan, 13 years)

Ewan's mother confirmed this independently in her interview by talking about the hours that she had spent in the past trying to help him learn his spellings. Again children spoke of the worries they had about exams and tests; these centred on not being able to read the questions accurately and fast enough and not being able to write fast enough:

> I don't like tests. I get very nervous and I don't do well, because there isn't enough time to get things down.
>
> (Stephen, 14 years)

> I get really nervous about exams because of reading the questions.
>
> (Sam, 11 years)

What this did emphasise was the need to see dyslexia as a developmental disorder that manifests itself in different ways at different ages and stages in a child's development. Although early intervention and support for reading are of vital importance for most dyslexic children it is important that the longer-term difficulties with areas such as writing and spelling are not overlooked. It is also important that we have a good picture of how the difficulties appear from the child's perspective. Children were particularly concerned about visible public indicators of their difficulties such as finishing last or being required to read out loud. This was underlined by their responses to a further question which asked if there was anything in school they really dreaded having to do. Seventy per cent of the children said that there were things that they dreaded having to do in school. We don't know from this data what percentage of 'non-dyslexic' children also dread doing certain things in school but what was striking was that all the activities mentioned were related to their specific learning difficulties. The most frequently mentioned were reading aloud in class, spelling tests and exams:

> Reading in front of the class; anything that shows me up and makes me different.

> I get upset in exams when I can't read something, my palms go sweaty.

Underestimating difficulties?

What was noted both in the children's interviews and independently by mothers was that some of the younger children in particular tended to underestimate their difficulties and appeared reluctant to acknowledge them. So, for example, Mark when asked what difficulties he had with his work at school started by saying:

> I don't really have any problems.

And when asked how much he wrote compared to other children he said: 'I just write the same.' Whereas his mother said:

> Spelling is the bane of our life, it's horrendous. One or two times they've had this thing like dictation. Calling something out and the kids have to write it down. That's just like the horrors for Mark, because he comes out with something that's totally incomprehensible. Sometimes getting something down quickly, he can't get it down quick enough. And his short-term memory causes problems for him. I don't think he realises how far he has a difficulty.

Some additional evidence for the defensiveness of some children may be the smaller number of difficulties mentioned by primary-age children compared with their mothers and secondary-age children (Table 9.4), although other factors such as embarrassment or poorer ability to generate answers may be responsible.

Children were asked whether they wrote more, the same or less than other children. Their mothers were also asked the same question. Several mothers commented spontaneously that whereas they thought their child wrote a lot less than other children their

Table 9.4 Total number of named difficulties with work because of dyslexia

	Primary (n = 10)	Secondary (n = 11)
Children	24	34
Mothers	34	33

child probably wouldn't agree and would be more likely to say they wrote the same amount as other children. In fact all the mothers thought that their children wrote less than other children, whereas only 50 per cent of the children thought that they wrote less than other children. Mothers' views were backed up with specific examples and corroboration from other sources such as school and the Dyslexia Institute. It also fits with Mosely's (1989) finding that children with spelling problems tend to write less. So for example Mandy on being asked how much she wrote said:

> The same as other children.

Whereas her mother said:

> I think she writes a lot less than other children, because she takes twice as long to write it.

This raises the question of why some children responded in the way that they did. Were they genuinely unaware of the extent of their difficulties or were they personally aware but not willing to admit to them, or had they consciously or unconsciously minimised their difficulties in order to keep their self-esteem intact? Returning to the case of Mark his mother made the following comments:

> The reason he started getting some extra help in the primary school was because at that point his self-esteem and confidence was rock bottom. And that's why they recognised the need to do something. Not specifically, I don't think, because of the academic side of things, because as a child he had no confidence or self-esteem.

As indicated in Chapter 3 some researchers have suggested that children may progress from a more global self-esteem to a more differentiated one as they grow older and there may also be individual differences in how self-esteem is structured. It could be argued that, where children are operating at the level of more global self-esteem, any difficulties may be threatening to that self-esteem, whereas if their self-esteem is differentiated into different areas they can afford to admit to specific difficulties without this affecting all areas of their self-esteem. This is highly speculative at present but more understanding of how and why children construe their difficulties in the way that they do is an important area of future research. Another reason why this is an important area to consider is that there is probably a relationship between the feedback that children receive on their performance and the way that they perceive their difficulties. Both mothers and classroom teachers spoke about the dilemma of how to point out mistakes without demoralising children and damaging their self-esteem. One experienced primary classroom teacher spoke about her bewilderment when confronted by the first piece of free writing of the year from a 10-year-old dyslexic boy:

> Well I just didn't know where to start. I'd never seen anything like it before. I had to get him to come and read it to me, because I couldn't make a lot of it out.

This teacher like many good teachers decided on a strategy of giving as much positive feedback as she could on the content of the story and just picking up on a few of the most basic errors. She admitted herself that she relied mainly on 'common sense' in deciding on what errors to pick up on and that this was a somewhat arbitrary strategy. This strategy appeared to work in terms of encouraging this boy to write and giving him the confidence to say what he wanted to say, but didn't really tackle his underlying difficulties in any systematic way. As Pollock *et al.* (2004) point out, arbitrary spelling and grammar corrections are of little use to the child who needs to be given structured coherent feedback. Another classroom teacher who had been on a specialist dyslexia course described the feedback she was giving to a dyslexic child:

> Well I try and turn the whole thing on its head. Rather than pointing out mistakes I try and put it in a positive light. So I'll say, 'Now you're doing so well, I think you could try and have a go at putting "-ing" and "-ed" endings on your words" [something this girl rarely did]. I'll give her some structured work to do to practise it first and then say she can have a point for each time she uses them in her free writing. I try and encourage her and make it fun.

Mothers also spoke about the difficulties of giving feedback both on specifics and at a more general level:

> It was very difficult choosing your words. Trying to say that although he was doing very well . . . you try to build him up . . . but! and how to put this 'but' over as best you could. That he was having a few problems with his spellings and to try and help him . . . and we never said you know, 'You've got a problem with reading.' It's always 'You've got to have this help.' It was a case of being very delicate, picking your words extremely carefully so that he wouldn't object to it.

This does raise some important questions. How far do children need to be aware of their difficulties in order to progress or to accept help? What appears to be important is the framework and the context in which difficulties are considered. It can be argued that difficulties need to be presented within a highly positive framework whereby the child is given explicit strategies for dealing with them so that they can feel they have some control over them. Reid (2007) discusses the importance of meta-cognitive approaches which encourage the child to be aware of their learning strategies. It also raises the question of how far children should be viewed as having difficulties and how far the environment should be seen as 'disabling' the child. Writers on disability have argued strongly that it is the environment that produces 'disability'. Others would argue that in a highly literate culture it is very difficult to completely avoid the need for literacy skills and that it would equally be doing the child a disservice not to try and improve their skills as much as possible. What seems important is that there should be a balance between these two points of view and that they work together in harmony to provide the best possible outcome for the individual. These arguments may seem rather abstract and removed from the nitty gritty of the everyday classroom but they do have a direct impact on the type of special needs interventions that take place. Much of the interest in early interventions such as reading recovery is based on the assumption that children's difficulties can and should be remediated. Although few would argue with the desirability of early intervention it is important that this doesn't lead to an exclusive focus on remediating early within-child difficulties. No doubt arguments will continue about the efficacy of various forms of early intervention but what seems clear is that some children will have longer-term difficulties. For example Wheldall *et al.* (1995) claim that, in a 1-year follow-up study of the reading recovery programme in 10 primary schools, 35 per cent of the children were not 'recovered'. This then raises the question of what sort of support these children are offered and how far the focus should be on improving difficulties and how far environmental changes should be considered. Mrs Slatter felt that even though her son Dean had improved considerably environmental changes would be of additional help to him:

> I think it's a very biased system, all the tests he's going to have are going to be written tests. They should be given an option. I still feel that orally he's a lot better than his writing. I think also the testing early on should be like that. The junior one he scored very low on the written test, and she gave him the same test orally, and he scored on the right line. I think there should be a lot more oral tests.

Although a whole range of environmental adaptations such as extra time in exams, taping work and photocopied notes are possible these, as many teachers will know, are not without their difficulties. Many children with special needs, especially as they grow older, try to cover up or disguise their difficulties, especially from their peers. Not surprisingly, anything that they think will show them up or make them different from their peers can be threatening and unacceptable. Environmental interventions have to be handled with skill and delicacy and need where possible to be negotiated on an individual basis with the child. What might be quite acceptable to one child may be highly unacceptable to another child and much might depend on how obtrusive or unobtrusive the intervention is. Sophie, a thoughtful and articulate 16-year-old interviewed in a later study, spoke about her experiences of being given extra time in exams:

> Yes, that's helpful. I would say that's helpful. I didn't think it . . . well, in some things it isn't, but then in others it's been really helpful.

She continued by explaining:

> I have to go and do it in the Sixth Form so everyone knows. It's awful really. They don't consider your feelings that much. They made us get up, we had to walk out of an exam and go into another room, and there was like a hundred people watching us walk out.

On a longer-term basis there are also questions about how much time and energy an individual should devote to overcoming their 'difficulties' and 'improving' themselves. Tim, a third-year university student, was asked as part of a pilot interview if he had used the new literacy support centre at the university. Tim had been identified as dyslexic whilst at primary school and had received support over a number of years. He said he hadn't used the new centre because this would only involve him in more work and that he felt he'd spent enough of his life doing extra work. He added that he'd got to a point where, although his difficulties still limited his performance to some extent, he was prepared to accept this and felt that he wanted to concentrate on other more positive aspects of his life. Pollock *et al.* (2004) also stress the importance of teachers highlighting what children can do rather than what they can't do. One mother talked about the difference in attitude between her daughter's primary school and the secondary school she was about to transfer to:

> At her primary school they never really acknowledged that she had dyslexia. It was always homilies about 'be more careful,' don't be lazy, don't be careless. It was like she wasn't valued; she was never picked for anything. I couldn't believe the difference when I went up the comprehensive to tell them about her problems. They took the problems seriously, they didn't try to sweep it under the carpet. They had specific plans about what they would try and do. They said it sounds like she's got a lot to contribute to this school. It was so positive, it was just such a different way of looking at it.

How children felt about their difficulties

When children had talked about the various difficulties they had with their work, and other people's response to their work they were asked how they felt about these difficulties. Many of them also added comments at other times during the interview. The children described themselves as disappointed, frustrated, ashamed, fed up, sad, depressed, angry and embarrassed by their difficulties.

Children's strategies for dealing with difficulties

Children were asked what strategies they used to try and deal with the difficulties they had described. Because in its abstract form this was a difficult question for children to answer they were asked some specific questions about how they dealt with their writing and spelling difficulties. In this case they were presented with a list of strategies such as avoiding difficult-to-spell words or getting help from a classmate. This list was compiled from strategies already documented in the literature, such as avoiding difficult-to-spell words, and strategies named in the pilot interviews, such as putting off writing. It was not thought that the children were simply agreeing with the interviewer in answering the list because children were quite selective and quite emphatic about which strategies they did and did not use. So, for example, when asked whether they avoided certain words several children gave a similar answer:

> Every day.

> I avoid lots of words I can't spell.

> Yes, all the time.

> Yes I do that nearly all the time like 'was' and 'because'.

> Yes, I try and make a different sentence out of it.

Whereas a small number of children were quite certain that they didn't avoid words in their writing which they found difficult to spell:

I just give it a try.

No, I just carry on. I try and use like my A and E [sounds].

The information in Table 9.5 on avoiding difficult to spell words fits well with research which shows that both children (Mosely 1989) and adults with spelling difficulties restrict their vocabulary because of this. What is not clear is how far these difficulties exacerbate any difficulties that children may already have with sentence structuring or how far they may be producing difficulties with sentence structuring. It is not hard to imagine that if a child is constantly trying to construct sentences without using words such as 'was' and 'because' this will lead to difficulties with sentence structuring. Pollock *et al.* (2004), who are experienced teachers of dyslexic children, highlight the dilemma that children face. If they are very careful in choosing words they can spell then they will often appear to be immature in their vocabulary and mode of expression. If on the other hand they ignore their spelling and get on with writing what they want to say they are in danger of being accused of being careless, especially as they may be able to correct their mistakes when they have been pointed out. One of the mothers in the study gave an example of this:

> She [class teacher] said she tells him not to be careless. When he brings her a piece of work she tells him, 'Don't be lazy. Go away and do it properly.' She says well he can do it because he brings it back with less mistakes.

This mother was very concerned because in past years when her son had sympathetic and supportive teachers he had been willing to write even though it was a struggle for him. Now he appeared very unhappy and had said all year that he couldn't stand school any longer. The boy himself when interviewed said:

> I dread having to do writing. I draw pictures instead if I can.

Another girl commented about writing:

> I'd choose to do anything else.

Table 9.5 Children's reported coping strategies for dealing with spelling and writing difficulties

Coping strategies	Primary (n = 10)	Secondary (n = 11)	Total (n = 21)
Avoids hard-to-spell words	5	11	16
Writes less	3	8	11
Gets classmate to help	4	6	10
Puts off starting or avoids doing writing	2	6	8
Total number of strategies named	14	31	45

Numbers are small so any conclusions have to be tentative. What does seem clear is that for whatever reason older children are more explicit about their difficulties and the strategies that they use to cope with them. By secondary age all the children claim that they avoid difficult-to-spell words and over half of them claim that they put off or avoid doing writing. It has been suggested that, whereas primary school teachers are basically optimistic about children with special needs and still expect them to improve or overcome their difficulties, by secondary school, teachers are more pessimistic in their attitudes and no longer expect children to show substantial improvements. It seems that by secondary school the emphasis of the intervention is based on teaching children to cope with or circumvent their difficulties rather than directly tackling their difficulties. It could be argued that the increased number of strategies named by secondary children is partly a response to this shift in ethos. The children themselves, in consciously writing less, avoiding writing and limiting their written vocabulary, appear to be adopting coping and avoiding strategies. Nearly all the secondary children had been put in bottom sets for some or all subjects. Many of them spoke of feeling rejected and ignored and resented the low expectations that they thought that many teachers had of them; these sentiments were also reiterated by their mothers.

Best and worst teachers

Although children were asked what sort of things they generally found helpful and unhelpful in school, it was found in piloting the interview that this was a difficult question for many children to answer; whereas they responded quite enthusiastically to the more personal question of describing the best and the worst teachers that they had encountered. Similarly with parents it was found that they responded in more detail and more confidently to the question about best and worst teachers. As was discussed in Chapter 7 this is probably because parents and children often don't have insight into the many structural and organisational issues which impinge on a teacher's role and they therefore have to judge teachers largely independent of context and on their face-to-face performance. Parents did temper their comments in the more general question and many of them showed awareness and expressed sympathy for the context in which teachers were working:

> It's not so much the worst teachers, he's had very interrupted teaching through his school career. He's been first of all in a very big class that had like the top number that you can have. So obviously they were pressurised with coping with that. And then just throughout the whole of infants as well he had like somebody was off ill for a long time, and then there was the supply. Somebody was off pregnant, and then there was another reason, and it went on and on . . . I think they generally did care. I don't think anybody knew exactly what it was and as he got higher up the school I think they did try to work around him. Well I know they did try. I don't want to write them off. They did try to help him.

There was close agreement between mother and children pairs in describing the best and worst teachers they had encountered. In the case of four pairs it was thought that there had been no 'best' or 'worst' teachers, with all the teachers described as fairly supportive or alternatively as fairly indifferent. So one mother when asked about the best teacher her daughter had encountered said:

> Nobody in particular. There's not one who's really thought about it.

Both mothers and children thought there were close links between the ways in which teachers related to children and how they coped with their dyslexia at a personal level. Mothers in particular emphasised the close relationship between their child's self-esteem or confidence and the way that teachers treated the child:

> He had one who made no allowances. She gave them twenty hard spellings a week. He was worrying himself sick before the spelling tests. In fact he started bedwetting because of the pressure of the spelling tests and other things. She destroyed his confidence completely, she used to systematically put red lines through everything.

> The second year juniors he had a very good class teacher, she really took him under her wing. It was her project to get him up and going by the time he left her class. She took a great interest in him, yes and she dwelled on the positive aspects of everything good he could do. He had very low self-esteem before that but his confidence seemed to really start to build in her class.

From Table 9.6 it can be seen that both children and mothers underline the importance of giving praise and encouragement allied to understanding as key qualities of the best teachers. Mothers in particular emphasised the support and encouragement offered by these teachers and often spoke of the teacher 'believing' in their child:

> She was so supportive, and she was aware of Mark having problems, and she you know recognised that, and she tried to help us. But apart from that if you ask Mark he'll tell you she was his favourite teacher anyway.

> His year tutor last year picked up on David's problems. He was really committed to helping David. He encouraged him with his marking and takes a personal interest.

> Mr H. He was the chap that really built his confidence up and encouraged him. He was great.

Mrs Salter and her son Graham, as can be seen in the next two quotes, were both very positive about the 'best' teacher to have taught him:

> She was wonderful, she encouraged him, praised him and rewarded him. She boosted his self-esteem and he progressed a lot with Mrs M. She enjoyed teaching him.

> Mrs M. She knew I was intelligent. She used to encourage me and she used to help me with my work.

Table 9.6 Children's and mothers' perceptions of the best and worst teachers they had encountered

Best teachers			
Children's perceptions (n = 18[a])		Mothers' perceptions (n = 18[a])	
Encourages/praises	9	Encourages/praises	12
Helpful/adapts work/explains	7	Knows strengths	8
Understanding/doesn't show up	6	Positive/supportive	7
Doesn't shout	2	Believes in child	7
Sense of humour	2	Boosts self-esteem	7
Knew child was dyslexic	1	Understands dyslexia	7
Treats as intelligent	1		

Worst teachers			
Children's perceptions		Mothers' perceptions	
Cross/impatient/shouting	7	Doesn't understand difficulties	6
Criticises or humiliates	6	Puts down or humiliates	5
Not helpful/negative	5	Negative attitude/no praise	5
Ignores/thinks useless	4	Low expectations/ignores	7[b]
Not understanding/insensitive	4	Lacks tolerance/no allowances	3
Blames you/thinks you are lazy	4	Shouts at child	3
Red lines through work	3	Red lines through work	4

Notes
a   As 4 out of the 22 mother/child pairs said they hadn't encountered any best or worst teachers only the remaining 18 pairs are represented on this table.
b   6 out of 7 at secondary school.

Malcolm and his mother were in agreement that his current teacher was one of the best he had encountered:

> The relationship is quite good with her because she knows when to encourage him when he's done well, and she does. And she can see areas where Malcolm's quite good at, like, model building and things like that, and she'll get him to show the other kids in the class how to do things like that. So he does feel, 'Well, I mightn't be good at that, but I am good at this.' . . . She's really good with him.

> She's really kind to people, she's encouraged me a lot.

Both children and mothers mentioned the importance of not being shown up or humiliated by teachers:

> Like she makes allowances for me and she doesn't show me up. She praises me and gives me gold stars.

She's understanding. She encourages you and always smiles at you. She's nice even when you get something wrong.

Some children as well as commenting on these supportive attitudes also mentioned more practical aspects of support. Kathy in her first year at secondary school when asked about the qualities of the best teacher/s she'd had so far named several of her subject specialists and added:

If the work's hard they help a lot.

When it came to worst teachers there was close agreement again between children and mothers on who fell into this category and why. Mrs Salter described what happened when her son Graham entered the first year of junior school after a year spent in America:

He had this bad teacher for two years who humiliated him for two years. She had on the second day we had come back from America, prodded him in the stomach and told him to go down to the kindergarten to get a book to read, right in front of the whole class. She found it an irritation having a child who couldn't read in her class. She had no tolerance at all.

Mrs N. She never noticed anything. She just liked the ones who knew everything. It was very off putting.

There was one in the primary school I won't mention her name. She said I was useless at everything and I couldn't do anything. My mum was very angry.

His second teacher was a battleaxe. There was red writing all over his books and no praise at all.

She had no understanding at all. She put him down for the least little thing and put red lines through all his work.

She kept saying 'You're lazy.' It's awful to say to a kid all the time 'You are lazy.' I think he lived up to expectations. I don't know how if you down a kid all the time you expect to get any good work from them.

I don't like being shown up in front of the class. The spelling tests are the worst. I'm not frightened of the shouting, but I don't like it when they get the class to laugh, like one teacher used to do.

By secondary school both mothers and children felt that on top of teachers who criticised and humiliated them there were teachers who ignored them and had low expectations of them.

Several mothers commented that irrespective of IQ and motivation their children were put in the bottom set for most subjects. Stephen (14) despite being well behaved and well liked by his teachers and having an IQ of 113 was in the bottom set for all subjects:

> At school they think he's great, but he's in the bottom set for everything. He's not being given any homework, he's probably not being stretched enough. Some of the teachers think that because they're in the bottom set that they don't matter, they ignore them and give them less attention.

Mrs Andrews reported similar problems despite her son having an IQ of 119 and according to his school reports being a quiet thoughtful boy who was well behaved:

> His present maths teacher is the worst I think . . . She said, 'Josh won't be able to take O level [GCSE] you know.' He says she doesn't like him. I said, 'Well, why do you think that?' And he says that she doesn't take any notice of him.

Sian's mother also commented on her 13-year-old daughter being put in the bottom set for everything and continued by saying:

> She's had teachers who've yelled at her, crossed everything out, labelled her slow and had low expectations of her.

In summary, the worst teachers were thought to be negative in attitude, critical, humiliating and lacking in understanding; in addition, especially at secondary school, some worst teachers were thought to ignore or underestimate children. As stated before, the best teachers were seen as positive, encouraging, understanding and helpful. These results are similar to those found when children in general are asked about good and bad teachers (Burns 1982) and the more negative aspects are similar to those reported by children who are failing or having difficulty in school for a variety of reasons. Burns (1982) has also reviewed a wide range of literature which suggests there is a link between how supportive and encouraging a teacher is and how positively they are rated by a child. In addition it has been suggested that there is also a strong link between the teacher's attitude and the child's level of self-esteem. Opie (1995) looked in detail at the practice of five exceptionally successful teachers of reading in terms of both their personal qualities and their teaching approaches. In her summary she gave the following description:

> All the teachers studied emerged as valuing positive and trusting relationships with their pupils and having high expectations with regard to progress. They stressed the importance of enabling their students to experience success, improving their confidence and raising their self-esteem.

These teachers were also reported to be well organised and prepared and enthusiastic in their approach.

They all stressed the importance of structured phonics teaching and a multi-sensory approach allied to keeping children on task as much as possible as well as making lessons enjoyable. One teacher who worked with a class of children with special needs emphasised that children have to believe they can be helped in order to progress.

Edwards (1994) in her interviews with eight adolescent dyslexic boys at a specialist boarding school found that the boys emphasised the need for a warm trusting relationship with their teachers and that many of them stressed the importance of an 'outstanding' teacher with whom they'd had a special relationship. It may be that the 'best' teachers identified by children and parents are not necessarily the 'best' or most effective teachers in terms of children's educational performance. But it can be argued that there appears to be considerable overlap in the qualities described by parents and children and those describing effective teachers of reading.

Discussing 'best' or 'worst' teachers or effective and ineffective teachers is a difficult area. The first point is that different children may have different views on who best and worst teachers are. A second point is that negative feedback or criticism is often threatening and difficult to handle. To look at it more positively, research (Rix *et al.* 2006, Galloway 1985) suggests that individual teachers and how they interact with children has more influence on their progress than organisational differences such as whether they are in a mixed ability class or not. Mok (2002) found in a statistical analysis of quality of school life factors for over 8,000 grade 12 children that children's experience in the classroom was the most important factor in their overall quality of school life rating. Ainley and Bourke (1992), in their quality of school life research, point to large differences in how fair and helpful different teachers are perceived to be by children. Galloway (1985) also suggests that these teacher differences in classroom interaction may have the greatest impact on children who are experiencing difficulties in learning. In the present study there were several instances where children and their mothers felt that they were in 'the firing line' because of their specific difficulties:

> He says she shouts at all the children and so on. But he probably gets more of it, because she's always telling him off for being untidy or being slow or getting his spellings wrong.

A difficulty for teachers may be that some children with specific learning difficulties are more sensitive than usual to criticism. So that a comment which is intended to be helpful such as praising a piece of writing but telling the child to put capital letters in may be seen only as criticism. This may sometimes be the result of cumulative criticism that the child has received over the years and from a number of quarters. Meryl, an outgoing and positive 16-year-old, talked about this in relation to her written work:

> I get really exasperated people never comment on the ideas first. They say, 'Oh look, you've spelt this wrong and this wrong.' My best friend at school does it; she leans over and points out my mistakes. I could kill her sometimes! The teachers are just the same and my mum's no better. It really bugs me.

Edwards (1994) detailed over sensitivity to criticism as one of the common features in the eight boys that she interviewed. One question that arises is whether at an objective level children with dyslexia do receive more criticism about their work than other children or they simply perceive themselves as receiving more criticism. It may well be that both factors are in operation, although parents and children strongly felt that they did receive more criticism. Robert, for example, by his first half term in secondary school had received negative written comments on the untidiness and supposed carelessness of his work from a range of subject teachers. It was found that half the homework he had done so far had negative comments of this kind and in some cases a subject teacher had given negative comments on several occasions. Many of these comments were tempered with 'good but . . .' and teachers may well have intended their comments as helpful feedback. But Robert was already becoming upset by these criticisms and wrote the following at half term in an account of his new school:

> The science teacher only marks for neatness and tidiness. I liked science, but I don't now.

Robert, like several children, stressed that what upset him was the 'unfairness' of this criticism and from his point of view the impossibility of doing anything about it:

> I already write as neat as I can.

To be fair to Robert's teachers his writing was appalling and his frequent attempts to correct his spelling added to the messiness of his work. He attended a school with a good special needs department and a generally positive approach to specific learning difficulties. But his experiences of marking do emphasise the need for all the teachers involved to be aware of a child's difficulties and to be aware of the cumulative effects of the feedback they are giving.

Some of the children in the study described in this book had displayed many of the features of depression when at their lowest point. It has been found that depressed individuals are more likely to remember negative rather than positive feedback (Cole and Jordan 1995) and are therefore more likely to be adversely affected by it. The need for appropriate feedback has already been discussed in Chapter 3, and the views of children and mothers in this study support the importance of giving careful consideration to how feedback should be given. With older children it may be possible to discuss with them the kind of feedback they find most helpful and the form they would like to receive it in. One difficulty appears to be that particularly when children are in a negative frame of mind it can take years of encouragement to get them to view themselves more positively:

> It's taken years to convince him that he's not stupid and to be more positive about things. When he was really low nothing seemed to be able to shake him out of it. He'd come home with praise for a piece of his writing and still be negative about it. One day he came home and complained that he'd only got 49 out of 50 for a maths test! He blamed himself because he'd got one sum wrong.

What was encouraging in this study was that when teachers did have positive and warm relations with children they were reported to bring about big improvements in children's self-esteem. Archer (2004) in a study of exceptionally skilled and effective teachers of reading in the US observed that they always displayed respect and had positive interactions with children and never used sarcasm or scorn but would use laughter to promote a positive learning environment. Opie (1995) suggests that it is important that teachers set aside time for building up good relationships with children when teaching them to read and that factors such as self-esteem and motivation are kept in mind. Where classes are large and teachers already overworked this obviously becomes more difficult for them to do. On the other hand in this study there was no indication that 'best' teachers spent appreciably longer helping the dyslexic children than 'worst teachers'. It was the way they related to the children that was seen to be of greatest importance.

In conclusion, best teachers appeared to combine a warm positive outlook with good specific understanding and skills.

Summary

1   Late primary age children as a group see writing about things as their greatest difficulty.

2   Secondary age children show increased concern with the speed and accuracy of their work.

3   There was a fair amount of agreement between children and mothers on the kinds of difficulties they had.

4   Mothers of primary age children placed more emphasis on maths and reading problems and several thought that their children tended to underestimate their work related difficulties.

5   Children were particularly concerned with visible public indicators of their difficulties such as finishing work last.

6   Children reported using a range of coping and avoiding strategies to deal with written work.

7   Both children and mothers thought that individual teachers had a big influence on their self-esteem and ability to cope with difficulties.

Children's views on dyslexia

> They said I would always be dyslexic cos they can't cure it, but I can be great at my work.
> (Darren, 12)

> Well, people think you're being stupid to be quite honest. That's the whole attitude of it.
> (Sophie, 16)

In Chapter 6 children's reactions to being labelled dyslexic were discussed, as this was felt to be a critical part of the labelling process. It was concluded that, whereas the majority of children found the label 'dyslexia' helpful at a personal level, half of them didn't find the label helpful at a public level. This chapter looks in more detail at their views on dyslexia and the ramifications of these views for various aspects of their life. Children were asked a number of questions that explored their understanding and attitude towards both their difficulties and the term 'dyslexia'. They were asked, for example, what dyslexia meant, who had explained it to them and whether it made sense to them. They were also asked if they met other children with similar difficulties, and whether this was helpful or not to them. In addition they were asked if they'd had adult dyslexics pointed out to them and again asked if they found this helpful or unhelpful. Another series of questions overlapped with their views on school but focused specifically on social issues such as whether they thought other children noticed their difficulties and if so how they tried to explain their difficulties and how other children reacted to them. Finally their long-term expectations were questioned by asking if they thought they would still be dyslexic when they were an adult.

In order to ask children about their understanding of the term 'dyslexia' in a non-threatening way the question was put in the following form: If somebody asked you what dyslexia meant, what would you say? Children responded to this question with a wide range of answers which could be divided into the categories in Table 10.1.

Only two children (one primary and one secondary) characterised dyslexia primarily as a reading problem. Given what is known about the long-term difficulties accompanying dyslexia and the priority that children of this age had given to problems with school work other than reading, this is perhaps not surprising:

Table 10.1 Children's definitions of the term 'dyslexia'

	Primary	Secondary	Total
Reading, writing, or spelling problem	5	5	10
Learning difficulty	2	3	5
Slow at work/learning	1	2	3
Can't explain or doesn't know	2	2	4

> It's when you find it hard to read and things like that. It takes a long time to overcome.

In contrast to this answer most children in the first category mentioned reading in combination with writing and/or spelling and one child described it solely as a spelling problem. 'You have trouble with reading and writing.' 'Not good at reading and spelling.' 'Somebody who can't spell as good as the rest.' Children in the second category rather than mentioning specific literacy difficulties referred in some way to the learning disabilities underlying these difficulties:

> I tell them like it's problems with learning words, it's a learning difficulty. Like the other way I use to describe it is, like, my memory, my short-term memory is like a broken camera, like the flash isn't working.

> People who have to learn in a different way.

Perhaps not surprisingly given that 'keeping up' was a major preoccupation of many children, two children actually described dyslexia in terms of slow speed:

> Basically a bit slow at your work.

Another child who said he didn't really understand what dyslexia was described himself as a slow learner:

> Just probably I don't know or a slow learner or something.

This boy had been very demoralised by his experiences at school and scored low on self-esteem.

In contrast the boy who scored highest in self-esteem and also had good verbal fluency was the only child to mention intelligence:

> Intelligent, but can't read and write.

It has to be born in mind that these comments only give a snapshot of children's views on dyslexia at a given moment in time. It may also be the case that what you choose to say in explaining dyslexia to others may not fully reflect your own understanding. One boy looked very frustrated and said:

I know what it is, but I can't really explain it.

Trying to explain dyslexia in brief, concise terms is quite a difficult task and much might depend on the verbal fluency and confidence of the child. One child pointed out that it's difficult to explain dyslexia to children who are basically hostile or disbelieving. The mother of another child talked about a recent incident at school. Her son was in the last year at primary school:

> They had to fill out this form describing themselves for the next school to look at. He'd put this bit about how he was slow at his work but he didn't know why. I asked him why he hadn't said he was dyslexic. He said he was worried that he might be asked to explain what it is, and that he wouldn't be able to.

This boy was able to explain what dyslexia was quite adequately to the interviewer and thought that knowing he was dyslexic was helpful. His mother felt that he had picked up on the critical and disbelieving attitude of his primary school and that this combined with his lack of confidence and poor verbal fluency made him very defensive and wary of any situation which might expose him to critical questioning or ridicule. This again reinforces the idea that whereas children find the concept of dyslexia helpful at a personal level they don't necessarily find it helpful at a public level, especially if the public level is seen as hostile or critical of the concept. Those educationalists who argue that labelling is harmful are right in a sense, in that labelling children in a public situation, especially one that is critical of the label, probably is harmful. But where they are probably wrong is to go on and deny the use of the label altogether. As argued before, labels have to be used in the right context and only when they are of help to the individual concerned. It's important that both parents and teachers discuss with children as they get older if, when and where they want a particular label used. It should also be accepted that children's views on this might sometimes be complex and contradictory and that as children change and develop so might their views. It can be argued that children's understanding of dyslexia is probably heavily influenced by how it is explained to them. In order to examine this issue children were asked who had explained to them what dyslexia meant and whether the explanation had made sense to them (Table 10.2).

Table 10.2 Who, according to the children, explained dyslexia to them

Mother	12
Mother + father	2
Mother + father + dyslexia teacher	1
Mother + dyslexia teacher	2
Mother + dyslexic friend	1
Mother + doctor	1
Dyslexia teacher	2
Assessing psychologist	1

It can be seen that in over 50 per cent of cases mothers alone explained dyslexia, and in another seven cases mothers explained dyslexia in conjunction with someone else, in three cases with the child's father, and in four cases with a professional. Thus in over 80 per cent of cases mothers were primarily involved in explaining dyslexia to their child. In three cases a professional was seen as the primary explainer. In these last three cases the children in question were all of secondary age and it may be that judgements about the appropriateness of who should explain change with age. What emerged from the interviews was that in some cases there was an ongoing dialogue between the mother and the child and/or specialist teacher about what was meant by dyslexia whereas in other cases children were reluctant to speak about the subject so there was little opportunity to clarify or discuss with the child what dyslexia meant. What was striking was the heavy responsibility that mothers had and the total absence of any explanation from within the mainstream school environment. This may be a function of this particular sample; in areas where schools and local authorities are more supportive of the concept of dyslexia, more explanation might come from within the school setting. Children's recollections of who explained dyslexia to them may not necessarily be accurate in a strictly objective sense but they do reflect their perceptions of who was significant in this process. Given that the manifestations of dyslexia change over time and the types of difficulties encountered change with time, it may be important for some children that they can revise or update their understanding of dyslexia. So a child in early primary school may understand dyslexia as a difficulty in learning to read whereas by secondary school they may see it as a difficulty in spelling. In addition to having dyslexia explained to them by an adult, two children mentioned that watching a television programme on dyslexia had increased their understanding:

I once saw a programme on dyslexia, that helped me to understand it.

Following on from the question of who had explained dyslexia to them children were also asked if this explanation had made sense to them. As can be seen from the figures in Table 10.3 the majority of children thought that the explanation given to them made sense. Sian (13 years), who said 'I suppose I'll never fully understand it', was the child oldest in age when identified as dyslexic. She said that knowing she was dyslexic was helpful but was resentful of her mother having her assessed even though this was at the school's suggestion. She went on to say that she would like to talk about it more but not with her mother:

Not to my mum, because she's my mum like.

Table 10.3 Children's understanding of the explanation of dyslexia they had received

Did it make sense to you?	Primary (n = 10)	Secondary (n = 11)	Total (n = 21)
Yes	9	9	18
No	1	0	1
Not completely	0	1	1
Forgotten	0	1	1

Luke (13 years), who as mentioned previously had been called lazy throughout his primary school and was very demoralised by the whole experience, said that although he'd probably had dyslexia explained to him he'd forgotten what it meant and that he would like to ignore the whole thing anyway.

Harry (8 years), the youngest child to be interviewed, when asked if dyslexia made sense to him, said:

> No it doesn't, it's a funny word.

Despite this response, Harry had in fact given a good explanation of dyslexia. It seemed more the case that he, like Sian, was responding more to the question of whether the idea of dyslexia made personal sense to him. He and Sian had been receiving specialist support for only the last 3 months and they both appeared to be grappling with what it meant for them. All three mothers of these children commented independently in their own interviews that their children were still coming to terms with the idea of thinking of themselves as dyslexic. Harry's mother had in fact written down verbatim some of Harry's thinking on the subject.

As a result of many of the poems/prose in the 'as I see it' book produced by the Dyslexia Institute, Harry and I had a long chat about 'getting to know' and I asked if he would mind if I wrote down whatever he said. These are Harry's words:

> When I was told I had to go and see a man about my reading I was gob smacked. But then I supposed I had to get used to the idea. On the journey there I felt funny: I didn't know this man . . . When we got there, we sat in a waiting room. Then the man came and called mummy and daddy. He came back and asked for me. After a while of doing lots of tests – I was very bored – he asked to speak to mum and dad. Much later mum and dad came back to the waiting room and we went outside. I said, 'What did all that mean?' When we were outside the building and in the car mummy said that it meant that I was dyslexic . . . I didn't like it . . . I didn't like the idea of seeing a specialist [Dyslexia Institute teacher] every week either, but mum and dad said not to worry and, 'Let's go to McDonalds to celebrate.'
>
> After a few days I began to feel a bit better about being dyslexic. Dyslexic people can't remember words, and they don't know how to use words on paper. They can't do writing and spelling very good either. They may not be very good at all those – reading, writing, spelling, but some things they are good at, like, they're intelligent and can do other things like maths . . . and swimming.

Harry's mother independently in her own interview gave an account of how they first told him he was dyslexic:

> We told Harry immediately. He wanted to know everything. We told him in a very congratulatory way that we were delighted. We're so pleased because we know what the problem is and we can help you.

Sophie, a 16-year-old who was interviewed in a later study, also commented on the difficulty of coming to terms with thinking of yourself in a new way. She had been assessed as dyslexic at the age of 13 at the instigation of her new school:

When I found out I was really upset because I thought it was incurable like. Like if you were a bit slow, you think 'Oh well, I can do this and then I'll catch up.' But when I found out like, everyone was saying, 'Oh I thought you'd be happy,' but I wasn't, I was shocked. Because everyone had been saying for so many years that I'm not dyslexic, I'm just slow. And it was frustrating that they'd never picked it up and I might have been able to get a bit better than I am now.

Sophie's mother confirmed these views in her interview, when asked how she felt when it was confirmed that Sophie was dyslexic:

Relief. Sophie didn't. I felt, 'Oh great! That's found it!' I thought Sophie would be pleased. Sophie was disgusted. 'Oh no!', you know. I think she'd rather have been a slow learner.

Given Sophie's initially negative reaction to the label it was interesting to check on how she felt about it 3 years later:

INTERVIEWER: How do you feel about the label now? Does it help you understand or do you resent it for making you feel different?
SOPHIE: Yes it does, it helps me. Because there's things about it and stuff you can relate to, and that makes you feel a bit better that there's someone out there going through the same thing.

At a speculative level it could be suggested that, whereas the majority of mothers had suspected for some time that their child was dyslexic and had been gradually seeking out information on it, for some children the idea may have been much more a bolt out of the blue. Sian, who, as already illustrated, was still coming to terms with the label 'dyslexia', made the following comment:

The first I'd heard of it was in January when I went for the test.

Alternatively some children may have built up a very negative image of dyslexia based on the attitude of the school to it. Sophie felt very strongly that the children in her school had a negative image of dyslexia:

Well, people think you're being stupid to be quite honest. That's the whole attitude of it.

In summary, it appears that the majority of children feel that they do understand what dyslexia is even though some find it hard to describe it to others. When children don't think that they understand dyslexia this appears to be related more to how they feel about the label than to any simple lack of understanding.

Telling other children

When children had been asked about the kinds of difficulties they had with their work at school, they were then asked if they thought other children noticed the difficulties they had. As can be seen from Table 10.4 only two children definitely thought that other children didn't notice their difficulties:

A major reason given for other children noticing their difficulties was their slow work speed:

Cos I usually finish work last.

Another reason given was that other children noticed when they were withdrawn for specialist support either within school or out of school:

Yes, because I went to see a special teacher.

This then raised the question of if, and how, children explained their difficulties to other children. As can be seen from Table 10.5 over two-thirds of children either didn't explain their difficulties to other children or explained them only to their closest friends. The overwhelming, and in fact only, reason given for this reticence was their fear of being teased by other children:

I don't want to tell anyone, because I think they'll tell everyone else, and then everybody might tease me.

Emma's mother made comments quite independently in her interview that underlined what Emma had been saying:

She doesn't like going in school time. She doesn't want anyone to find out. In fact she tells them she's going swimming, she really doesn't want other children to know. It's the same in class, she doesn't want any obvious help in class.

Table 10.4 Dyslexic children's thoughts on how aware other children are of their difficulties

Do others notice?	Primary (n = 10)	Secondary (n = 12)	Total (n = 22)
Yes	6	8	14
Not sure	3	3	6
No	1	1	2

Table 10.5 Children's explanation of their dyslexia to other children

	Primary (n = 10)	Secondary (n = 12)	Total (n = 22)
Doesn't explain	5	3	8
Only tells best/close friends	4	4	8
Teacher explained	0	1	1
Yes will explain	1	4	5

The next reply, by Graham, was typical of those given by children who just told their friends:

Some people I do tell, some I don't. Most of them would just make fun of me.

Some children, such as Mark, said they only told their best friend.

Only my best friend knows.

Sean (8 years), who had experienced considerable teasing at school, said he had started by telling other children to mind their own business. With support from his mother he had told some of his friends. Because of the negative attitude of his class to dyslexia, his mother had recently asked if someone from the Dyslexia Institute could come in and talk to the children about dyslexia and was waiting for this to happen. Among those children who said they did explain their difficulties some limited themselves to brief practical explanations. So Robert, for example, said that when other children asked where he was going he would reply:

I'm going for a bit more English help.

Only three children claimed that they directly explained what dyslexia was to children in general. As has been noted earlier in this book, the two boys in question scored highest on self-esteem and verbal fluency out of the children in this sample and the girl in question went to a school that was highly supportive of dyslexia. In several cases mothers had discussed with children the issue of whether they should tell other children about their difficulties, especially if their child was being teased about them. What clearly emerged was that nearly all the children were left to fend for themselves with mothers offering what support they could in the background. The one boy who said that his teacher had explained about dyslexia to the class was appreciative of this support:

Well, the teacher said a bit about it. That was helpful.

In another case, although the boy in question didn't mention it, his mother mentioned that a class discussion on dyslexia had taken place:

They have discussed it in the class [secondary school] why David comes here, which I think is a good open attitude. I was really pleased with that.

Interestingly, David was one of the few children who said he was willing to talk to children in general about dyslexia. Although there would be issues about how and in what context dyslexia is explained and it would need to handled with great sensitivity, it is important that, if children wish, they are given help and support, and are not left solely responsible for explaining their difficulties to other children. In some cases children need not be singled out, but the school could inform and educate both teachers and children about dyslexia and create a more informed and sympathetic environment. This in turn could be part of a school's overall special needs policy and would be treating dyslexia not as a special case but as part of an inclusive approach to special needs. Sophie (16), who was interviewed in a later study, spoke of her frustration at the negative attitude of children in her comprehensive school to dyslexia. She felt that the school should have been educating children about dyslexia and changing their attitude towards it. She said that her secret dream was to give a talk in her school about dyslexia:

> I've always wanted to do like a big talk on it. Just to tell them what it means and everything. They don't understand at all.

Teasing

Half the children in the sample said they had been teased specifically about difficulties with their work related to dyslexia:

> She kept saying I was thick because I was always last on our table [to copy things down].

> They said I was dumb and a nerd because, like, I couldn't spell things.

Edwards (1994) reported that all eight of the boys she interviewed said they had been badly and frequently teased in their mainstream schools and she saw this as one of the main reasons for them ending up at a boarding school for dyslexic boys. Singer (2005) interviewed 60 Dutch dyslexic children aged 9–12 years about their experiences of teasing in school; 85 per cent said they had been teased because of their dyslexia and 25 per cent said they were teased or bullied once a week or more. Singer commented on the finding that even children who were not teased reported putting a lot of effort into covering up their difficulties in order to avoid being teased. What was noted in the present study was that many of the children lived with the constant fear of being teased about their difficulties and put a lot of their energies into covering up their difficulties or trying to divert attention away from them.

Dyslexic friends

Several children made spontaneous reference to friends with dyslexia during the interview and towards the end of the interview all the children were asked if they met other dyslexic children, and if so was this helpful to them (Table 10.6).

In fact, all the children had teaching sessions in pairs at the Dyslexia Institute so in this setting they all met at least one other child with dyslexia. Although exact figures are not available, what was clear from the interviews was that for some children this was the only opportunity they had to meet another child with acknowledged dyslexia. It appeared that, particularly in schools where dyslexia was not acknowledged, children could feel very isolated. In some cases they suspected that certain other children might be dyslexic but because the school didn't recognise dyslexia and children tended to keep it secret this made it difficult for children to identify each other:

> But they tend to keep it hush hush . . . Where at my school, like, you don't meet each other and stuff. It's like private.

Table 10.6 Meeting other children with dyslexia

Do you meet other children with dyslexia?	Primary (n = 10)	Secondary (n = 12)	Total (n = 22)
Yes	10	12	22
No	0	0	0

Table 10.7 Children's views on meeting other children with dyslexia

Do you find it helpful to meet other children with dyslexia?	Primary (n = 10)	Secondary (n = 12)	Total (n = 22)
Yes	9	10	19
No	0	0	0
Not bothered	1	2	3

Following on from this question about meeting other children, they were then asked if they found this helpful or not. The figures in Table 10.7 would suggest that the large majority of children in this sample did find it helpful to know other children who were dyslexic or had similar problems. Children's answers gave more details on the kind of contact they valued:

It's helpful knowing there's someone else.

It's more enjoyable knowing someone else has the same problem.

Because then I feel it's not just me.

Children appeared to particularly value either having someone in the same class with similar problems, whether these were recognised as dyslexia or not, or having a close friend with dyslexia. Jason and Malcolm, for example, both mentioned boys in their own classes who had similar problems:

It's OK, cos there's someone with your own difficulties.

I'm not very embarrassed now because there's someone the same as me.

Other children mentioned the positive value of having close friends who were dyslexic:

Two of my friends are dyslexic, we're like closer friends because of it.

Well my friend Tim's dyslexic you know. We joke about it and call each other names and that, but it does help us [me].

Some children also made positive mention of sharing their session with another dyslexic child at the Dyslexia Institute:

I share a lesson with Rachael. I like that better.

The Dyslexia Institute teachers in their interviews also spoke of the positive advantages of children being able to share their problems and talk them over in these sessions.

In summary there appeared to be three major aspects to knowing others with dyslexia:

1   Having a close friend/s with the same problem.
2   Having other children in the class with the same problem.
3   Sharing specialist support with children with the same problem.

As well as this face-to-face type of contact, some children and mothers spoke of more distant types of 'knowing' which gave support. As has been previously mentioned in discussing the issue of labels, children spoke of the advantage of knowing at a general level that there were others with the same problem and of seeing illustrations of this on television or in books.

Whereas having a friend with dyslexia seemed to focus on positive factors such as supporting each other and sharing experiences, knowing there was another child in the class who did as badly or worse than you sometimes appeared to be based on the more negative strategy of simply comparing yourself with someone the same as or worse off than yourself.

Although the majority of children said that knowing other dyslexic children or children with similar difficulties was helpful, they varied considerably in how helpful they seemed to find this, so that responses varied from the highly positive, through the more lukewarm, to the frankly indifferent:

Yes, yes, definitely.

Yes, it's a little bit helpful.

I'm not really bothered.

The variation in responses may be partly a function of children's mode of expression and the experiences they were reflecting on. But, as we know from many areas of disability, people vary considerably in how helpful they find it to align themselves with others with similar experiences. Whereas many derive great benefit from doing so, some people do not find this at all helpful and have no wish to do so. These individual differences need to be borne in mind in any plans to enable dyslexic children to meet or support one another and would suggest that they need to be optional and responsive to feedback from children. Having said this, the majority of children in this sample did find that knowing other children was helpful, especially in their own school. This would suggest that ways of enabling dyslexic children to meet either individually or in groups should be considered as part of special needs support. Meryl, another 16-year-old interviewed in a later study, described how dyslexic children tended to know one another and informally get together in her comprehensive school. This school had an open and supportive attitude to dyslexia as part of a wider special needs policy which appeared to enable this personal support to flourish. Schools, it can be argued, can by their ethos and organisation either facilitate or hold back various types of peer support.

Adult role models

Both children and their mothers were asked about the significance of adult role models. Of the 22 mothers, 21 said that they pointed out adults with dyslexia to their children. The one mother who didn't do this was the one who had already said that they didn't use the term 'dyslexia' at home. The children were asked if they had heard of famous or successful adults with dyslexia. They all said that they had, apart from the boy who didn't discuss dyslexia at home. Following on from this children were asked whether they found this helpful or not (Table 10.8).

Some children responded to this question at a general level whereas others named specific role models:

Yes, it's encouraged me a lot.

Yes it does, if they can do it, so can I.

Yes, Duncan Goodhew, cos I used to like swimming.

Tom Cruise, Cher, Michael Heseltine. Yes, it helps, like Michael Heseltine is an MP. It's nice to think you're not the only one.

This 13-year-old girl was keen on pop culture and wanted role models that she saw as current and relevant to her:

Einstein, Roald Dahl wrote the *Vicar of Nibbleswick,* and Michael Heseltine.

This boy was very keen on politics and wanted to be leader of the United Nations when he grew up. He was therefore particularly pleased that there was a role model from the political world that he could refer to. He was also interested in science and, as described earlier in the book, said that he sometimes defended himself when teased, by referring to Einstein:

I brag at school actually . . . like Einstein was dyslexic . . . so that means dyslexics can't be thick, that stops that.

Apart from Einstein, who according to a recent survey is a popular cult figure with young people, all the role models were of living people recently or currently in the public eye (Table 10.9). (These were all people that the children believed to be dyslexic, whether this was the case or not.) Some children described people whose names they

Table 10.8 Children's views on adult role models

Does this encourage you or not?	Primary (n = 10)	Secondary (n = 11)	Total (n = 21)
Yes	10	9	19
No/not bothered	0	2	2

Table 10.9 Role models named by children

Duncan Goodhew	(Olympic swimmer)	6
Tom Cruise	(film star)	5
Einstein	(scientist)	4
Michael Heseltine	(politician)	4
Cher	(pop singer/actress)	2
Ruby Wax	(comedienne)	1
Susan Hampshire	(actress)	1

had forgotten. 'That presenter on children's TV, the one with peroxide hair, she said she was dyslexic.' What appeared to be important was that role models were relevant to children's values and interests.

One girl complained about the lack of current women role models, and one of the mothers mused on the lack of current sporting role models:

> Duncan Goodhew is quite a long time ago now. It doesn't mean that much to him. Now if it were Kevin Keegan [ex-captain of the England football team and recently manager of Newcastle United], that would be a different story.

Luke, when asked if he had heard of famous or successful adults, replied:

> There used to be some people on the notice board [at the Dyslexia Institute]. Duncan Goodhew I think was one, and there were a few other people.

When asked if this encouraged him or not he said:

> LUKE: Not particularly . . . I somehow don't think . . . what's swimming got to do . . . Duncan Goodhew I mean . . . what's it got to do with dyslexia. It's like you learn it off by heart.
> INTERVIEWER: He said the reason he started swimming was because he wasn't any good at most of his school work, so it was like a way of proving you know that he could be really successful, and that's how he got into swimming.
> LUKE: That's a bit like me that . . . I sort of like bikes.

Luke was classified as one of the two children who didn't find role models helpful, but his comments do raise questions about how role models are introduced to children. He was critical of the idea of simply learning a list of names, and the conversation with him suggests that talking about role models in more detail may be of more value. It may well be that there are individual differences in how children identify with and use role models. At a general level it seemed to be the case that role models served two purposes. One was to encourage children and improve their self-esteem; the other was to give them a way of defending themselves when teased by other children. Several children spontaneously mentioned a dyslexic parent or relative as a positive role model, despite the fact that a question was not directly asked about this.

Mark commenting on his dad's difficulties said:

If he can get past it, I can get past it.

Given that half the children in this study had a parent with similar difficulties and several more had uncles and aunts or older cousins with similar difficulties the importance of family members as role models should not be overlooked. Children didn't seem to be concerned with their parents having prestigious roles: what seemed to be important was that they could relate to an adult whom they saw as competent at coping with dyslexia who had survived school! Two children mentioned their dyslexic mothers who had left school early because of their difficulties and had been largely housewives with occasional part-time work:

Like me mum's dyslexic and she's survived it.

A girl interviewed in a later study spoke of her delight when one of the teachers at her comprehensive school also admitted to being dyslexic.

It may well be that a range of more familiar everyday role models would be helpful to many dyslexic children. At present this process is hampered because of the underidentification of adults with dyslexia. In this study several of the fathers were not openly acknowledged as dyslexic and examples of dyslexic adults in a range of local jobs were not available to children. Lewis (1995) talks about a unit set up for dyslexic children within a comprehensive school. He points out that one of the advantages of this is that older pupils and pupils who have left have acted as positive role models for younger children. Criticism is sometimes made of famous adult role models because, as with physical disability, it is suggested that it encourages the notion of the 'super cripple' and gives children unrealistic goals and expectations to live up to and also gives the public at large unrealistic expectations of what should be achieved. Although this has to be taken seriously there was little evidence from the interviews that children viewed role models in this light. For most children they appeared to be a minor but important part of the elaborate defences that they used to survive school and also gave a small but much needed boost to their self-esteem. It can also be argued that giving children a wider range of more everyday role models would counterbalance the influence of 'super' role models.

Do your parents understand what it's like to be dyslexic?

Children were asked this question and were then asked to choose between three categories. As can be seen from Table 10.10 the majority of children think that their parents do understand at least to some extent. This might reflect the nature of this particular sample of parents, in that the parents had to believe in the concept of dyslexia sufficiently to send their child to the Dyslexia Institute for extra support. Whether children who were initially identified by the school system would feel similarly understood only further research can tell. Perhaps not surprisingly primary age children felt more understood than their secondary age counterparts:

My dad does most, because like, he used to go through a hard time because like there was no help around. So I think he knows what it's like.

My mum's dyslexic so she knows what it's like.

Yes they definitely do, because my mum used to have difficulties.

Those children who chose the 'some extent' category were more ambivalent in their answers:

To some extent. Sometimes I think they do and sometimes I think they don't.

I'm not sure if they know what it's like, although they know what it is.

My mum might think she knows what it feels like, but she doesn't fully understand it.

In several cases it was thought that mothers were more understanding than fathers:

My mum understands a bit more than my dad.

Only two children felt that they weren't understood at all:

She thinks she knows what it's like but she doesn't.

As well as the six children in the 'definitely do understand' category who specifically mentioned a dyslexic parent another two of the children in this category also had dyslexic parents. Therefore eight out of the nine children who felt definitely understood had a dyslexic parent. Although more research is needed to verify this, it would suggest that children are more likely to feel understood by a dyslexic parent, especially in families where the parent openly acknowledges their difficulties. Darren's mother, who had been identified as dyslexic as an adult, spoke about what happened when she helped him with his homework:

Well he dictates it to me and I try and type it out on the computer. He thinks it's really funny when I'm damning and blasting because I've spelt something wrong or

Table 10.10 Children's perception of whether their parents understand how it feels to be dyslexic

	Primary (n = 10)	Secondary (n = 11)	Total (n = 21)
Definitely do	6(4[a])	3(2[a])	9(6[a])
To some extent	4(1[a])	6(1[a])	10(2[a])
Not at all	0	2	2

a   Denotes the number of children who spontaneously and specifically mentioned feeling understood by their dyslexic parent.

I don't know how to spell it. I ham it up a bit because I reckon it's good for him to see that a grown up makes mistakes and that I have to struggle and work at it. We have a good laugh, it's something we can share.

Darren had spoken of feeling definitely understood by his mother and had also cited his mother as a positive role model. Darren's mother thought that, although her non-dyslexic husband was basically sympathetic, especially before Darren had been identified, he used to get more exasperated with him:

> I felt that because I had some inkling into the problems he was having, so I was a bit easier with him. I think as far as Mike's concerned he used to get annoyed because sometimes it appeared that he could do it.

In this sample it was almost entirely mothers who helped children on a day-to-day basis but despite this some children still felt more understood by their dyslexic fathers. Mark, as already shown (first quote, this section), felt especially understood by his father even though his father worked away from home for long periods of time and he valued the day-to-day support that his mother gave him. Another boy whose dyslexic father worked away from home said:

> Aye me dad's alright, he understands. He works on the oil rigs.

This is not to say that children didn't value the support and understanding of their non-dyslexic parent and much might depend on the general quality of the relationship that a child has with their respective parents.

There has been little discussion in the literature on the role of dyslexic parents and what there was in the past tended to view them rather negatively as adding to children's difficulties (Ravenette 1985, Thomson 1990). This appeared to be based on speculation and assumption rather than firm evidence and, it could be argued, fitted with the general tendency to pathologise families (Falik 1995). Evidence from many dyslexic adults and children on the positive role of their parents (including dyslexic parents) indicates that where dyslexic parents have come to terms with their own difficulties and have a positive relationship with their children they can be of considerable support. Although more research is needed, the evidence from this study suggests that dyslexic parents can be a positive asset in providing role models and understanding to their dyslexic children. Some of the mothers in this study who also had dyslexia or literacy difficulties said they felt guilty at passing their 'defective' genes on to their children. Most of them said they had a miserable time at school and found it especially painful to watch their child going through the same experiences. It may be helpful for dyslexic parents to be aware of the positive aspects of their dyslexic status in relation to their dyslexic children. Appreciation of this is starting to permeate support literature as in the following example addressed to dyslexic parents: 'you will have developed strategies for coping with dyslexia which you can share, and you can be an excellent role model who has a natural empathy with your children's difficulties' (Being Dyslexic 2009).

Telling parents

Children were asked if they talked to their parents about any problems or difficulties they had at school because of their dyslexia. They were then asked to rate their responses according to four categories (Table 10.11).

It is commonly held that children in general vary considerably in the amount that they want to talk about school and especially any problems that they are having at school. Research on bullying (Smith *et al.* 2004) suggests that children often don't tell their parents about this, especially as they grow older. In this sense these figures may not represent anything out of the ordinary. What may be more significant is that, when schools were unaware of problems such as a dyslexic child being teased, having difficulty copying down homework, dreading spelling tests or reading aloud, it was often parents in this sample who brought these problems to the attention of the school. Obviously parents can only bring problems to the attention of the school if they are aware of them in the first place. At the same time children's need for independence has to be respected as they grow older. It can be tentatively suggested that children seemed to take this issue into their own hands by becoming more selective about what they told parents as they grew older but it has to be borne in mind that these results are from a small sample of children.

Those children who sometimes told their parents stressed that it depended what it was and how important they thought it was:

Sometimes not if it's not important.

It depends what it is.

Five of the seven children who said that they rarely told their parents said that this was simply because they didn't like talking about school and not because they deliberately wanted to keep things from their parents, although this may have sometimes played a part:

I don't like talking about it unless I have to.

I don't like talking about school.

I usually say school's boring all the time and I think it is, so when I come home, I usually just forget about it.

Table 10.11 Degree to which children tell parents of dyslexia-related problems

	Primary (n = 10)	Secondary (n = 10)	Total (n = 20)
Usually	5	0	5
Sometimes	2	4	6
Rarely	2	5	7
Never	1	1	2

Luke went on to explain that because he found much of school boring and stressful the last thing he wanted to do when he came home was to talk about it and that his way of coping was to blank it out of his mind as much as he could.

Luke's mother when asked if he talked about his problems simply said 'no.'

Mark on the other hand seemed more concerned about the reaction of his mother:

> I would keep it to myself, because I don't want my mum to know because I think she would say, 'Why don't you do the proper work?' and things like that.

Mark's mother, when asked whether he would talk about problems at school or she had to drag them out of him, said:

> Drag it out of him. I know there's something wrong by his mood, and I sort of like, I don't go on at him all the time. I ask him. But I mean, the more you go on the more he won't say anything. So I sometimes leave it and then he will eventually sort of like say, 'Mum, I've got like . . .'.

The majority of mothers appeared to be aware of the degree to which their children were communicating or not communicating with them. The problems arose when a mother thought something was wrong but had to wait until their child was ready to talk about it. Several mothers spoke of their children bottling things up. Ewan's mother recounted an incident in which her son in his first year at secondary school had been having problems with his homework that she was not aware of, although she was aware that something was wrong:

> Ewan bottles it up. He didn't really talk about it. He got quieter and quieter and it all boiled to a head before last Christmas. About the October half-term I got an official letter from them saying Ewan had seven defaults and they were for not doing his homework, and every single night I'd been saying are you alright with your homework, I'd no idea this was going on. So I asked for a homework book because I thought this would help him. Next thing Ewan comes in from school absolutely distraught, in a dreadful state because some teacher had said to him, 'Here's a homework book for you, Bell, because your mum's asked for it.' What I didn't know, was that they were often given as punishment. So he thought I'd asked for him to be punished. When he came in it was the worst night of my life. He cried and he was upset; he couldn't believe that I'd asked for this punishment.

It transpired that Ewan was struggling with the written work at his new school and was having particular problems in copying down homework and had gradually become overwhelmed by the difficulties he was having.

Ewan, in his interview, said that he rarely or never talked about his problems at school with his parents, when asked why he said:

> I just didn't want to talk about them.

Ewan did go on to say that on rare occasions he did talk to friends at school about his difficulties. Edwards (1994) noted in her study that five of the eight boys she interviewed said that they had great difficulty in talking about their feelings of distress and unhappiness to anyone and often hid their problems at school from their parents. Although there may be no easy solutions for children who are reluctant to talk about their problems, it can be suggested that, particularly as they get older, opportunities at school should be made for them to discuss any difficulties. One comprehensive school arranged a contact teacher for special needs children who met them regularly on an individual basis to check on any difficulties or worries that the child had. The use of peer counselling or peer support groups might be another way of enabling some children to talk about their problems.

The future

The final question that children were asked was whether they thought they would still be dyslexic when they were an adult. The purpose of this was to get more information on how children were viewing both themselves and dyslexia. Some critics have argued that voluntary organisations such as Dyslexia Action give both children and parents false expectations by implying that dyslexia is something that can be 'cured' if given the right treatment. This criticism seems at variance with the definitions given by such organisations which emphasise the constitutional basis to the cognitive deficits underlying dyslexia. The organisations, in their defence, would probably argue that they set out to improve and not to 'cure' dyslexics. Nonetheless this debate does raise the question of what sort of expectations children should be given and what sort of balance between optimism and realism should be struck.

Although with small numbers such as these, evidence has to be interpreted cautiously, there was some indication that children became more realistic about the possibility of long-term difficulties as they got older. The two youngest children in the sample both replied with vehemence to this question of whether they would still be dyslexic when they were an adult:

No definitely not!

No way!

Two other primary children replied 'no', on the basis that they would improve with help:

Table 10.12 Children's responses to the question, 'Do you think you'll still be dyslexic when you're an adult?'

	Primary (n = 10)	Secondary (n = 11)	Total (n = 21)
Yes	1	3	4
Not sure/don't know	5	5	10
No	4	0	4
Hope not	0	3	3

I don't think so, cos I'm getting a lot of help.

Children in the 'not sure' category varied from those who thought they probably would be dyslexic as an adult, through those who thought they probably wouldn't, to those who felt they had no idea:

I might be, I'm not sure.

I don't know, probably not, cos I'm not that bad.

I don't know, I'm going to try to get rid of it.

I don't know whether it gets better or not.

By secondary age some children seemed to realise that there was a possibility that they would have difficulties as an adult despite the fact that they wished it to be otherwise:

I hope not, I want to overcome it but I don't think I can.

Some of those children who thought that they would still be dyslexic when they were an adult framed this in positive terms. In fact the two boys highest in self-esteem and verbal fluency both thought that they would be dyslexic as an adult, but were positive about their ability to cope with it:

They said I would always be dyslexic cos they can't cure it, but I can be great at my work.

More than likely, but I think I'll learn to cope with it.

Whereas some children were less positive about the idea of still being dyslexic:

Well, my mum says you cannot grow out of dyslexia, like, you've got it. You've got it twice as hard as anybody else, to be able to catch up with everybody at work. It would be nice not to have it. Like, for it to wear off. Like, to find a cure, you drink enough diet coke and it's gone!

As can be seen there were a wide range of responses to this question; only further research can tell whether this variation is largely due to individual differences in personality and experience or it indicates various points on some sort of developmental process in coming to terms with a possible long-term disability. It may also be the case that children's expectations vary with the severity of their difficulties and/or all these factors combine to provide a distinctive developmental history for each child. What does seem to be important is that a clear distinction is made between the difficulties underlying dyslexia, which may persist, and the ability to develop positive coping strategies and improve performance. The two boys who expressed positive opinions on being dyslexic as an adult appeared to already be doing this. McLoughlin *et al.*

(2002), in counselling adults with dyslexia, argue that awareness and understanding of one's difficulties are the first step in taking control of them and developing effective compensatory strategies. They suggest that four levels of awareness can be identified:

1   no awareness – no coping strategies
2   aware – no coping strategies developed
3   aware – unconscious coping strategies
4   aware – conscious coping strategies.

One of the important aspects of specialised support for children may be that it gives them the belief that they can apply effective strategies to their work and that over time they can gain more control over their difficulties:

> He was writing something recently, and as usual he'd left several words out. When he read it to me he realised what he'd done. At one time he just wouldn't have noticed or he'd have got upset and gone off in a state. He was a bit exasperated, he said 'I'm always missing words out, but I'm trying to think of a way of not doing it anymore.' I was really pleased: a few years ago he would never have said that. It's as if he's getting more insight and more confidence that he can tackle things.

Summary

1   Over two-thirds of children could give a reasonable explanation of dyslexia.
2   In 80 per cent of cases mothers had a major role in explaining dyslexia to their children.
3   The majority of children felt that the explanation they were given of dyslexia made sense to them.
4   The majority of children thought that other children noticed the difficulties they had with their work.
5   The majority of children were not willing to explain their difficulties to children in general because of fear of teasing.
6   Fifty per cent of children said they had been teased because of their work-related difficulties.
7   Knowing other children with similar problems was rated as helpful by most of the children.
8   The majority of children said that role models were helpful.
9   Most children thought that their parents understood at least to some extent what it was like to be dyslexic.
10   Children may become more aware as they grow older of the possible long-term nature of their underlying difficulties.

Chapter 11

Mothers' views on dyslexia

But the real costs are to the spirit, the sorrow of observing a child's bleak despair, the anguish and alarm when the despair turns to rage.

(Donawa 1995)

Various aspects of mothers' views have already been presented in several chapters in this book. The purpose of this chapter is to look more closely at their overall views on living with a child with dyslexia and how they think this has affected them and the rest of their family.

Responsibility

At a day-to-day level all the mothers in this sample thought that they had the major responsibility for dealing with their child's dyslexia. This may be partly because this was an atypical sample with several fathers working away from home for long periods of time and several more regularly working away from home for shorter periods of time. In addition there were three single-parent mothers. Van der Stoel and Osmond in their interviews both document detailed views from fathers on their dyslexic children; Edwards on the other hand also notes the lack of input from fathers in the eight case studies of dyslexic adolescents which she presents. Scott, Scherman and Phillips (1992) found in their research that mothers were the most likely adults to support their dyslexic children. Several mothers in this case study said that their husbands gave them support on specific occasions such as open evenings or an important meeting in school and generally felt that their husbands supported what they were doing despite their lack of regular involvement. It may therefore be that some fathers have a higher profile in the public arena than they do on a daily basis at home. Edwards wonders if some fathers are less involved because their own experiences of dyslexia make this a painful area for them to cope with. Although this is a possibility there was no direct evidence from this study to support this hypothesis. There appeared to be no consistent difference in involvement between dyslexic and non-dyslexic fathers in this sample and dyslexic mothers were just as involved as non-dyslexic mothers in supporting their children. In the health area we know that mothers are often the 'guardians' of the family's health and take the responsibility for monitoring family health. Stace and Roker (2005) interviewed a cross-section of 50 parents of 11- to 16-year-olds about how they monitored and supervised their children's lives. Most parents said they regularly checked their child's emotional well being and adjustment especially at times of transition or stress. Mothers said they were more involved than fathers in every-day monitoring and that this was often time-consuming and stressful. In the sample described in this book, within the family it was exclusively mothers who first realised something was wrong and took the initiative in identifying the problem. For many of them their day-to-day support appeared to be an extension of this early initiative:

> Dave [husband] says, with him not being sort of like academically inclined at all, he didn't realise at the beginning that Mark really had a problem. He just thought, 'Oh well, maybe Mark's slow to pick it up like I was.' And I says, 'Well, I think we should do something about it as soon as we could.' And so we did. I mean, I help with his homework and everything like that . . . and sometimes I think he has difficulty understanding what Mark's supposed to be doing, so it's difficult in a sense because it's always me that has to do it you know.

Mrs Thomson had commented in her interview that she was the only one for a long time who had suspected her son might be dyslexic. She was asked what her husband thought about this:

> I don't think he'd been able to give it a thought. Like most husbands, although they love their children and they try to be around it's you who are there and who have the dealings with the children. You're the one when they bring homework and whatever. So I don't think he was really that much aware.

Mrs Knight felt that she and her husband were in fairly close agreement but that she saw more of the day-to-day difficulties:

> He's much the same as me really I suppose, although he's not so much of a worrier as I am. He tends to be a little bit more philosophical and optimistic at times, although he does have his moments when he worries about it. Well, it's me that does everything with him as well. So it's me that sees him when he's had a bad day and he's getting his spelling pack wrong and so on.

Several mothers in this sample pointed out that their husbands either worked away from home or worked very long hours so with the best will in the world they were not able to give the level of support that their wives gave to their dyslexic children:

> Well he [husband] does what he can, but he has to work away from home. I think people don't always appreciate that you have a lot on your plate when your husband isn't there you know.

> My husband is supportive, but he basically leaves it to me. He works long hours.

Other mothers, even when their husbands were at home, made it clear that they saw it as their role to deal with this kind of issue. A few of the mothers who worked did express resentment that the major responsibility seemed to fall on them. Despite this the majority of mothers were at pains to point out that their husbands were very concerned for their children. Again this may be an atypical sample, because given the cost of the Dyslexia Institute lessons it could be assumed that fathers would have to be committed enough to agree with their wives that this was an appropriate use of family funds. Mrs Schaffer was typical in emphasising her husband's interest:

> I think I had closer contact with the school and what they were doing. It's not that he's not interested. We both constantly went up the school.

Other mothers whose husbands were not involved with helping their dyslexic children on a day-to-day basis nonetheless valued the general emotional and social support that their husbands gave. Mrs Street, who had struggled with dyslexia at school herself, valued her husband's support if she went up to school to talk about any difficulties that her son was having:

> The only thing is I find I get quite emotional about it because I had experienced it in the past. So sometimes my husband comes with us.

In the three cases where mothers reported differences of opinion between themselves and their husbands these were not over their child's being dyslexic but over what should be done about it and the degree of concern that should be expressed:

> He [husband] does care, but he doesn't see the state he comes home in after school. He doesn't worry about it as much as I do.

> He [husband] hated school from day one, you know, and he can understand how he really feels. Part of him lets him backslide you know, so the trouble is it's always me that has to make him do it.

Some mothers felt that even though their husbands were supportive at one level they still didn't fully understand the problem and could still get impatient and exasperated with the specific difficulties that their dyslexic child had:

> Well he's the same as me. He was a bit annoyed really that it had taken all that time to find out. But then he's so busy with the business to be honest. I mean he gets frustrated with Sophie. He thinks she doesn't try and that's not the case, she can't do it.

Sophie, when asked if her parents understood what it was like to be dyslexic, replied:

> I don't think my dad does. But my mum is more understanding. My dad thinks I'm lazy.

Some mothers therefore felt that as well as shouldering the major responsibility for helping their dyslexic child that they also had to mediate between their husband and child or between their dyslexic child and their non-dyslexic brothers and sisters:

His younger sister's always correcting his reading or telling him if he's spelt things wrong; you can imagine how that goes down!

Uncertainty

For all parents their thoughts on their child cover the present, the past and the future. It is also the case that all parents and children face some degree of uncertainty in envisaging the child's future, even when it is limited to school and the first few years beyond. It can be argued that for many children with special needs there is often greater uncertainty and apprehension about what the future will hold for them. Several mothers commented at various points in the interviews about the uncertainty and anxiety that they felt about their child's future:

> It's like steering a ship through uncharted waters really, you just don't know what rocks you're going to hit next.

The mothers in this sample were asked a short series of questions focusing on their child's future. They were first asked whether or not they worried about their child's future progress at school. They were asked to rate this on a five-point scale.

> Do you worry, or not, about (Emma's) future progress in school?

> a lot 5   4   3   2   1   not at all

The average score for mothers of primary age children was 4.6 and for mothers of secondary children was 4.4, with 65 per cent of mothers overall scoring a 5. Without comparing these scores to mothers' ratings of non-dyslexic children it could be argued that all mothers worry a lot about their children's future development. Only further research can answer this point but at a qualitative level several mothers claimed that there was no comparison between the concern that they had for their dyslexic, as opposed to non-dyslexic, children:

> There's no comparison really, it's just not the same. With her sister we've never really had to worry. She's had her ups and downs, teachers she doesn't like, friends she's fallen out with, but nothing serious. She's just average but she seems to just sail along. There's none of that misery and despair that her sister's had, none of that dreading going to school, feeling sick every morning crying and so on.

Another mother commented:

> I don't think until you've had a child with a problem you've any idea what it's like. It's totally different, it's this constant worry. Oh, please God give him a nice teacher, don't let him get that depressed again. How will he cope at secondary school? How on earth will he do the homework or manage in exams? With my other children I just don't have those sort of worries.

Perhaps as a hangover from not wanting to be seen as neurotic or overanxious many of the mothers were apologetic or fearful that the degree of worry that they expressed would be seen as inappropriate. Typical responses were:

Yes, I'm afraid I do worry a lot.

I know I shouldn't but I do worry a lot.

It thus appears that some mothers, in addition to worrying a great deal, were also made to feel that this was inappropriate or not legitimate.

Mrs Salter said that when she had tried to discuss her concerns with the school:

They just laughed at me.

The kind of things that mothers worried about obviously varied with the age and stage of the child. Mrs Forest, whose 8-year-old son was still learning to read and had had a difficult start in school, said:

I try not to think about it.

Mrs Salter felt that her son's school had a particularly competitive ethos:

I do worry about it a lot, they're so competitive there.

The mother of a primary-age girl listed the following worries:

I worry about whether she'll be able to get things down quick enough, whether she'll be able to spell things, copy things off the board, learn her tables, be able to play skipping in the playground without being laughed at or told she can't join in. All those sorts of things. They may sound silly but she's been told off or laughed at for all these things already. It's not that I want her to do them for me, I want her to keep up so she's happy in school, so she can enjoy it.

Mrs Kerslake in the following comments encapsulated many of the worries that mothers of secondary- or near to secondary-age children expressed:

I worry about him going to secondary school. I worry about the amount of work he's going to have to cope with. I worry about how he'll cope with exams when these come along. I worry that he'll sort of lose interest in school, and not want to go. Playing truant. I worry about everything!

It can be argued that the worries that Mrs Kerslake has expressed are quite reasonable and legitimate. Evidence suggests that poor readers are more likely to play truant at secondary school and are more likely to display disruptive behaviour (Bynner *et al.* 2007, McGee *et al.* 1992). Other evidence suggests that dyslexic children often do take longer to complete written work and the time concessions for public exams are an open acknowledgment of the difficulties that these present to some dyslexic children.

Concern over exams was a major concern at secondary level, although mothers stressed that this was on their children's behalf:

> I suppose I worry in the sense of the exams. That's the part that bothers me. If he can't get his exams and it stops him doing what he wants to do.

Another major concern especially for boys was that they would become disruptive and alienated at secondary school. Mrs Bell had already had experience of this when her son Ewan started to struggle badly at secondary school:

> Because in the other class they say he was misbehaving and then he was one of the naughty boys and that's not really him. I mean he's often been a clown as a means of distracting I think, but he was really naughty.

Mrs Carter was worried in case something like this should happen in the future:

> I think the only thing that really gives me cause for concern, I mean, like, I say Malcolm's never been disruptive or anything like that, but I know it can get to a stage where they feel totally isolated and I wouldn't want to see any decline in his behaviour when he goes to senior school.

Several mothers also pointed out that the degree to which they worried fluctuated depending on how things were going at the time and what picture they had of future provision:

> It varies really, it's very up and down. Sometimes things go well for a while and you start to get more optimistic about the future, then something will happen at school and you feel right back where you've started. You can never completely relax and say right that's that sorted, its like a long-term campaign.

> I feel sad for him. It varies for me between the depths of pessimism to feeling if he's had a good day quite optimistic for a time, and thinking things aren't going to be so bad, he's going to manage.

Mrs Graham's son David had been put into a special needs class when he entered secondary school as he could barely read. The school hoped that with special help his literacy skills would improve and allow him to do himself justice. Mrs Graham felt uncertain how things would go and what her expectations should be:

> I'm never sure for myself, at school they have great hopes for him, they say whatever happens he'll get on.

Mothers' worries it appeared were based on past experience of the difficulties their children had encountered and realistic projections about the difficulties they were likely to face in the future. Allied to this, several underlined their degree of uncertainty about their child's future academic progress. Some mothers were at pains to point out that, although they worried, they did their best to keep these worries from their dyslexic child. One mother who was dyslexic herself said:

> I think it's affected me more than him. I don't let him know I'm worried. Graham's quite oblivious as yet. He's got a very easy going temperament; he doesn't mind too much about it.

> The trouble is, I think some teachers think that because you talk about your worries to them that you've made your child all anxious and neurotic. It's not like that at all. It's him that comes home from school with the worries, we tell him not to worry, that it's not that bad, that we'll help him sort the problem out.

> We never talk about our worries for her in front of her.

> The problem is getting the balance right between not making him worried, but at the same time acknowledging his worries and not dismissing them.

> He's due to start secondary school in a few months. He's full of optimism, he seems to think that because he's going to a new school all his problems are going to disappear. I think that's what he wants to believe because he's had such an awful year at school. I haven't let him know about my worries. I'm in a quandary though, I mean I don't want to put ideas in his head, but should I prepare him just a little bit otherwise it might be an awful shock to him?

> Well, the thing is, you only talk to teachers when things have reached a crisis, when you are really upset and worried. They don't see you the rest of the time. I think they get a distorted view.

Although worry and anxiety are used widely in informal explanations for the detrimental effect that parents can have on their children, there is almost no formal research on this issue. The assumption often seems to be made that, where you have an anxious, worried child and anxious, worried parents, it is the parents' anxiety which has led to the child's anxiety. Of course the opposite assumption, that the child's anxiety has led to the parents' anxiety, is equally plausible. A third possibility is that there is an interactional cycle with both fuelling further anxiety in the other. As discussed in Chapter 7, the belief that anxious parents are responsible for the anxieties and unhappiness displayed by dyslexic children seems to be based more on myth than on reality. Dewhirst (1995) reports that the parents that she spoke to argued that the best way to overcome family stress is to acknowledge dyslexia and give effective support so that children don't become anxious in the first place. Some of the mothers in this sample said that they had been called overprotective by teachers. This is a term which is widely used to comment on the behaviour and attitudes of parents of children with a wide range of disabilities. MacKeith (1973) has argued that this is a judgemental term and that we should talk instead of very protective parents, a term which he feels does not necessarily imply criticism. In the same vein it can be argued that it is more appropriate to talk about very worried or very anxious parents. Another implicit assumption appears to be that worry or anxiety is automatically harmful, whereas, in reality, worry may lead to a number of different outcomes. Worry that leads to seeking information and help and leads to forward planning is very different from worry that leads to pessimism and lack of action. A certain level of worry, it can be argued, is an integral part of parenting and a parent who didn't worry would be equally criticised for not showing the appropriate concern for their child. Mrs Knight's 11-year-old son had in the past been refusing to go to school, bed wetting and falling a long way behind on his reading and spelling. Both his teachers and the educational psychologist had expressed concern about his academic performance and his emotional response to it:

> Given the state he was in you'd have to be a very odd mother not to worry.

It can also be argued that when worries are dismissed or not taken seriously this is more likely in the long term to exacerbate them, whereas acknowledgment can at least be the starting point for dealing with difficulties. Mrs Knight went on to discuss what happened when she talked to Jason's class teacher at the end of his fourth year in primary school:

> He still couldn't read or write properly then, so I asked her whether I was right to worry about how he'd cope when he got to secondary school or was I just making a fuss about nothing. She said that speaking as another mother she would be concerned about him. In a funny sort of way I was pleased she said that because I knew he'd got problems and at least it gave me confidence in my own judgement, made me decide I must carry on doing what I could.

Meryl, a 16-year-old girl with dyslexia, was asked whether she worried about her work because her parents worried about it or her worry was related to school:

> No, it's definitely not because they worry about it, I worry because of school.

Goodnow and Collins (1990) talk about parenting as a public performance with many different onlookers who feel that they have the right to judge or comment on the quality of the performance. Whereas this applies to all parents, it applies even more strongly when something is thought to have gone 'wrong':

> Even my mother-in-law started asking if I was reading enough books to him.

Hannon (1995), in discussing parents' involvement in their children's literacy development, talks about the myth of the 'bad parent'. He goes on to say, 'but the myth is pervasive and its power should not be underestimated for it can lead well meaning teachers to treat perfectly able parents with suspicion.'

The future at work

Mothers were asked a similar question about whether they thought having dyslexia would affect their child's career choice and were again asked to rate their degree of concern on a 5 point scale.

a lot 5   4   3   2   1   not at all

In this case, the mothers of primary school children scored an average of 4.5, and the mothers of secondary children 4.2.

Mothers felt that having dyslexia would restrict their children's choice of job either because they wouldn't be able to do the job or because they wouldn't be able to pass the exams needed for the job:

> I often think 'Ee, I wonder what he'll do eventually.' Jobs are so hard to come by now. Nowadays they're so fussy, people with 'O' and 'A' levels can't get jobs so it will be a big impact.

> Obviously there are jobs she won't be able to do because she's dyslexic.

Some mothers felt that their children were already limiting their expectations to jobs which required no literacy skills:

> Oh definitely, he'll go for something totally mechanical.

> I think she wants a job in Sainsbury's packing shelves.

> He sees himself leaving without an examination to his name. If he could leave school tomorrow I'd let him.

Whereas in some cases mothers were worried about children limiting their expectations, in other cases mothers were worried that their children were going to be disappointed:

> I worry about his future. He won't be able to choose what he wants to do. He wants to go to university and he wants to do this, that and the other and I know it probably won't be possible, or you know, perhaps he'd find it very difficult.

Mrs Glover, the mother of 16-year-old Sophie who was interviewed in a later study, made the following comments:

> I think she puts too much emphasis on the fact that she might not be able to go to university. That she might not get A and O levels, and I say they're not the criteria for success in life. I mean they are for some but not for everyone.

Research on the careers of adults with dyslexia or learning disabilities has come up with mixed results but does suggest that overall they don't do as well as non-dyslexic adults from the same background (PACFOLD 2007, Price *et al.* 2003). This would suggest that mothers' worries are well founded. Maughan (1994) points out that low achievement motivation is commonly correlated with poor reading. Oka and Paris (1987) claim that, whereas low achievement motivation is usually seen as a negative factor, it may be that some children use this as a coping strategy. In this case it is suggested that they pick 'safe' goals that they can attain in order to keep their self-esteem intact.

Maughan (1994) argues that evidence from adult follow-up studies (Bruck 1985) suggests that poor readers may use these same strategies when it comes to choosing careers or further education. Again though, it can be argued that this could sometimes be seen as a positive strategy which minimises the risk of disappointment or failure. What is not always clear when looking at these adult follow-up studies is what degree of support, if any, children received for their dyslexia whilst in school, nor do we know if or how this might influence career choice. In the present studies several mothers suggested that their children were limiting their choice of future career because of their dyslexia. Both Sophie (16 years) and her mother spoke independently about how she had already restricted her career choice:

> I think it's limited her to what she'd like to be. I think she would have liked to have been a lawyer or something like that you know; and I think she would have been good, because she's quite articulate and she loves arguing, and she loves nit-picking.

> If I wanted to do acting I couldn't. Like at school I would like to have had a go. But I've never had the opportunity because it would have taken us [me] longer to learn the lines and everything.

The issue is whether Sophie has been realistic in limiting her choices or she and those factors that influenced her have limited her unnecessarily. The question of career choice is highly complex for anyone and it can be argued that a great many children have their career choices influenced or limited by a wide variety of factors. What is at question is how far dyslexia interacts or adds to the limitations or influences on career choice. McLoughlin et al. (2004) give a useful summary of the different theoretical approaches to career choice and their particular relevance to dyslexic individuals. They maintain that dyslexics often choose or exclude certain career choices because they make incorrect assumptions about the skills required, especially in terms of literacy. They point out as examples that dyslexics often assume that they cannot enter the legal profession because it involves too high a demand on literacy skills (as Sophie had), whereas they assume that video production work doesn't involve literacy skills. They advise that dyslexics should not automatically exclude themselves from jobs that require literacy skills and that career counselling should not perpetuate the idea that there are a lot of jobs that dyslexics should avoid. They also claim that many dyslexics are surprisingly unaware of their own strengths and weaknesses and that as well as dealing with the primary cognitive difficulties that they have they should be given insight and support for their frequent lack of confidence or low self-esteem. Miles et al. (2007) suggest that is important for dyslexics to develop self-knowledge. McLoughlin (1990) also argues that there is no evidence that dyslexics as a group are better at either spatial tasks or working with computers than are non-dyslexics although this assumption is often made. What is not clear at present is whether dyslexics are overrepresented in some fields of work and if so if this is because they are less good at other types of work and therefore avoid them. McLoughlin concludes that: 'Essentially, dyslexics should pursue occupations and careers for which they are appropriately equipped in terms of their abilities, aptitudes and interests.'

Although in theory this is sound advice, the problem in practice is that by the end of schooling many dyslexic children have been negatively influenced in terms of both expectation and opportunity. As illustrated in an earlier chapter, one mother found that even when her son was at primary school he was limiting his expectations to jobs such as being a lollipop man on the grounds that this involved no reading and writing. Nearly all the secondary children had been placed in the lowest ability groups for some, or in many cases all, subjects, thus limiting both their expectations and their chances of exam success. Maughan (1988) and Fogelmann (1988) both report in follow-up studies that the outlook for most severely dyslexic children is poor with few of them obtaining educational qualifications. Andrews (1990) followed up 50 students aged between 14 and 19 years who attended the Barts Dyslexia Clinic for assessment. These students were found as a group to be above average in intelligence and to have average levels of reading although their spelling was still nearly a standard deviation below the average and their writing speed was slow. Of this group 23 went on to take A levels. It was noted that all but three of this group took A levels in maths or science. This is not the distribution that would normally be expected even when taking the predominance of boys in the sample into account. This suggests that, even when children are seen as 'successful' in formal examinations, for some their choice of subject has been curtailed. One mother whose son had an IQ in the superior range on the WISC, with similar scores for the verbal and performance scales, made the following observations:

> He's a good all rounder really. In a funny sort of way I actually think he's quite good at English! He chooses like the best word to express something and his comprehension has always been excellent. He got almost a 100 per cent for comprehension in the SATs [at 11 years old], but of course his writing and spelling let him down. But I've noticed he gets marked down for things like history and geography because his writing's so poor, anything really where he has to write he's disadvantaged. So the thing is what he gets the best marks for is maths. He's not really that interested in maths and he says he doesn't like maths. But I can see him ending up doing maths simply because he won't manage anything else. I know in a way it's lucky that at least he can do maths, but I think it's a shame if he ends up without a real choice and without doing something he's really interested in.

Even in science subjects some mothers thought that their children's poor literacy skills held them back:

> I think he seems to quite understand them, but it's always the presentation. He can't put it down and he can't describe what happens in the experiments and all the rest of it.

It thus appears that by the time some children with dyslexia come to make career choices that a number of factors, over and above those normally operating on children, have already influenced the choices that they can make.

Several mothers emphasised that what they wanted was for their child to reach their potential and be happy in what they were doing:

As long as Graham can achieve to his potential and do something in life that he's happy in that's fine. That's all I want at the end of the day. I don't want him to be a physicist or whatever! I just want him to be able to get where he wants to be . . . and I said to my husband the other day, 'If he wants to work on a production line making cars, as long as he's happy, what's wrong with that?'

Present feelings

One of the last questions in the interview asked mothers how they felt at the moment about their child having dyslexia. Not surprisingly mothers' answers varied depending on the progress their child was making, the stage they were at in their schooling, the attitude of the school, the age at which they were identified, the severity of their problems and how the child was coping with them at a personal level. Mrs Carter in answering this question summarised several themes that had arisen during the interview:

I don't know really now . . . I think I'm relieved like I said before, that you know what it is and you can do something about it. But I don't think, you know, that there's a magic cure. I think he'll be as dyslexic at seventy as he was at seven. But as long as he learns to cope with it. Probably when he was in the infants, I probably thought there was no hope at all, but when you come here and you see them progressing. I'm quite happy with things the way they are as long as he continues to make progress.

Right now I'm not as worried as I was originally. He was really down and low, now he's coping well. He's catching up quick. He's more positive he's enjoying life a bit more.

I feel sorry for him that he's had to struggle.

I just wish she wasn't!

Just something that we have to get on with.

I admire him the way he deals with it. Considering the problems he's had he's been very strong.

I've given up trying to push him, but now I feel guilty. I can get very negative at times, it's all left to me.

I'm quite concerned with coming up to GCSEs. I can't see him getting anything. People have made comments to his sister, 'Your brother's simple.' It must be very hard for him.

These comments reflect what mothers feel at a particular point in time, but what also emerged from the interviews is that, for both the children and their mothers, they were dealing with the difficulties related to dyslexia on a long-term basis. The nature and extent of the problems changed with time and circumstance and they all had to learn as they went along to make sense of their current difficulties and try and find the best way of dealing with them:

> I suppose I've come to accept now that she's always going to have difficulties and that I'm always going to have to support her, at least while she is at school.

Donawa (1995), an educationalist herself, reflects on the difficulties of bringing up her son Gabriel, who has dyslexia, in what she describes as the formal and competitive school system of Barbados:

> Much of my energy of the last 15 years has been devoted to negotiating a safe passage for my son.

Donawa goes on to talk about both the financial and emotional costs of bringing up a child with special needs:

> Even at the least painful level, that of financial cost, there is an unending stream of lost thermoses, books, shoes, glasses; the extra tuition; the jettisoned career.

> But the real costs are to the spirit; the sorrow of observing a child's bleak despair, the anguish and alarm when the despair turns to rage.

Although few of the mothers in this study had encountered such severe difficulties as Gabriel's mother, the majority could point to a time when their child had been deeply unhappy because of their difficulties and many mothers had in turn been distressed or worried by their child's unhappiness. Half the mothers in this sample described themselves as feeling 'sad' for their child during their interview, even if they were basically optimistic in outlook. All of the mothers said that they would have liked more support, especially when their children were younger.

Support for parents

> Initially I would have liked more support. I'd have liked help in sorting out what the problem was and I'd have liked to talk to other mothers.

None of the mothers in this sample named school as a source of support, and therefore all the significant support that they received was seen to have come from outside the school system. Some mothers specifically mentioned that they would like more support from school:

> I'd like the school to be a lot more supportive.

The most frequently mentioned source of support was from voluntary organisations such as the Dyslexia Institute. This was on either a direct or an indirect basis. Indirect support in the form of meeting other parents in the waiting room whilst children were having their tuition was the most frequently mentioned form of support. This was also considered one of the most valuable forms of support and many mothers spoke in very positive terms about it:

> Oh definitely. Talking to the other parents is a big plus, they understand how you feel.

Direct support would include support from specialist dyslexia teachers and arranged parents' groups. Both parents' groups and specialist teachers were again seen as a valuable source of support by some mothers:

> It really helped at the parents' group to talk to other mothers.

> Mrs G. [dyslexia teacher] has been very supportive.

Mothers of older children and working mothers who didn't use the waiting room and therefore didn't have the chance for informal contact with other parents often regretted this:

> I just drop him off unfortunately, but I came to a parents' course, I found that a great help.

Some mothers pointed out that as well as giving them personal support meeting other parents also had an educative function:

> Meeting other parents and having informal chats with them. You get ideas, suggestions, it's made me more patient.

Hannavy (1995) describes the piloting of a simple reading and writing programme which can be followed by parents of children who are progressing slowly in these skills. She comments that an unexpected outcome of the parents' meeting together is the considerable amount of help and support they give each other, especially in solving problems about how to get their children to work. Apart from two mothers whose daughters both attended the same highly supportive school, none of the other mothers had the opportunity to meet other parents whose children had similar problems through the school. Another major source of support for mothers was from friends or workmates who had similar problems:

> I talk to this woman at work who's got a grown up son who's dyslexic. I do find it a help to talk things over with her.

In summary, the mothers in this sample drew on a wide range of support largely outside the school. This may not be typical of what happens in all areas but Dyson and Skidmore (1994) also found in their survey of 27 Scottish secondary schools that only one instance of support for parents was recorded. Reid et al. (2008) noted that even when good identification and intervention procedures were put in place for dyslexic children the needs of parents were not always being met. Schools may well argue that with all the pressures upon them there isn't time to offer support to parents as well. But if dyslexia/specific learning difficulties are taken seriously then it does raise legitimate questions about how parents can best be supported. The support that mothers most wanted from school was help and understanding in identifying their child's difficulties and acknowledgement of their worries and concerns:

> I just want recognition of the nature of his difficulties. I don't expect magic.

Given that parents draw much of their support from voluntary organisations outside the school it is also important that they don't feel criticised by the school for doing so, as happened to several of the parents in this sample. When schools don't feel they have sufficient time, resources or expertise to offer support, they can encourage parents to contact parent support groups or voluntary groups or perhaps consider any form of organisation which will enable interested parents to meet and support each other. In England this is advocated by the SEN Code of Practice and by the BDA Dyslexia Friendly School Pack. Part of what parents derived from support was information and understanding on how to help their child in a variety of ways. As the role of parents is seen as critical in how children cope with their difficulties it is important that parents be educated and informed about their difficulties and given support and encouragement when needed. The mothers in particular in this sample made it their business to be well informed. There may well be cases when difficulties are first identified by the school where parents will not be as well informed and this raises the question of how such parents can best be informed and supported.

Overall, many mothers in this sample had found that as well as dealing with their child's difficulties they had also had to deal with the hostility, disbelief and blame of others. Edwards (1994) comments that: 'The parent of a dyslexic faces the continual strain of having to watch helplessly, while your child suffers, often while the authorities blame you for the problem, which would be unthinkably brutal with any other form of handicap.' Far from blaming parents it can be argued that educationalists should be thinking about how best to support parents in a constructive and enabling manner.

Summary

1   The majority of mothers felt that they had the main responsibility within the family for supporting their child, especially at a day-to-day level.
2   Mothers had legitimate worries about their children's future academic progress in school.
3   Mothers said they worried a lot about their child's specific learning difficulties narrowing down their future career choices.
4   There were indications that some children were already restricting their career choices as a direct result of their specific learning difficulties.
5   Mothers obtained support for themselves entirely from outside the school system.
6   Mothers found the support of other parents particularly helpful.

7   Many mothers would have liked more support from the school especially in initially identifying and understanding the problem.

8   Given that parents are a major source of support to children with dyslexia, it is important that they in turn be given the information and support that they need to enable them to support their children as effectively as possible.

9   Many parents had supported their children over a number of years and had gained insight and understanding of their children's difficulties; it is important that this 'expertise' be recognised and utilised.

Chapter 12

Case studies

> People jump to the wrong conclusions and they should be educated about what dyslexia means. It's just been one of my dreams to tell them all what it means.
>
> (Sophie, 16 years)

One of the problems with using the case study approach to any issue has been in deciding how 'typical' or 'representative' the case studies described are. As was discussed in Chapter 3 this is especially difficult in the case of dyslexia or specific learning difficulties because in many areas identification is still patchy and variable in nature. This means that a representative sample of all the children in a given population with dyslexia is almost impossible to obtain as not all children are identified. It has to be borne in mind that identification in a loose sense is not an all or nothing phenomenon. Teachers, like parents, may think that something is wrong and offer some level of support even though they don't recognise the child as having specific learning difficulties. In looking at the case studies presented by the likes of Osmond, Van der Stoel, Miles and Edwards it is easy for the unconvinced in particular to say 'Yes, but aren't these exceptional cases? Perhaps these children are particularly vulnerable, or particularly severe or particularly unlucky in the experiences they've encountered.' These are valid points but the sheer weight of case studies reporting similar experiences makes it hard to consign them all to the category of exceptional cases. In reality we do need to know more about the range of experiences that dyslexic children encounter and the range of responses that they make to these experiences. The present study, although still open to criticism of sampling bias, tried to go some way to addressing this problem by selecting a representative sample of children who attended the Dyslexia Institute. It can still be claimed that these children are not representative of dyslexic children in general but given that they were selected from 80 children attending over 70 different schools in six different local authority areas they do represent a wide range of experiences and degrees of difficulty. These children may well be typical of the dyslexic children who are recognised by either the school or their parents as having a specific problem, but the sample excludes an unknown proportion of children whose parents cannot afford private tuition or whose problems go unrecognised. A particular aim of this study was to look at a group of children whose parents had explicitly chosen to understand their children's difficulties in terms of the label 'dyslexia' and had chosen to seek extra support outside the school system for their children. The three case studies looked at in more detail were again picked not to show exceptional or extreme responses, but merely to flesh out the range of experiences that children and their families came across. If anything, in presenting two of three case studies that have had good outcomes so far, these represent the positive end of the spectrum of children interviewed and don't dwell on the more negative experiences of many of the children. Some of the comments made have already been quoted in other chapters but are included here when they are an important part of a wider picture or part of an ongoing thread or theme running through an interview. These are shortened extracts from the full interviews.

Sophie Glover, age 16

Sophie had been fully assessed by an educational psychologist when she was aged 14 years 5 months and the results in Table 12.1 had been obtained. These test scores confirmed the results of more informal testing at school which had put her literacy levels at around 9 years of age.

Thus at the age of 14 years 5 months Sophie was clearly over 5 years behind in her reading and spelling.

Mother's account

Sophie has attended her present comprehensive for 3 years. Before that she attended a middle school. She had two older sisters who had no problems at school. Her mother thought that Sophie's father, uncle, niece and nephew had all had similar problems, although less severe.

> I suppose my husband was a slow reader you know. He used to be in front of the telly and he couldn't read it, and he didn't read books till he was in his mid teens, and also my husband's brother was a very poor reader and needed specialist help.

When asked when she had first realised Sophie had a problem she simply said,

> Straight away . . . There was no question about it.
>   She found it so difficult to read and she didn't like it. She had trouble with the first teacher as well . . . she didn't like Sophie, and she smacked her on the leg the

Table 12.1 Sophie's assessment results

WISC-R Standard: High Average	Full Scale IQ	111
	Verbal Scale IQ	105
	Performance Scale IQ	115
Macmillan Graded Word Reading Test:	Reading age	8:9
Neale Analysis of Reading Ability	Accuracy	7:6
	Comprehension	8:11
	Rate	9:6
BAS Spelling Scale	Age	9:3

second day there. And she was always saying she was lazy and stupid. And she was straight away put in a class for slow children. I didn't think she was slow, I just thought she couldn't read.

Mrs Glover said that looking back with hindsight Sophie was probably clumsy as a young child and had difficulty with skills such as learning to tie her laces. She hadn't learnt her alphabet until about 12 and at 16 still didn't know her times tables. Mrs Glover thought that she'd probably read about dyslexia in magazines and newspapers and when Sophie was about 7 she started asking the school if she might be dyslexic. She was asked what happened when she suggested this to the school.

MRS GLOVER: They tested other kids! That's what got me. I just couldn't understand it. Probably because they knew the other daughters were OK they couldn't accept that Sophie could be different.
INTERVIEWER: So how did they explain her problems to you?
MRS GLOVER: Well they just said, 'You get children like that. She's a bit slow. She'll catch up.'

Sophie's middle school accepted that she had problems and gave her additional help but according to her mother were still emphatic that it was not dyslexia.

They were always, 'No, no, no. We don't believe in that, it's not recognised.'

It was only when she entered her comprehensive school at 13 that it was recognised by the school that she was dyslexic. In fact the special needs department at the school took the initiative and phoned Mrs Glover to suggest that she might be dyslexic.

I said, 'Well, thank goodness.' You know, someone at last had listened!

The school told Mrs Glover they would make a programme for Sophie but she felt that despite good intentions they had done very little. Finally out of desperation she talked to Sophie about going for sessions at the Dyslexia Institute. Sophie was reluctant to do this because the only vacancies were during the school day; she went a few times but stopped going when she'd run out of excuses. Although the school thought that Sophie was dyslexic and actually suggested to her mother that she had some private tuition they were very negative about her attending the Dyslexia Institute.

They thought it was a waste of money, the school. I'll tell you that now. She shouldn't go because they take your money and they take you. He got this tutor for me, Sophie goes there on a Thursday, and I think she only goes there for a natter and a cup of tea . . . She's got no idea about dyslexia this woman, she admitted it.

Mrs Glover then talked about the sorts of difficulties Sophie had.

If you ask her to read something, she'll die. She says, 'Don't ask me to read or write anything,' because she'd rather die than do anything like that.

This had led to particular problems at school because on several occasions she had been asked to read aloud to the class.

> And they've done it time and time again. I've got so cross I've nearly threatened to get her out of the school. And when she comes home she's so upset. She gets stressed out. She cries. The first few times she did it she was so frightened she just burst into tears and was completely humiliated. Everyone laughed. I think that's awful. Before the term's started I've always rung up and said, make sure she's not allowed to read aloud. But it's part of the curriculum. They seem to pick on her now because I've told them not to.
>
> But really when I've got cross at this, at the end of the day it's not really made much difference. They've still done it again about two weeks later and you just despair, and you think I've made all that fuss and palaver and they do it again!

To be fair to the school, Sophie's general willingness to talk in public may have made her understandable fear of reading aloud less obvious to those who weren't fully aware of her problems.

> Now if you said to Sophie, 'Oh, tomorrow you've got to stand and talk on something,' oh, she'd love it. She'd stand in front of the class and she'd do it. She'd revel in it. Yes, it seems that one thing is different from the other. In fact a school mistress said she would have made a good television reporter.

Something that arose several times during the interview was the extra amount of time and effort that Sophie put into her work.

> If she's doing her work she can start at six and she can still be doing it at eleven. She'll hardly have done anything. It's like having teeth pulled out without an anaesthetic. I mean the older girls are saying 'Oh, Sophie's got homework, I'm going out. Bye. See you later.' It takes her for ever to do anything. She's miles behind now with everything.
>
> They just have to work doubly hard really . . . I mean, she puts 10 times more effort into everything than the other girls did.

Another issue that arose was that, like nearly all the secondary-age children in the main study, she was in the bottom sets for everything and allied to this, no attempt was made to explain the specific difficulties of dyslexic children to other children in the school.

> Well, she's in all the low groups and everything which she doesn't like. Some of the kids in her class are really you know, bad. I think there's six boys who have extra time a week. We're presuming they might be dyslexic as well but none of them discuss it. I would have thought the school could do more by bringing it out in the open . . . Like them six children that are in Sophie's year. I mean they could all get together, and there might be a few more who are as well. You could have like, say, a

half an hour free period to discuss your problems . . . They should explain to other kids that it's not their fault that it's a handicap. It's no big deal. But they don't tell the kids this. And then the kids just say 'Oh she's dyslexic, she's stupid.'

Despite these criticisms, Mrs Glover was appreciative of the efforts that the school were making on Sophie's behalf.

It's quite a good school. They're doing OK for her.

She talked about various forms of support that Sophie had been offered such as some-one to read exam questions to her and write things down, and also extra time in exams. Mrs Glover felt that the difficulty was that as Sophie had hidden her problems from all her peers she was reluctant to accept any form of help that would single her out. She described what happened when Sophie was offered extra time in an exam.

MRS GLOVER: Of course, it was an absolute trauma trying to get her to do that. But in the end she did. Because she had to go and sit the exam in the 6th form. She'd told none of her friends she was dyslexic, with them all being in different grades, she could get away with some of it. But one of them she couldn't. She had to tell one girl she'd got extra time. But I think the girl was quite sympathetic. But they should tell them you're dyslexic.

INTERVIEWER: So she doesn't tell her friends?

MRS GLOVER: No, not even her best friend.

INTERVIEWER: Has she talked to you about why she doesn't tell others?

MRS GLOVER: Well I think she thinks that they'll think she's stupid, if she's dyslexic. She has said to me 'Oh, so and so were discussing someone that they thought was really thick and stupid, and they said they must be dyslexic or something.'

In contrast, although Sophie hadn't been recognised as 'dyslexic' at her middle school her difficulties were openly acknowledged.

All the time she was in middle school she had special tuition. A lady she went to two or three times a week, and Sophie accepted it. I mean all her friends knew she had learning difficulties and helped her, you know, with her assignments or whatever she was doing.

Mrs Glover mentioned several times during the interview that Sophie was more concerned about doing well at school, formal examinations and further education than she and her husband were.

She's just took her mocks. She was really upset when she didn't do well. You know, she got some bad marks. So I've said, 'So what?' You know we're not one of those parents who thinks they've got to have a bit of paper and that's going to be success for life.

Mrs Glover was asked how she felt at the moment about Sophie having dyslexia.

Well I'm sad that she's got it. I'd sooner she didn't have it really! But she can cope with it. She's coping with it alright. I think she does quite well . . . She's got quite an outgoing personality, and she's got, like, the support of her family which a lot of kids might not have . . . I mean them advantages more outweigh, you know the fact that she's a bit dyslexic.

She was finally asked if there was anything else that she thought important or relevant that she wanted to add.

Just the negativeness that I was bit worried about. If you come across more of that, if there's anything you can do to get her out of it? Feeling so negative about things.

Sophie's account

Sophie presented in the interview as a pleasant and articulate 16-year-old with a good sense of humour. Understandably given the degree of her literacy problems she appeared depressed and frustrated when talking about some of her experiences and was close to tears on occasion. Despite this, at the end of the interview, she said she hadn't minded talking about her experiences and was glad to have the chance to give her point of view.

Sophie was first asked about what sort of interests she had out of school.

Well, I've just started making clothes and things. I find that interesting. And art. But really that's the only thing. I don't like reading books. Not at all. I don't mind magazines and things like that.

She went on to say that the only thing she enjoyed at school was art. She then talked about the difficulties of going for Dyslexia Institute lessons during school time.

SOPHIE: It's school. Because it's one thing learning to read, but you're missing out on the other things. It's like fighting a losing battle really.

INTERVIEWER: How did you explain it to other people?

SOPHIE: I used to make up all lies and stuff. I was going to get my eyes tested, going shopping. I would say anything . . . It was stressing us [me] out trying to think of excuses.

INTERVIEWER: Would it have made a difference if it had been out of school time?

SOPHIE: Yes, I would do it after school like. That's what I'd like to do. But there's no space really.

Sophie was then asked about what difficulties she had in school because of her dyslexia.

SOPHIE: Reading out. In lessons they make you read out all the time. My mum does complain sometimes but the school doesn't listen. They don't know how much it affects you. I think it, like, frightens you, it really frightens you. Being put through the traumas of it. And like sometimes you have to read like paragraphs and stuff, and you're not as fast as other people. You feel embarrassed, it's not easy.

INTERVIEWER: When you're writing, do you find that's all right?
SOPHIE: Well if they dictate to you it totally confuses me.

Sophie then went on to say that she wrote less than other children, and that she avoided words she couldn't spell and that in consequence she got less marks for her projects. She was then asked how she felt about having these types of problems.

SOPHIE: I hate it. I really hate it. It's frustrating.
INTERVIEWER: Do you think other children notice the difficulties you have?
SOPHIE: I think some of them do. Some of them close round me. Like some of them know now, and they've said, 'Oh well it explains a lot of things you've done.'
INTERVIEWER: Have you told them, or have they just found out?
SOPHIE: They found out. I wouldn't never really have told anyone.
INTERVIEWER: How do you feel about them knowing?
SOPHIE: Well, people think you're stupid, to be quite honest. That's the whole attitude of it . . . I try not to let them notice, as best I can do.
INTERVIEWER: What about the teachers at school? Do you think that they understand the difficulties you've got?
SOPHIE: No. Not all of them. No, I don't think they're aware of it at all. They don't understand what it is. They don't know what it's about, they don't. I think they think things are backwards. That's what everyone thinks. Some of them are more understanding though.

Sophie was then asked if she thought she'd had a best teacher, and if so what this teacher was like.

Mrs F. I had her for a year, and she never asked me to read once. She used to be very helpful. If I couldn't hand in a project or something, she would say 'Well Sophie, I understand, I'll give you some extra time.' She was nice. But it's just because she was probably a nice person.

By contrast she was also asked about the worst or least helpful teacher she'd encountered.

SOPHIE: Like the head of department I didn't think he was very helpful. I think it's because he hasn't much time . . . it's only, like, him running the whole thing. I understand, like, there's a lot of people that he's got to help. But he's just not helpful at all.
INTERVIEWER: Is that because of his attitude or what?
SOPHIE: I think it's mine as well, because I don't want help probably. Because he wanted to take me out of lessons to help us, but it's like the same thing. The embarrassment and I'm missing out on other things I need to learn.
INTERVIEWER: So has he talked over the way you'd like the help?
SOPHIE: Yes, I told him the way I would like it to be, but he says, 'you can't have that way, it's impossible.'

Sophie was then asked about teachers' attitudes towards her

> SOPHIE: Teachers have called us lazy. Because I'm slow. Like homework; I hate
> doing it because I can't do it. French is my worst. I can't do French at all.
> INTERVIEWER: Do you find homework in general a struggle, or is it this in
> particular?
> SOPHIE: Everything, I, think is hard going. I'm so wrecked. Tired after the day,
> and just worn out from all the effort.

Sophie was then asked what she thought about being called dyslexic.

> SOPHIE: When I found out I was really upset because I thought it was incurable
> like. Like if you were a bit slow, well you think, 'Oh well, I can do this, then I'll
> catch up.' But when I found out, like, everyone was saying 'oh, I thought you'd
> be happy' but I wasn't, I was shocked. Because everyone had been saying for
> years that I'm not: I'm just slow. And it was frustrating that they never picked
> it up and I might have been able to get a bit better than I am now.
> INTERVIEWER: How do you feel about it now?
> SOPHIE: It helps me. Because there are things about it and stuff you can relate
> to, and it makes you feel a bit better that there's someone else out there going
> through the same thing.

Sophie was asked if she would or would not like the chance to talk to other dyslexic
children.

> I think I would to be quite honest. Because they're the people who are going
> through the same thing as you. Because no one can know until they've actually
> been through the trauma of it. But they tend to keep it hush hush. Like at my
> school you don't meet each other and stuff. It's, like, private.

Sophie was finally asked what sort of help would be most useful for people with
dyslexia.

> Just to make people more aware of it so that you don't feel like you've got some
> horrible disease. People just jump to the wrong conclusion and they should be
> educated about what dyslexia means. It's just been one of my dreams to tell them
> all what it means.

Key points to emerge

Many of the points that arose have already been discussed in other chapters, so just a
few of the main ones are commented on here. Both Sophie and her mother thought
that there was a negative attitude towards learning difficulties including dyslexia on
the part of other children at Sophie's comprehensive. This meant that the attempts of
the special needs department to provide her with support were undermined to some
extent by the overall ethos of the school, and this underlines the importance of having a

whole-school policy, which as part of its remit considers the general ethos of the school and the opinions and attitudes of others.

Another point of note is that even though the school took the lead in identifying her as having a specific learning difficulty they were still dismissive, according to Mrs Glover, of the idea that the Dyslexia Institute could offer appropriate support. Although there may be valid concerns about the effectiveness of out-of-class support, the school itself wished to withdraw Sophie for support and had suggested an out-of-school tutor to help with Sophie's literacy. It appeared from Mrs Glover's account that it was more ill informed prejudice rather than rational criticism that led to the school's comments. All the Dyslexia Institute teachers have a recognised specialist diploma in teaching children with dyslexia on top of their ordinary teaching qualifications. It was also the practice of this branch to advise parents to try and first get a free assessment by a local authority psychologist and to try and get support in school. Again it may be that schools have genuine concerns about parents having to pay for tuition, but Mrs Glover, by her own account, could comfortably afford the fees. Given the degree of Sophie's literacy problems and the obvious concern of the school, it appears that it was mistrust of specialist dyslexia organisations and the general 'mythology' that surrounds dyslexia that was influencing the school.

A more general problem that this did raise was how best to offer support to a secondary school child who was very behind in her literacy skills because of a specific learning disability. In a case such as this it is hard to imagine that within-class support alone would be sufficient and yet Sophie herself was reluctant to miss out on her 'normal' school timetable. If there had been a much more positive attitude to dyslexia and special needs in general on the part of other children and Sophie had been able to miss one of her least favoured subjects such as French, it is possible that withdrawal could have worked combined with good in-class support.

In many ways Mrs Glover fitted the stereotype of the 'dyslexic' parent that some educationalists seem to hold. She was middle class, articulate, financially well off, a successful business woman and a graduate. Yet like many parents in this study she stressed that she had not pressurised her daughter in terms of academic success and that she felt relatively powerless in trying to influence the school. Although it may be true of parents in general that some do put pressure on their children for academic success it is important that this is not used as an automatic explanation for the anxieties that some children display and it is especially important that it is not overused as an explanation for the anxieties of children with dyslexia. It could be argued that what parents do and what they say may be two different things and that some may unintentionally convey certain expectations. This is hard to prove either one way or the other but in the present study not a single child mentioned pressure from their parents for academic success as an issue.

A problem that can arise for any child with a specific learning difficulty, but may be more frequent among girls, is one of isolation in terms of meeting others with a similar problem. Given the much smaller numbers of girls with dyslexia there is more risk of this happening, as in Sophie's case where she didn't have anyone she could share her problems with.

The fear that many dyslexic children have of reading aloud has been well documented (Edwards 1994) and some children like Sophie become highly anxious about it. Reading aloud especially to the whole class is a totally public performance which clearly reveals all your deficiencies, real or imagined, to a large audience. It is important that all teachers be aware of the misery and humiliation that reading aloud can cause some children. In the case of Sophie's school, the educational psychologist concerned thought that this was probably an organisational problem rather than wilful intent on the part of the school. She collaborated with the special needs department in briefing all the subject specialists about children with special needs at the beginning of each term. She pointed out that, in the case of Sophie's year, seventeen different supply teachers had been used in the space of one term, and that under such circumstances it was easy for important information not to get passed on to everyone. Whether or not this was the reason why Sophie was asked to read aloud on several occasions, it is easy to see that this situation may be seen as one of personal fault rather than organisational difficulty by Sophie and her mother. It also highlights the need for all classroom teachers to be responsible for special needs and to review their own approach to asking children to read aloud. A child like Sophie needs to feel safe that she is never going to be asked to read aloud in public as living with the fear, dread and anticipation that this might happen can by all accounts seriously affect a child's well being, ability to learn and overall attitude to school.

This case clearly highlights the point that other people's reactions to difficulties can be as much or more of a problem to an individual than the difficulties themselves.

David Graham, age 12 years 10 months

At 12 years 3 months David was assessed by a chartered clinical psychologist (Table 12.2).

At 11 years 10 months David was assessed by the head of the special needs department at his secondary school (Table 12.3).

He was estimated by his teachers to be of average intelligence and was considered weak in reading, spelling and arithmetic compared with his age group. Under special abilities it was noted that he was verbally intelligent, and had many interests.

His behaviour in class was deemed to be co-operative, friendly, responsive and oversensitive. His attitude to work was considered to be enthusiastic, and his attitude to adults as obedient and normal. His attitude to others was considered to be friendly and normal and he was popular with other children. In summary it was stated that David had extremely good general knowledge and excellent verbal skills. He was thought to be a very friendly boy who still worked well despite his problems. David presented in

Table 12.2 David's clinical assessment results

Wechsler Intelligence Scale	Full scale IQ	113
	Reading Age	6:10

Table 12.3 David's special needs assessment results

Reading age Holborn	6:9
Reading age Blackwell	6:0

his interview as outgoing and highly articulate with a generally positive and enthusiastic approach to life. He was the only child of a single mother although an extended family network gave considerable support. Money was tight and he was only able to receive tuition at the Dyslexia Institute through its bursary fund for low- or no-income families. He was attending a Roman Catholic secondary school which, although it had reasonably high academic expectations, was considered to have a caring ethos and a good special needs department. At the time of the interviews David had been attending the Dyslexia Institute for an hour twice a week for the previous 8 months.

Mrs Graham

Mrs Graham, like many of the mothers in the larger sample, thought something was wrong during David's first year at school. She felt that far from progressing he seemed to be deteriorating and had lost some of the spark and enthusiasm that he had prior to going to school:

> At his first school they kept saying he was sensitive. But I suppose you would be sensitive if you kept being treated as a moron and you're not.

Like most of the mothers in the sample, Mrs Graham encountered considerable problems when she tried to help Graham learn to read:

> Oh terrible. I used to sit with him to learn him to read, I even bought him all the reading books [the school had no reading scheme]. I was so close to him I was really getting angry with him. He used to go round to my sister. One time he'd read it fine and the next page he couldn't. I used to say, 'David, that's the same word.' It was a continuous struggle.

David made no progress in learning to read and could write nothing legible when he entered the junior school. Mrs Graham eventually suggested to the primary school that David might be dyslexic:

> I mentioned it a long time ago at primary school. He was checked by the local authority but they thought it was mainly an emotional problem because he was from a one parent family, which I disputed because he was a happy-go-lucky kid, he was a social child.

Mrs Graham had several meetings with David's class teachers and the head of the school:

> I felt I was always being fobbed off. I always felt with the primary school, that they thought I was blaming them. But I mean you go to see different doctors for different kinds of things so why not different kinds of teachers.

After Mrs Graham had persisted it was agreed that he should have 'special needs' support at school. By the time David left primary school Mrs Graham thought that they had realised that he wasn't 'slow' and his difficulties weren't all attributable to emotional problems:

> So we discovered he wasn't emotional and on leaving primary school they apologised that they'd always had him down as a slow learner.

> David is interested in Watergate and what it's all about. He's mad on J.F. Kennedy and wants to know all about him. At the moment he's mad about Malcolm X. He loves history. He's interested in politics. He knows who the president is and he wants to know the difference between the Democrats and the Republicans. He's not a dull child and why they couldn't see that at primary school I do not know. They're in charge of your child's future, it's kids' lives they're playing with.

As soon as David entered secondary school at 11 years of age it was recognised that he had serious difficulties and, in consultation with David and his mother, plans were made to try and deal with these. At this point David was approximately 6 years behind in his reading and spelling and was thus barely able to read and write at all:

> His year tutor at high school was the first to realise there was a problem. He wanted to know why he couldn't read as he was obviously intelligent. I was thinking about the Institute, I'd got information on it. I said, 'Do you think I should get David tested?' and he said, 'Yes I would.' So it was all my worst fears confirmed really . . . I felt guilty I hadn't followed my own instincts in the first place. I feel really guilty about that, but you know if you're talking to professionals you expect them to know.

Mrs Graham was very pleased with the support that David's secondary school had provided. It had been agreed to keep him in a small special needs class where he could be given help with his literacy skill. He was also given some individual sessions at school by someone trained in dyslexia as well as the sessions at the Dyslexia Institute. The hope was to return David as quickly as possible to a mainstream class. Mrs Graham felt that in the 9 months David had been receiving special support he had made considerable progress:

> Since he's been to secondary school the support he's had has been unbelievable . . . It wasn't till he came here he could really read. I mean this time last year he was picking up real little books.

> I think his year tutor last year was a big influence on both of us; he commented straight away. Those teachers seem to really strive for them kids. They're great, their attitude towards them is really good. The headmaster takes them for history and he keeps saying he has high hopes for David.

Mrs Graham was asked how she felt about David having dyslexia:

I think it's a damn shame he's got it. We're always positive, and I always talk positive to David about it. But, you know, academic achievement is so much these days, I'm really frightened.

She was also asked how she felt David had responded over the years to his difficulties:

We have quite a close relationship, we're quite pals. He's quite open about any difficulties he has unless he's hiding it from me very well. He's quite a happy go lucky kid. I don't think there's much gets him down for long.

Mrs Graham rated her son's self-esteem as fairly high and added to this:

He doesn't seem to let himself be put down at all.

Mrs Graham also noted that he was friends with children in the top grade although a couple of recent incidents suggested that David did encounter some difficulties. He'd recently experienced some resentment from the other children in the special needs class because of his general enthusiasm and keenness to answer questions:

He's stopped going to circuit training at lunchtime, because they're all in the top grade. So he is really aware.

But overall Mrs Graham felt the school had done their best to counter any negative attitudes:

They have discussed in class why David comes here, which I think is a good open attitude. I was really pleased with that.

Mrs Graham emphasised that both she and David had a lot of support from a large extended family. She was asked whether or not meeting other mothers of dyslexic children was helpful:

Oh definitely. You talk to other girls and you think, 'Oh, good I'm not the only one who's going through this, I'm not neurotic,' and sort of getting it confirmed that you are not neurotic.

Mrs Graham talked about the fact that without the bursary fund it simply wouldn't have been possible for David to have tuition at the Dyslexia Institute. She strongly resented people making the assumption that parents of dyslexic children were all wealthy neurotics. She also felt, like many mothers in the sample, that she had been forced into the role of being 'pushy':

How many have fallen by the wayside. How many parents aren't pushy. I suppose in some ways I have been pushy, but you've got to be.

David

David was positive about all the support he was getting. He said he liked his sessions at the Dyslexia Institute and thought that they had helped him to sound words out and read more fluently. He said that at school he still had difficulties with reading and spelling and that he got frustrated quite often, especially with words that he couldn't read. He said that he wrote less than other children, avoided writing if he could and avoided words he couldn't spell on a regular basis. David appeared to be able to transfer what he was learning in his specialist sessions to the classroom situation, because when asked what kind of things he found helpful in school he first said:

> Me cards help [systematic sound cards taught in specialist sessions]. Like I use them to remind me, like, I say, 'Has "h"'.

He valued specific practical help given to him by various teachers in his secondary school such as being given the spellings of various words for his geography lessons. He felt that on the whole his teachers had quite a good understanding of his difficulties. When asked what sort of thing he didn't find helpful in school he said that copying off the board was the biggest problem and that he got frustrated because he was too slow. He said that in the past in particular he had been frequently called slow and lazy. He said that what particularly annoyed him was being told to hurry up when he was already going as fast as he could, especially as he liked to be tidy and knew that if he went any faster he would then be told off by one teacher in particular for being untidy. When asked about how he felt about these criticisms he said 'angry'.

David said that the thing he most dreaded doing in school were exams and that he worried about these for weeks in advance:

> It's the reading of the questions and I generally worry about them.

In his last exams it had been arranged for someone to read the questions to David and he had been happy with this arrangement. David was asked what he thought about being called dyslexic. He said he was pleased to have this label and to know what his problems were. When asked if he didn't resent it for making him different he replied:

DAVID: Like some people are ill, like me mum's got arthritis and people like arthritics, they're not really bothered about having a label . . . It's helped us get me own back on some teachers. No teacher now brands me as thick, cause I've told them I was dyslexic.

INTERVIEWER: So did you think that some of your teachers in the past thought you were thick?

DAVID: Yes, very much so.

INTERVIEWER: How did you feel about that?

DAVID: I felt like punching them, because I was feeling like, I'm not thick cause I know these things. They wouldn't believe that I knew them but I did. It was like one great big knot and, like, the knot's now starting to come undone.

David was asked if he explained his difficulties to other children and what effect, if any, this had on his friendships. David said he was willing to explain his difficulties to other children and said that he still had friends in nearly every class in his year:

> Two of my friends have got it as well. We're closer friends because of it.

David said that he just ignored or told other children to shut up if they tried to tease him. He said there had been some teasing but that this had stopped since the teacher had explained to the class about dyslexia.

When asked how he thought he compared with his classmates in terms of intelligence, David said:

> Like more for talking, cause like with being dyslexic it's not really shown through.

David was enthusiastic about the various adult role models he had heard of. He was particularly keen on Michael Heseltine because of his own interest in politics and his ambition to be leader of the United Nations one day. David was finally asked if he thought he would always be dyslexic:

> More than likely, but I think I'll learn to cope with it. Although I think I'll still get stuck on things.

Postscript

Soon after this interview a statementing process was started and 9 months later Mrs Graham received a proposed statement. This said that David would be best remaining in his mainstream school but needed to receive highly structured and sequenced learning in a one-to-one or small group situation in addition to following much of the national curriculum. It was acknowledged that his literacy difficulties made it difficult for him to access the national curriculum at a level matching his intellectual abilities but that this should be done as far as possible. It was pointed out that David was already responding well to a multi-sensory approach (programme followed by the Dyslexia Institute). It was also recommended that his self-esteem should be monitored and that he should be given the chance to talk about his difficulties or strategies for dealing with them if he so wished.

Key points

It is interesting to contrast the experiences of David and Sophie because they are similar in IQ and also in the extent of their literacy difficulties and were both considered to have good verbal skills. On the other hand any comparison has to take into account all the variables on which they also differ; these include gender, class, age, personality, schooling and family circumstances, to name a few. It also highlights the importance of having more systematic longitudinal research which can give us more idea about how different variables influence a child's long-term adjustment. Is David's confident attitude to telling others about his problems an outcome of his personality and relatively high self-esteem or in part due to a more receptive and sympathetic environment? Does having close friends with similar difficulties help? Will David retain his optimism as he gets nearer to public exams and to making decisions about his future? Is the fact that David was properly identified and given the structured support he needs at an earlier age than Sophie of significance? Did David's strong verbal skills and confidence in speaking up plus his friendly and enthusiastic manner give teachers a more favourable impression of him than a shy tongue-tied dyslexic child who might have greater difficulty in convincing teachers of their intelligence? This is all speculation, but research and observation, which tells us about those children who cope well and in which circumstances, is important in informing future practice.

It was interesting to note that David's school had good relations with the Dyslexia Institute and collaborated with them on his support. This was reflected in his statement, which commented on the value of the multi-sensory teaching he had already received.

Malcolm Carter, age 9 years 9 months

It was noted in Malcolm's report that his low average IQ indicated that he should be reading and spelling at an age level much closer to his chronological age, which would indicate that he had specific learning difficulties. He attended his local primary school and had been attending the Dyslexia Institute for 18 months. He was the middle of three children and his father worked away from home on the oil rigs.

Mrs Carter

> Well I wasn't worried until he was about six, I would say. But even at nursery Malcolm never wanted to bring a picture home. He never wanted to do a Mother's Day card or things like that you know. Things where he would have to write.

> Well, the school weren't too concerned, because it was all the new ideas, they learn through play. You know, they're never concerned about reading and writing really until junior school. But, I mean, having said that there were three years in the infants school.

Mrs Carter felt that Malcolm was making no progress at all and had difficulty with tasks such as saying the days of the week in order. She accepted that Malcolm probably wasn't one of the brightest children in the class but felt as she put it 'he was intelligent enough' to learn to read. She said she made several visits to the school to discuss Malcolm's difficulties. Malcolm was then seen by an educational psychologist; according to Mrs Carter she didn't receive a written report:

> He just said he was immature, and that as he got older he would make progress.

When Malcolm entered junior school he was still not reading so he was given some remedial help, but Mrs Carter felt that this was not specific enough and Malcolm still made poor progress. After the first two terms she decided to contact the Dyslexia Institute:

Because I got absolutely sick of going up and down the school. I mean, it had got to the stage where I was in tears and I was frustrated by it. And I felt that there was no one you could really turn to. Nobody was pointing you in any direction. So he wasn't getting the help and you knew there was something wrong.

But the only thing was every time I mentioned dyslexia it was like a taboo word. It's like, 'Well, I've taught for 30 years, and I've only ever come across one child you know.'

And I think I was so concerned because in the earlier days, when it was just being made public about dyslexia. There were people having to risk their homes and everything just really to get help for their kids. I mean it's all right for people who come where you can afford it. For them to have the lessons. But I mean there's lots of kids out there who are just getting wrote off and I don't think that's right. People say 'Well, there's a lot of dyslexics who've succeeded,' but probably for every one that's succeeded there's these twenty behind who haven't.

I mean I know a lot of people are against them being labelled, but to me it makes no difference, because if you're blind you're blind. If you're dyslexic you're dyslexic, and there's not much you can do . . . so long as you get help and you learn to cope with it, why worry about it? And to me being statemented is just as bad a thing in my eyes. But they can accept that and not the label 'dyslexia'. And I think when they do say 'special needs', I think that's a big umbrella, and they can sort of fit everything into it.

Mrs Carter thought that having dyslexia had influenced Malcolm quite a lot and she rated his self-esteem as fairly low:

He was fine until last year. I think he knew then that there were a lot of the kids getting ahead of him, and I think the other kids were starting to realise that Malcolm wasn't the same as them. And I think he had a few little hassles at school, which he hadn't come across before: a bit of name calling and things like that.

He said the other day, 'Well, I'm never going to do what the others do in class.' You know, I just says, 'There'll always be things that other children will go on and be able to do that you can't but, there again there'll be things you can do that they can't.' But I think what hurt the most with Malcolm was last year, he was even thinking about what he was going to do when he leaves school. He was coming home and saying things like, 'I think I'll be a lollipop man because you'll not really have to do much written work,' or things like that. And I thought, you know, 'You shouldn't even have to worry.' You know, really your school days should be happy.'

Mrs Carter was pleased with the general attitude of teachers in the school and thought that the majority of them had been encouraging in their approach:

Well certainly last year and this term, he's had such a lot of help from some of the teachers, and they've given him awards for certain pieces of work that he's done. It'll be completely mis-spelt in a case like that, but for him it's a good piece of work. So they have encouraged him to do a lot better, and the last open evening I was really impressed on how well he had done.

It was a bit difficult last year; I had a bit of a to-do with one of the teachers because I wasn't very happy with what she had written in his report at the end of the year, saying that he hadn't tried, he hadn't worked, that as well. Like a lot of teachers have said, he does try, it's just he can't get through that brick wall type of thing . . . I rang the head and he said, 'Well, she said he'd only worked to 40 per cent of his capacity.' I says, 'Is that 40 per cent of his capacity or what the rest of the class are capable of?' Because if she's saying 40 per cent of what the rest of them are capable of, that is what Malcolm will be functioning at. I just don't think teachers realise what efforts these kids put in.

Mrs Carter was disappointed because this teacher had expressed an interest in having some information on dyslexia and had been taken in several pamphlets:

I knew from the report that she'd written that she hadn't taken on board anything that was in the leaflets.
    I mean, he's got a teacher now, who if he's not trying, she tells him. She's not sort of soft on him or overly sweet to him because he's got problems. I mean she knows if he's trying or not, and it seems to have worked. The relationship with her is quite good because she knows when to encourage him when he's done well, and she does.

Mrs Carter was aware that Malcolm often kept things to himself and was not one to talk about his problems:

I would say he misbehaves a bit more. If you know he's been having problems he can come home and take it out on the family type of thing.

Mrs Carter thought that some parents and teachers did think she was making excuses for Malcolm by calling him dyslexic. She'd also felt a bit isolated from other parents on occasions such as open evening:

Because you see all the mothers going to see their nice paperwork on the wall.

It had also been suggested to her by some teachers that Malcolm should go to special school:

I don't see that as an option because Malcolm is bright enough. I mean I don't want anybody to think he's above average, he's not. He is just an average child. I mean he's got his problems, and if he overcomes them, great, but I don't want him to be sort of like a university graduate if he's not capable of it.
    You do feel a bit neurotic and pushy because you're always up at the school. But I've always felt it was important to sort it out in junior school.
    If schools would listen to you the way that doctors do sometimes, because doctors often think, 'Yes, Mum knows best: she's with them 24 hours of the day type of thing,' and you know your own child. Whereas, like, teachers think, 'Oh well, we've been trained, we know what's happening with your child,' and I don't think they always do.

Mrs Carter then spoke about a course for parents which she had been to recently at the Dyslexia Institute:

> I think it makes you realise you're not the only one with problems and that children vary a lot. But it made you realise about the whole scope of the things and not just the reading and writing.
>
> I think the only thing that gives me cause for concern, like, I say Malcolm's never been disruptive or anything like that, but I know it can get to the stage where they might feel totally isolated and I wouldn't want to see any decline in his behaviour, when he goes to senior school.

Mrs Carter was asked how she felt at the moment about Malcolm having dyslexia:

> I think I'm relieved, like I said before, that you know what it is, and you can do something about it. But I mean, I don't think there is a magical cure. I mean I think he'll be as dyslexic at seventy as he is at seven. But as long as he learns to cope with it. Probably in the infants I thought there was no hope at all, but obviously when you come here [Dyslexia Institute] and you see them progressing, I'm quite happy with things the way they are. As long as he obviously continues to make progress.'

Malcolm

Malcolm presented in his interview as a calm sensible boy, who was quite happy to talk about practical things connected with his work but found it much harder to comment on how he felt about things. This could be put down to the interview situation, but his mother also found him the same at home.

Malcolm said his main interests were football, and anything else active; this was similarly reflected in his interests at school where he said he liked PE, football and playing. He was positive about his specialist sessions and gave a detailed account of the specific things he learnt; he said he didn't mind coming even though it was extra work. When asked why he thought coming to the Dyslexia Institute was 'good' he replied:

> I've learnt how to do more joined up writing. I've learnt spelling, all sorts of stuff as well, and it helps us [me] with my reading. I think it helps us a lot. It's better than being like stuck, and at school it helps you a lot, you know how to get on with your work, and you don't go to the teacher all the time.

When asked about what difficulties he had at school because of his dyslexia he said that his difficulties had been mainly before he started having specialist help:

> Like writing about things we did . . . like to write a sentence out because I didn't know what to write and like I didn't know how to spell.

He spoke about how he used to watch other children go up and say they had finished, when he had just started writing. Malcolm mentioned several times during the interview that he felt better because there was another boy now in the class who also had difficulties:

Because there's another boy like me, but he's got more problems now because he hasn't been doing sounds and stuff.

Malcolm said he used to feel embarrassed by his difficulties and blame himself:

I'm not very embarrassed now because there's someone the same as me.

Malcolm thought that his teachers were generally positive and supportive and that he had never been unfairly criticised by them.

Malcolm had to leave school early for one of his specialist sessions and said that he avoided telling other children where he was going and why.

He said he wouldn't know what to say if someone asked him what dyslexia was, although his mum had explained it to him and he thought he did understand at a personal level what it was.

When finally asked if he thought he would still be dyslexic as an adult he said:

I don't know. I'm going to hope to try to get rid of it.

Key points

Even though Mrs Carter felt that she had had to push to get Malcolm's difficulties recognised both she and Malcolm thought that the school had been largely supportive in their attitude to him and that he had experienced no direct humiliation or unfair criticism from teachers. This, combined with the good progress that Malcolm had made in his specialist sessions, appeared to be giving him a good all round level of support to which he was responding positively.

It was notable that Malcolm had quietly compared himself to other children over the years and drawn his own conclusions. Again this brings into question how far the ethos and organisation of the school and the nature of the personal support a child receives can help prevent them from building up a negative self-image. In relation to this the importance of having another child in the class with similar problems was emphasised by Malcolm as a way of coping.

Both Mrs Carter and Mrs Graham described themselves as having to be 'pushy' in order to get their children's difficulties properly recognised. It perhaps says something about the power relationship between parents and school that when parents put forward legitimate concerns this is seen as 'pushy', whereas if the schools had put forward the same concerns it's hard to imagine that this would have been seen as 'pushy'. In all three cases the children received two to three sessions a week of 'remedial' support at school before they were identified as having dyslexia. Their lack of progress in terms of reading and spelling scores would seem to support their mother's contentions that this support was not specific enough to their difficulties to have a significant impact on them. In a more positive light this does suggest that in some cases schools don't necessarily need to be giving more support but need to have a better understanding of specific learning difficulties so that support can be more appropriate and effective.

Chapter 13

Conclusions and recommendations

I don't give a damn for a man that can only spell a word one way.

(Mark Twain)

Written language is a social convention with astonishingly strong sanctions to even the smallest aberrations from the norm.

(Solvag 2007, p. 87)

In thinking about the experience of living with dyslexia it is useful to consider three main spheres of influence, namely the home, the school and wider society, and how they might interact with each other. Bronfenbrenner (1979), when examining the influences on children's development, stressed the importance of bringing together psychological, sociological, economic, educational and political factors and considering them with an ecological perspective. He termed relatively closed systems such as the family or the classroom 'micro-systems' and the interaction between them 'meso-systems'. These meso-systems were affected by what he termed the exo-system, in other words factors that impinged on how parents or teachers carried out their role such as the training that teachers received. Finally all these systems interacted with the wider socio-cultural context or what Bronfenbrenner termed the macro-system. Bronfenbrenner and his followers have revised this model over time; however, the fundamental point that we need a comprehensive and interactional model to fully understand a child's development still remains. Shakespeare (2006) in writing about disability argues that a bio-psycho-social model is needed that does justice to the intricacies of people's lives. Truss (2008) comments on the sparse literature on the perspectives of parents and children with SENs and the need for a whole system perspective which transcends the rather narrow educational perspective in which they are often viewed.

Child and family

A bio-psycho-social model suggests we need to consider for an individual child how their underlying processing skills interact with the learning demands placed upon them and the support they receive. An important part of this explanation is to understand the role of psychological factors such as attribution style and self-esteem in mediating between underlying processing difficulties/differences and learning demands. This is a complex interactional process with past experiences of learning influencing current attribution style, self-esteem and coping strategies. By listening to children's perspectives we are gaining a clearer perspective of how they view themselves as learners, what they see as important influences and ultimately how they are learning to live with dyslexia. The views of children and adults with dyslexia have underlined the supportive role that parents can play and fleshed out what kinds of parental attitudes and actions are particularly helpful. They have also given us information on the kind of teaching practices and learning experiences in school they find helpful and unhelpful. The attitudes and context in which teaching practices take place may be important but many children named specific practices such as being asked to read out loud or having to give or receive test scores in front of the class as particularly distressing. It appears that visible public indicators of their difficulties are particularly humiliating and difficult to come to terms with.

Although the child or young person in question is our main concern, particularly with younger children their experiences are embedded within a family context. Parents or other carers as well as observing children's development and learning within the home will often interpret children's school learning experiences through both what children say and how they behave. As this and other studies illustrate, parents can act as advocates when their children are experiencing difficulty at school and co-supporters in helping with their children's learning and well being. They can also play an important role in helping children cope with learning failure at school and in helping children to invest their self-esteem in alternative activities outside school. It is therefore essential that we research and attend to the experiences of parents and it is somewhat surprising that this is one of the few studies to systematically consider the views of parents in relation to bringing up a child with dyslexia.

The relationship between home and school

An important thread that runs through the debate on dyslexia is the relationship between parents and teachers. This was discussed in some depth in Chapter 7; here just some of the main points to emerge from that are reviewed. Riddick (1995a) has suggested that this relationship becomes critical when there are differences between the parents and the school on the nature and extent of a child's difficulties. Allied to this the powerful myth of parents as pushy, overambitious, and unrealistic was often invoked when parents questioned the accuracy of the school's perceptions and raised the possibility of dyslexia. In cases such as this it appeared that parents were treated as clients rather than partners and that no or little credence was given to their point of view. Parents in this situation found themselves largely powerless, whatever their social class. As Dewhirst also found in her study some parents felt that they had been labelled as 'pushy' by the school and blamed for their children's difficulties. There appeared to be an interaction between a school's attitude to dyslexia and their attitude to parents. In some cases where schools were more positive in their attitude to parents, they were willing to listen to parents' concerns even though they were initially dubious about the concept of dyslexia. In recent interviews updating the original ones parents were less likely to report schools or teachers completely denying the existence of dyslexia but they still found teachers often disputed that their child had such difficulties and would make remarks such as 'there's plenty worse than him in the class'. Teachers in schools with a high percentage of children needing literacy support and insufficient policies and resources to meet them may well be right that there are other children in the class who equally need support. Dyson and Skidmore (1995) found that in comprehensives supportive of the concept of specific learning difficulties there were generally good relations with parents, with little conflict. The message seems to be that conflict tends to arise when schools are not identifying and supporting children with dyslexia and that in such cases parents are entitled to feel concerned and that they could be seen as 'pro-active' rather than 'pushy'. There is no evidence that parents of dyslexic children are different from parents in general, and the same range of views and attitudes towards education are held. Although organisational issues may well impinge on how parent–school relations develop, from the point of view of parents these are very much down to the attitudes of individual teachers, and parents could point to marked differences between teachers within a school. It can be argued that a reduction in negative stereotypes, especially by teachers, would enable there to be a better understanding between teachers and parents and a better understanding of children's difficulties as a consequence. This again can be seen as part of good practice and not as something exclusive to children with dyslexia. Hannon (1995) argues that: 'It is professionals, by virtue of their institutional position, who have the greater power and responsibility for parent–teacher relations.'

School

Although many in the field of dyslexia would argue that dyslexia is more than a reading problem, most would agree that learning to read and write is usually where dyslexic children encounter their first serious problems. Although such children may have been late learning to speak or poor at learning lists such as days of the week, as this study and others indicate, these early signs rarely caused children distress. This may be partly because these occurred in the more accommodating environment of the home whereas the formal teaching of reading is in many countries inextricably bound up with a child's first few years in school. The fact that in most cases children are placed in classes with same-age peers and required to undertake the same learning tasks as their peers almost inevitably leads to a highly comparative and in some cases competitive learning environment even if this is not what is intended. The other central difficulty is that literacy mediates the learning environment of the school. If children don't develop strong literacy skills they cannot access the curriculum successfully because of their poor reading and they cannot display their learning output successfully because of their poor writing skills. Kame'enui (2006) suggests that after grade 3 the school is an unforgiving environment not because teachers are harsh in their attitudes but because the literacy demands of the curriculum are unforgiving. Reading sits at a complex intersection between the individual processing skills of the child, their early language and literacy exposure, the elaborate written language that has to be decoded and the methods by which the child is taught to do this. Mark Twain said 'to every complex problem there is a simple solution that doesn't work'. Kame'enui (2006) points out, when giving advice to a White House Conference on the training of teachers, that this is certainly the case in relation to the teaching of reading. He goes on to suggest that we need complex solutions to the teaching of reading and that we also need to appreciate that schools are complex host environments. At an international level there has been concern over the teaching of reading and moves towards more structured and systematic approaches to the teaching of reading based on research evidence. In theory this should lead to fewer children encountering difficulties in learning to read and with better monitoring of children's progress those encountering difficulties should be identified earlier and given the additional support they need. Theory and practice of course are not the same thing and progress is patchy, with insufficient training of teachers and insufficient resources for the additional specialist reading and literacy instruction that some children require. Nationally and locally, different funding formulas and different ways of apportioning resources have been tried but they all come up against the demanding reality that many hours of specialist tuition are required to help children with the severest difficulties progress, let alone catch up with other children. Depending on how such programmes are implemented there is a concern that the 'reading process' rather than the whole child becomes the centre of attention and that how a child feels about their reading difficulties or the wider range of problems related to their dyslexia can be overlooked. Vadasy and Sanders (2008) in the US suggest that if individual or small-group tutoring is seen as the 'gold' standard for reading intervention we need to consider alternative resources such as training large numbers of paraprofessionals to meet the level of need, especially in more socially deprived school districts. Wearmouth (2004) in the UK for similar reasons suggests that parents are an important resource that could be better utilised. Despite the considerable amount of research on the respective merits of different types of reading intervention programmes even the most successful ones have children who make relatively little progress. Reading remains a laborious task for such children and progress in spelling and written work is often equally affected. Many would also argue that dyslexia encompasses a wider range of difficulties, and poor short-term memory for example can lead to difficulties with aspects of arithmetic, following multiple instructions in school and organising oneself. For older children, even if reading improves, speed and accuracy in reading, writing and spelling often remain a problem and lead to challenges with keeping up with reading and written work at secondary level. It is therefore important that schools have comprehensive and systematic policies and practices which enable children and young people with dyslexia-type difficulties to learn effectively and feel a valued part of the school community whatever their age. In the UK the 'Dyslexia Friendly Schools and Local Authorities' approach sets out such policies and practices in detail under four main headings:

1   leadership and management
2   teaching and learning
3   classroom environment
4   partnership with parents and children.

It can be argued that aspects of teaching and learning, the classroom environment and partnership have all been informed by and can be further refined by listening to children and parents on how practices and policies impact on them. The hope is that the accounts in this book when combined with studies of specific aspects of dyslexic children's reactions and coping strategies in school (Riddick 2009, Coffield *et al.* 2008, Singer 2008, 2005, Nugent 2008, Ingesson 2007, Burden 2005, Humphrey 2002) have given us a more refined and detailed understanding of how children see themselves as learners and what can be done to best support them. There is not sufficient space here to give detailed practical advice on a dyslexia-friendly school approach and the promotion of good self-esteem and promotion of good parent–school partnerships. Pavey's book (2007) gives practical advice on dyslexia-friendly primary schools; the DCSF (DfES 2005) also offers practical advice and a DVD, as does the Scottish executive (Deponio (2007). Riddick *et al.*'s book (2002) give specific advice on parent–teacher partnerships and assessing and promoting self-esteem in dyslexic children. Humphrey (2003) also gives useful advice on promoting self-esteem in the classroom. Other practical guides are listed at the end of this book. Riddick *et al.* suggest (2002, p. 18) there are five key elements to effectively supporting dyslexic children in school:

- direct help with specific difficulties to improve basic skills
- ensuring good access to the curriculum and output from the curriculum
- encouraging effective and positive coping strategies
- maintaining or improving self-confidence or self-esteem
- creating an inclusive and dyslexia-friendly environment.

In reality there is considerable overlap between these elements but by separating them out it is possible to consider the balance and interplay between them both at the school level and for individual children and young people. In attending to children with a wide range of special or additional needs educationalists understandably want policies and practices that are equitable and give all children the support they require. One solution is to have a three-tier approach with inclusive practices that are relevant to all children, inclusive practices that are relevant to children with particular sets of needs, and practices that are relevant to the needs of individual children. Some schools are now developing autism- or deaf-friendly approaches and the issue for teachers is how to keep abreast of all these developments. It may be that schools need a rolling 3- or 4-year programme with a focus one year on updating policy and practice for a range of specific learning difficulties and language impairments including dyslexia, another year on social, emotional and behavioural difficulties and so on. All approaches to SENs involve a subtle and dynamic mix of inclusive whole-school practices and specific accommodations, adjustments and interventions to address particular needs. In all areas of special needs it can be argued that the voices of children and parents are important in helping to decide on an appropriate approach and it is to be hoped that this study contributes to thinking on how their views can be best considered across a whole range of special educational needs.

Dilemmas

An issue that runs through much of the discussion on inclusion and special needs is the dilemma of if and how differences should be attended to. Understandably children and young people do not want to be seen as 'different' or treated 'differently' even though some of their differences may need attending to if they are to successfully negotiate their way through school. This can lead to dilemmas for teachers, parents and possibly children themselves sometimes. The ideal of an inclusive approach in schools is that some of this can be addressed by whole-class or school practices, such as the way work is assessed, that meet the needs of particular children in an unobtrusive way whilst being good practice for all children. The BDA for example argues that many of the dyslexia-friendly practices that they advocate in school are helpful to a much wider range of children, and there is some evidence to support this position. Difficulties arise when children do need additional support such as extra reading instruction or extra time to complete written work. Even when adequate resources are available schools have the difficult task of deciding how best to organise and deploy them to meet children's differences without humiliating or embarrassing them.

Both parents and teachers face the dilemma of what allowances to make and what standard of work and effort they should demand of children with literacy difficulties. Parents were often in a quandary as to whether they should be getting their children to do additional work at home to improve their literacy skills, or whether home should be enjoyable downtime and a respite for their children away from the exhausting literacy demands of school. The reality is that if most children with dyslexia want to 'keep up' they inevitably will have to expend more time and effort especially when they are younger and their basic literacy skills are particularly weak. Part of living with dyslexia is coming to terms with this and developing effective and efficient coping strategies that can lessen this difficulty. One dyslexic student described how she successfully passed her GCSE in English literature by reading summary revision notes and key passages but never whole books as this would take too long.

A hidden disability

The problem is that because 'dyslexia' is physically invisible you have to know what it is before you can clearly see it. This explains why it was possible for teachers to claim they have been teaching for 30 years without coming across a child with dyslexia. As they knew nothing about dyslexia they never saw a child with dyslexia! Many of the mothers in this sample had known something was wrong with their child's learning but it was only when they came upon information describing dyslexia that they identified this as the difficulty. Similarly several specialist teachers also said that before they knew about dyslexia there were children in their class who mystified or puzzled them. It was only in retrospect that they realised that these children were dyslexic and many of them felt guilty that they had been able to do little for these children. It can be argued that a move to an interactional approach which stresses the importance of both within-child and environmental factors is needed if we are to do full justice to many aspects of special needs and inclusion. Research into the learning of children with severe learning disabilities shows that different groups of children have different cognitive profiles and different strengths and weaknesses in the way that they learn (Clements 1987, Dockrell and McShane 1993). This suggests that no child's learning should be described in vague terms such as 'slow'; far from threatening our overall approach to special needs, dyslexia can help us to improve the way that we think about and approach a whole range of special needs. It can be argued that if we take the 'whole' person as our starting point and listen to what a person with a disability or difference has to say we are less likely to do this, as such people have to grapple with environmental factors every day of their life and can tell us graphically how these affect them:

> They don't know how much it affects you. I think it, like, frightens you being put through the traumas of it. In lessons they make you read out all the time. My mum does complain sometimes, but the school doesn't listen.

The perceptive and articulate girl who told the interviewer this was near to tears as she spoke. This girl went to a comprehensive school with a supportive special needs department but, as with many children in the study, it appeared that teachers underestimated the emotional impact of the difficulties that she was having. It can be argued that, where teachers understand something about the difficulties involved in specific learning difficulties or dyslexia, this will inform and direct their perception of need. One mother in the study found that, although her son's secondary school was very sympathetic about his poor literacy, the school completely dismissed the idea of specific learning difficulties and thought that all his problems were caused by lack of confidence and would thus be solved by improving his confidence. His mother felt this was a partial solution which didn't take on board the specific nature of the literacy difficulties he was having at school. As more is learnt about dyslexia it is becoming clearer that there are different degrees of the problem and that individuals differ in the precise nature of the problems that they have, although there are enough commonalties to justify the overall label of 'dyslexia' or 'specific learning difficulties'. It may well be the case that those with mild to moderate difficulties will be helped by moves to more phonics-based systematic teaching of reading or the introduction of multi-sensory methods to the classroom. What is less clear is how far these approaches will alleviate the more severe difficulties that some children have. It may be that these more severely affected children will need more individual and specific teaching over a longer period of time. It is important that a developmental perspective be taken and that the long-term difficulties that some children have be acknowledged and planned for. It is also important that children be not only given academic help but also given personal support and that everything possible be done to maintain their self-esteem and to help them develop self-awareness and positive coping strategies. In this study it was found that that, for the majority of children, telling them they were dyslexic helped them make sense of their sometimes bewildering learning experiences and in some cases this led to an improvement in their self-esteem. It also enabled children and their families to access a whole range of support such as role models, literature, support groups and so on which they may not have otherwise had contact with. For this reason it is important that schools, even if they prefer the term 'specific learning difficulty', acknowledge the word 'dyslexia' and allow children and parents to feel comfortable in using it:

Every time I said it I could feel myself getting embarrassed.

It is also important that schools do what they can to promote a positive attitude towards dyslexia so that children are not teased or denigrated about their difficulties:

Basically it's [dyslexia] like a stigma in my school.

Educationalists have been understandably wary about labelling children because of fears this might stigmatise them; but many dyslexic children and their parents felt they had already been stigmatised and argued that at least the term 'dyslexia' allowed them to challenge the incorrect attributions that had been made about them. At the moment a crossroads appears to have been reached. The way ahead could be for educationalists to reformulate 'dyslexia' as an educational term or to consider what is needed to make an alternative term such as 'specific learning difficulties' or 'reading disability' a more meaningful term for parents and children. Rather than 'blaming' individuals for using the term 'dyslexia' we need to ask in a constructive manner why they choose to do so. At present it is suggested that 'dyslexia' provides more personal support for many individuals and that they often end up using this term because they perceive themselves as lacking support from the mainstream school system.

Teacher training

Most people would agree that teachers have a difficult and demanding job and that a great many different skills are expected of the ordinary classroom teacher. The move to a more inclusive approach to education across many counties has increased the knowledge and skills that classroom teachers and learning support assistants require to meet the needs of a diverse range of children. Given the complexities of researching and unravelling the underlying difficulties that characterise dyslexia it appears highly unreasonable to expect teachers to identify and remediate these difficulties without specific training. As teachers and parents know only too well, trying to teach a child without these insights can be a baffling and infuriating experience at times. Many have advocated the need for much wider training for teachers and other professionals in the area of specific learning difficulties or dyslexia (BDA 2009, DA 2009, HCESC 2006). All are agreed that there needs to be training at both the initial and in-service (INSET) levels. At present, according to the BDA, there is great variation in coverage on initial teacher training courses. An issue that runs across both initial and INSET training is what level of training should be compulsory and what level of training should be optional. MacBeath and Galton (2006) recommend three levels of training in special educational needs with all teachers and learning support assistants receiving core skills training, and some teachers in all schools receiving advanced skills training which would allow them to carry out screening, assessment and some specialist teaching. Finally some specialist skills teachers who could carry out diagnostic assessments and highly specialised teaching would be shared between a group of schools. Sawyer and Berstein (2008) in the US stress that all mainstream teachers need dyslexia awareness training so that the skills children learn in pull-out literacy programmes can be successfully integrated into classroom learning. All the leading dyslexia charities in the UK advocate that there should be one specialist dyslexia-trained teacher in every school. Dyslexia Action and the BDA both run and accredit specialist dyslexia training courses attended by many mainstream school teachers and the BDA has developed a quality mark for dyslexia-friendly mainstream schools. As noted in the introduction, the close liaison by the UK government with voluntary bodies over dyslexia support and training is something that has developed over the last 10 years. Although in a number of countries there have been reports, enquiries and initiatives related to children with dyslexia or specific learning disabilities the problem is that if they don't lead to mandatory comprehensive and persistent changes in practice the effects are partial and transitory. In England the DCSF has commissioned a report into the teaching of dyslexic children in all schools; this is not yet available but in interim comments Jim Rose (2008) notes that many parents have contacted him to complain of insufficient support. Many educational psychologists do have training in specific learning difficulties but the depth of this still varies from course to course and those that trained some time ago will not necessarily have covered this area and, like many practising teachers, are dependent on INSET for updating their knowledge. A particular difficulty appears to be that, because of the negative mythology that has surrounded dyslexia, some educationalists are very reluctant to take any in-service training on specific learning difficulties or dyslexia. In the present study it was found that, even in schools with a good overall approach to specific learning difficulties, there always seemed to be a few teachers who were dismissive of children's specific difficulties and openly hostile to the term 'dyslexia':

> The French teacher is a nightmare. She says there's no such thing as dyslexia.

At primary school the effects of a critical teacher could be particularly devastating and several mothers in this study gave graphic accounts of the distress their children suffered:

> It was making him so negative in outlook, especially that term with the bad teacher. I mean, teachers have a lot to do with outlook. I saw him completely change from enjoying school to the spark wasn't there, but then it came back, it's definitely who's teaching them at the time, it definitely makes an impact. When he had the bad teacher he was so frightened of her he used to wring his hands. The teacher after the bad one said, 'You can see him sitting at the table, working himself up into a frenzy as to whether he should come and ask us something, and he stands beside the table and he's wringing his hands.' That was all instilled by one bad teacher.

Griffiths *et al.* (2004) found similar instances and noted that even in local authorities with ostensibly good dyslexia-friendly school policies everything depended on the attitude of the individual teachers. Whereas some were very supportive others were hostile or dismissive of the idea that a child was dyslexic and unsympathetic in the way they treated the child.

Reynolds (1995) points out that whole-school policies for special needs may have very little impact in the classroom and ultimately much is dependent on the attitude of the individual teacher. This underlines the importance of all teachers having training in this area and not just those who are interested. Another important point is that training, as well as imparting specific knowledge, needs to help address teachers' underlying attitudes and develop their understanding of and empathy with children who have specific difficulties. In some cases mothers were disappointed because even when teachers had requested specific information this didn't always appear to make them more understanding of the child's difficulties. Long *et al.* (2007) reported in a survey of 25 dyslexic adolescents that 18 of them thought teachers lacked empathy and had little understanding of their specific needs even though they were being taught generic study skills ostensibly to address their needs. It may be that these teachers weren't given sufficient information or simply didn't have sufficient time to reflect on the information and think through its implications for classroom practice, but it may also be the case that some teachers need help in doing this. One class teacher reflected that what had really brought home to her how frustrating and tiring writing could be for dyslexic children was being asked to write with her non-preferred hand for the whole of a training day on dyslexia.

Wider culture

It has become clear that different written languages pose different degrees and types of difficulty for children with dyslexia. Regular languages such as Italian or Finnish, in which nearly all words are spelt the way they sound, are considered to be more phonologically transparent and therefore easier for children to learn. English unfortunately, because of its numerous irregularities and odd spelling patterns, is considered the most difficult language for children to learn to read and write. Critics such as Spencer (2002) have argued that English is a 'dyslexic' language and that if we are serious about inclusion we should consider simplifying English spelling so that it is more regular and phonologically transparent. To some degree this is analogous to providing better access to buildings and public spaces for people with physical disabilities in that barriers are being removed. Although this may sound an outlandish proposal, Turkey, for example, reformed its complex spelling system in the 1920s with an attendant improvement in children's literacy learning so that first-grade Turkish children generally outperformed third-grade American children on a word reading task (Oney and Goldman 1986). This is a complex issue; Siegel (personal communication, 2008) observes that at least English speaking dyslexics are forced by the irregular spelling to move on from phonological to more efficient (for them) whole-word strategies as soon as they can whereas Italian children may persist for longer and rely more heavily on their inefficient phonological skills. Despite this it is still the case that roughly twice as many English as Italian children encounter difficulties in learning to read and write which are not attributable to differences in socio-economic factors or general teaching factors.

At a cultural level there are also issues about attitudes to literacy standards particularly relating to spelling and some aspects of grammar. Do so called 'easy' languages such as Italian expect and demand greater reading and spelling competence and what is it like for those children who have difficulty learning to read and write Italian? There is virtually no research on whether there are cultural differences in the standards of literacy expected of children and how tolerant or intolerant different cultures are of children – or adults for that matter – who have literacy difficulties. As argued elsewhere, there is often the assumption that being literate and being 'well-educated' or able are one and the same thing (Riddick 2001). There is also the assumption that anyone who cannot spell or punctuate well is lazy, careless or stupid, or possibly all three! The quotes by Twain and Solvag at the beginning of this chapter query cultural attitudes to spelling and suggest we need to challenge or think about the purpose and appropriateness of certain literacy standards. In a literate society we need to do all we can to help children become literate but without demoralising and denigrating those individuals who struggle with literacy. With international concerns over literacy standards in education, schools and individual teachers are also under pressure to attain results and uphold certain standards. The difficulty for them is how to have rigour without harshness and how to have leeway without laxness. Especially for children with milder processing difficulties/differences, an environment that gives them good early literacy exposure with rigorous and well informed teaching of reading and a dyslexia-friendly approach may prevent such differences from becoming a problem. The line between intervention, prevention and a shift in wider cultural attitudes to literacy is a difficult one to draw and it could be argued that synergy between all three approaches is needed. An attempt has been made to draw together the many different strands that impact on how children and their families live with dyslexia. Historically it can be argued that the main impetus for recognising and supporting dyslexia has come from outside the educational establishment and at present we appear to have reached a transitional point at which increasing numbers of mainstream educationalists are taking an active part in identifying and supporting children with dyslexia or specific learning difficulties. Because of the past dominance of the clinical, individual child-centred approach, a major task for mainstream educationalists is to develop viable 'educational approaches' to identifying and supporting such children.

Appendix

Interview schedule – children

Warm-up questions

W1   What sort of things do you like doing at home?
W2   What sort of things do you enjoy at school?

Dyslexia Institute

1   I understand you've been coming to the Dyslexia Institute for the last . . . Can you tell me about the sort of things you've been doing here/there?
2   Can you give me some examples of the things you've learnt at the Dyslexia Institute?
3   What do you think about coming to the Dyslexia Institute?
     (probes) (a) fed up because it means more work
                  (b) pleased because it helps me with my work

School

4   When you're doing your work at school do you find that you use anything that you've learnt at the Institute?
     (probe) every day, once a week, never?
     Can you give me an example of this?
5   What sort of work do you have difficulty with at school because of your dyslexia?
     now
     in the past
6   How do you try and cope with these difficulties?

Writing

(probe)   Do you think you write the same amount as other children or do you think you write less?

	every day	every week	rarely	never
(a) write less than other children				
(b) avoid certain words				
(c) pick easy to spell words				
(d) try and get out of doing writing				
(e) not write clearly				
(f) try and get a classmate to help				
(g) put off starting work				
(h) other				

7 How do you feel about the difficulties that you have?

8 Do you think other children notice the difficulties you have?
 yes no not sure

9 Do other children ever tease you about the difficulties you have?
 no yes
 What sort of things do they say?

10 How do you explain your difficulties to other children?

11 Does your teacher/s (form tutor) understand your difficulties?

12 Does your teacher/s do anything to help you with your difficulties?
 (probe) Any support teaching?

13a In general what kind of things do you find most helpful in school?

 b Can you tell me about the best teacher you've had so far?

14a What kind of things do you find unhelpful or upsetting in school?

 b Can you tell me about the worst teacher you've had so far?

15a Have you ever been told you are any of the following because of the difficulties you have with your work?
 (a) lazy
 (b) careless
 (c) slow
 (d) untidy
 (e) not paying attention
 (f) other

 b How do you feel about being called————?

16 Are there any things in school that you really dread having to do?

17 Compared with your classmates are you:
 more intelligent than average
 about average
 less intelligent than average

Home

18 Do you read at home for your own pleasure? (probe) What sort of things?
 never (Go to 19a) less than once a week a few times a week every day
 (go to 19b)

19a   Why do you never read?
  b   Do you find any problems or difficulties with the things you read?
20   If somebody asked you what dyslexia meant, what would you say?
21   What do you think about being called dyslexic?
      (probe) Do you resent it for making you feel different or has it helped you understand your problems?
22a   Who explained to you what dyslexia means?
  b   Does it make sense to you?
23   Would you like the chance to talk about it more?
24   Do you meet other children who have dyslexia? (Is that helpful or not?)
25   Have you heard of any famous or successful adults who have dyslexia?
      (If yes, has this encouraged you or do you think they're irrelevant to your life?)
26   Do you think your parents understand what it's like to be dyslexic?
      definitely do
      to some extent
      not at all
27   Do you talk to your parents about any problems or difficulties that you have at school because of being dyslexic?
      usually   sometimes   rarely   never
      (probe) What sorts of things would you talk/not talk about with your parents?
28   Do you think you'll still be dyslexic when you're an adult?
29   Is there anything I've left out that you'd like to talk about?

Interview schedule – adults

Do any close family members have dyslexia or a similar problem?

Identifying the problem

  1   How old was N when you first became aware that N might have difficulties?
      (a) Was it you who first realised that N had problems?
      (b) Was it someone else who first realised that N had a problem?
      (c) What kind of problems did N display?
2a   Looking back, were there any earlier signs that N might have difficulties?
  b   Did you always feel that basically N was as intelligent as other children?
      Yes   No
  c   Can you give me some examples of what convinced you of N's intelligence?

  3   Who was it who first suggested that N might be dyslexic?
  4   Where had you learnt about dyslexia from?
5a   Who did you first discuss your concerns with?
  b   What was their response?
      (probe)   In agreement   Noncommittal   Dismissive
  6   If someone else first suggested N was dyslexic, what was your response?
  7   How did you feel when N was first identified as dyslexic?
8a   If the school first suggested N might be dyslexic or have a specific learning difficulty, what support did they offer?
      Primary

Secondary
b If you first suggested N might be dyslexic what support did they offer?
Primary
Secondary
c Were you satisfied with the support offered?
d Was N formally assessed by anybody?
e Did they think that N was dyslexic?
f What did they recommend?
g Were you happy with the recommendations?

Help at home

9   Were you involved in teaching N to read? (How did this go?)
10a What sort of practical support have you tried to offer N at home, or do you think it's best left to the experts?
 b Has this gone OK or has it caused any problems?
 c How did you decide what support to offer?
 d What support was most effective?
11 What sort of personal support have you tried to give N?
12 Have you discussed with N what the label 'dyslexia' means?
13 If someone asked you to define or describe dyslexia what would you say?

Problems at school

14 What sort of problems, if any, does N encounter at school because of her/his dyslexia?
    At present
    In the past
15 Does N freely discuss these problems with you or do you have to drag them out?
16 When N has problems at school is it easy for you to talk to the school about them and get them resolved?
17 Could you tell me about the best teacher that N has had so far?
18 Could you tell me about the worst teacher that N has had so far?
19a What influence if any do you think having dyslexia has had on N?
    none   some   a lot
 b Does N have any nervous habits which you think are associated with the pressure of being dyslexic?
20 How would you rate N's self-esteem compared to other children of the same age?
    very high   fairly high   average   fairly low   very low
21 Have you ever felt isolated from other parents because of N's problems?
22 Have you ever felt that teachers or other parents think you're making excuses for N by calling her/him dyslexic?

The Dyslexia Institute

23 Why did you decide to send N to the Dyslexia Institute?
24 How did you hear about the Dyslexia Institute?
25 How long has N been attending for and how often?

26   Has attending the Institute helped N or not? If it has helped in what way has it done so?

27   Has attending the Institute helped you at all?

28a Is there any direct liaison between N's school and the Dyslexia Institute?

  b Does N have to miss any school in order to attend the Institute?

  c Does this cause any difficulties?

  d If N attends after school are there any problems with tiredness?

29a Do the things that N learns at the Institute carry over to her/his work in school?
     completely   somewhat   not very much   no idea

  b Can you give me some examples of this carry over?

30a How long does a round journey to the Dyslexia Institute take?

  b Does this cause any problems to the family timetable?

31   Does paying the fees have any impact on the family budget?
     none at all   some impact   a considerable impact

32   Do you think that support of this nature or a similar nature should be provided in your child's school or do you think it is best provided by a private institution like the Dyslexia Institute?

33a Turning to the future, do you worry about N's future progress at school?
     a lot   5   4   3   2   1 not at all

  b What particular concerns do you have?

34   Do you think having dyslexia will affect N's career choices?

35a What do you think about the support you've had in coping with N's difficulties?

  b Would you have liked more support?   No   Yes

  c What sort of support would you have liked?

36   In general how do you feel at the moment about N having dyslexia?

37   Is there anything I haven't covered that you'd like to mention?

Suggested further reading

Biographies and case studies

Edwards, J. (1994) *The Scars of Dyslexia*. London: Cassell.

Frank, R. (2004) *The Secret Life of the Dyslexic Child*. US: St Martins Press.

Hampshire, S. (1990) *Susan's Story*. London: Corgi.

Innes, P. (1991) *Defeating Dyslexia: A Boy's Story*. London: Kyle Cathie.

Kurnoff, S. (2001) *The Human Side of Dyslexia*. London: Universal.

Osmond, J. (1993) *The Reality of Dyslexia*. London: Cassell.

Pollak, D. (2005) *Dyslexia, the Self and Higher Education*. Stoke on Trent: Trentham Books.

Riddick, B., Farmer, M. and Sterling, C. (1997) *Students and Dyslexia – Growing up with a Specific Learning Difficulty*. London: Whurr Publishers.

Sagmiller, G. and Lane, G. (2002) *Dyslexia My Life* (3rd edn). Lee's Summit, MO: Doubting Thomas Publishing.

Schmitt, A. (1994) *Brilliant Idiot: An Autobiography of a Dyslexic*. PA: Good Books.

Van de Stoel, S. (1990) *Parents on Dyslexia*. Avon: Multilingual Matters.

Advice on teaching/managing dyslexia

Backhouse, G. and Morris, K. (eds) (2005) *Dyslexia? Assessing and Reporting*. A Patoss Guide. London: Hodder Murray.

Deponio, P. (2007) *Dyslexia at Transition*. DVD+ supporting website. www.dyslexiatransition.org.

DfES (Department for Education and Skills) (2005) *Learning and Teaching for Dyslexic Children*. CD-ROM. Nottingham: DCSF publications. www.dcsf.gov.uk/publications.

Pavey, B. (2007) *The Dyslexia-Friendly Primary School*. London: Paul Chapman Publishing.

Reid, G. (2007) *Dyslexia* (2nd edn). London: Continuum.

Reid, G. (2005) *Dyslexia and Inclusion*. London: David Fulton Publishers/NASEN.

Riddick, B., Wolfe, J. and Lumsdon, D. (2002) *Dyslexia: A Practical Guide for Teachers and Parents*. London: David Fulton Publishers.

Shaywitz, S. (2005) *Overcoming Dyslexia*. New York: Knopf Publisher.

Pollock, J., Waller, E. and Pollit, E. (2004) *Day-to-Day Dyslexia in the Classroom* (2nd edn). London: Routledge.

General reading

Reid, G., Elbeheri, G. and Knight, D. (eds) (2009) *The Routledge Companion to Dyslexia*. London: Routledge.

Reid, G., Fawcett, A., Manis, F. and Siegel, L. (eds) (2008) *The Sage Handbook of Dyslexia*. London: Sage.

Snowling, M. (2000) *Dyslexia* (2nd edn). Oxford: Basil Blackwell.
Swanson, H., Harris, K. and Graham, S. (eds) (2003) *Handbook of Learning Disabilities.* New York: Guilford Press.

Useful websites

United Kingdom

British Dyslexia Association www.bda.org.uk
Dyslexia Action (formerly The Dyslexia Institute) www.dyslexiaaction.org.uk
Dyslexia Scotland www.dyslexiascotland.org.uk
SpLD forum. Discussion forum for SpLD Professionals and Researchers www.jiscmail.ac.uk/archives/spld.html
Dyslexia forum. Self-help information discussion group for parents, dyslexics and others www.jiscmail.ac.uk/lists/dyslexia.html

United States of America

International Dyslexia Association www.interdys.org
Learning Disabilities Association of America www.ldanatl.org

Australia

AUSPELD The Australian Federation of SPELD Associations www.auspeld.org.au

Canada

Canadian Dyslexia Association www.dyslexiaassociation.ca

Hong Kong

Hong Kong Dyslexia Association www.dyslexia.org.hk

New Zealand

Dyslexia Foundation of New Zealand www.dyslexiafoundation.org.nz

References

Ainley, J. and Bourke, S. (1992) 'Student views on primary schools'. In E. Wragg (ed.) *Research Papers in Education*, 7, 107–128.

Alessi, G. (1988) 'Diagnosis diagnosed: a systematic reaction'. *Professional School Psychology*, 3 (2), 41–51.

Allport, G.W. (1954) *The Nature of Prejudice*. Reading, MA: Addison Wesley.

Andrews, N. (1990) 'A follow up study of dyslexic students'. In G. Hales (ed.) *Meeting Points in Dyslexia*. Proceedings of the 1st International Conference of the British Dyslexia Association. Reading: BDA.

Archer, J. (2004) 'Characteristics of an effective teacher of reading in an elementary school setting'. PhD thesis. Louisiana State University.

Armstrong, D. and Humphrey, N. (2009) 'Reacting to diagnosis of dyslexia among students entering FE: Development of the "resistance-accommodation" model'. *British Journal of Special Education*. (In Press).

Atkin, J. and Bastiani, J. with Goode, J. (1988) *Listening to Parents*. London: Croom Helm.

Augur, J. (1985) 'Guide lines for teachers, parents and learners'. In M. Snowling (ed.) *Children's Written Language Difficulties*. Windsor: NFER-Nelson.

Bandura, A. (1997) *Self-efficacy: The Exercise of Control*. New York: WH Freeman New York.

Bannister, D. and Fransella, F. (1971) *Inquiring Man: The Theory of Personal Constructs*. Harmondsworth: Penguin.

Barnes, C. and Mercer, G. (2007) *Disability*. London: Polity Press.

Barton, L. (2007) *Society and Education: 25 Years of British Journal of Sociology of Education*. London: Routledge.

Bastiani, J. (1987) 'From compensation to participation? A brief analysis of changing attitudes in the study and practice of home–school relations'. In J. Bastiani (ed.) *Parents and Teachers 1: Perspectives on Home School Relations*. Windsor: NFER-Nelson.

Battle, J. (2002) *Culture Free Self-Esteem Inventories* (3rd edn). Austin, TX: PROED.

Battle, J. (1992) *Culture Free Self-Esteem Inventories* (2nd edn). Austin, TX: PRO-ED.

Battle, J. (1981) *Culture Free Self-Esteem Inventories for Children and Adults* (1st edn). Austin, TX: PRO-ED.

BDA (2009) British Dyslexia Association. http://www.bdadyslexia.org.uk/faq.html#q1.

BDA (2008) http://www.bdadyslexia.org.uk.

BDA/DfES (2005) *Achieving Dyslexia Friendly Schools* (5th edn). Oxford: Information Press.

Beck, J.S. (2005) *Cognitive Therapy for Challenging Problems: What to Do When the Basics Don't Work*. New York: Guilford.

Beck, A., Rush, A., Shaw, B. and Emery, G. (1979) *Cognitive Therapy of Depression*. New York: Guilford.

Being Dyslexic (2009) www.beingdyslexic.co.uk.

Blaxter, M. (1976) *The Meaning of Disability*. London: Heinemann.

Blaxter, M. and Paterson, E. (1982) *Mothers and their Daughters: A Three Generational Study of Health Attitudes and Behaviour*. London: Heinemann.

Booth, G.K. (1988) 'Psychologists' perceptions of children who have specific learning difficulties'. *Educational Psychology in Practice*, 13 (2), 46–51.

Booth, T. (1978) 'From normal baby to handicapped child'. *Sociology*, 12 (3), 302–22.

BPS (1999) *Dyslexia, Literacy and Psychological Assessment*. Leicester: BPS, Division of Educational Child Psychology.

Bradley, L. and Bryant, P.E. (1985) *Rhyme and Reason in Reading and Spelling*. Ann Arbor: University of Michigan Press.

Bridges, D. (1987) 'It's the ones who never turn up that you really want to see'. In J. Bastiani (ed.) *Parents and Teachers 1: Perspectives on Home–School Relations*. Windsor: NFER-Nelson.

Bronfenbrenner, U. (1979) *The Ecology of Human Development: Experiments by Nature and Design*. Cambridge, MA: Harvard University Press.

Bruck, M. (1985) 'The adult functioning of children with specific learning disabilities: a follow-up study'. In I. Siegal (ed.) *Advances in Applied Developmental Psychology*. Norwood, NJ: Ablex.

Bruck, M. (1992) 'Persistence of dyslexics' phonological awareness deficits'. *Developmental Psychology*, 28, 874–86.

Bryan, T. and Bryan, J. (1991) 'Positive mood and math performance'. *Journal of Learning Disabilities*, 24, 490–4.

Bryant, P. (1994) 'Children's reading and writing'. *The Psychologist*, 7, 61.

Bryant, P.E. and Bradley, L. (1985) *Children's Reading Problems*. Oxford: Blackwell Scientific Publications.

Bullock, Lord A. (chair) (1975) *A Language for Life*. London: HMSO.

Burden, R. (2008) 'Is dyslexia necessarily associated with negative feelings of self-worth? A review and implications for future research'. *Dyslexia*, 14, 188–96.

Burden, R. (2005) *Dyslexia and Self-Concept*. London: Whurr.

Burns, R. (1982) *Self-Concept Development and Education*. London: Holt, Rinehart & Winston.

Butkowsky, T.S. and Willows, D.M. (1980) 'Cognitive-motivation and characteristics of children varying in reading ability: evidence of learned helplessness in poor readers'. *Journal of Educational Psychology*, 12 (3), 408–22.

Bynner, J. and Joshi, H. (2007) 'Building the evidence from longitudinal data'. *Innovation: The European Journal of Social Science Research*, 20 (2), 159–79.

Callison, C.P. (1974) 'Experimental induction of self-concept'. *Psychological Reports*, 35, 1235–8.

Campling, J. (ed.) (1981) *Images of Ourselves: Women with Disabilities Talking*. London: Routledge & Kegan Paul.

Carugati, F. (1990) 'Everyday ideas, theoretical models, and social representations: the case of intelligence and its development'. In G. Semin and K. Gergen (eds) *Everyday Understanding: Social and Scientific Implications*. London: Sage.

Casey, R., Levy, S.E., Brown, K. and Brooks-Gunn, J. (1992) 'Impaired emotional health in children with mild reading disability'. *Developmental and Behavioural Paediatrics*, 13 (4), 256–60.

Cattell, R.S., Eber, H.W. and Tatsuoka, M.M. (1970) *Handbook for the Sixteen Personality Factor Questionnaire*. Champagne, IL: Institute for Personality and Ability Testing.

Chaix, Y., Albaret, J., Brasard, C., Cheuret, E., Castelnau, P., Benesteau, J., Karsenty, C. and Demonet, J. (2007) 'Motor impairment in dyslexia: the influence of attention disorders'. *European Journal of Paediatric Neurology*, 19 (2), 144–61.

Chapman, J., Silva, P. and Williams, S. (1984) 'Academic self-concept: some developmental and emotional correlates in nine year old children'. *British Journal of Educational Psychology*, 54, 284–92.

Chen, C. and Uttal, D.H. (1988) 'Cultural values, parents' beliefs, and children's achievement in the United States and China'. *Human Development*, 31, 351–8.

Chinn, S. (2009) 'Dyscalculia and difficulties in mathematics'. In G. Reid (ed.) *The Routledge Companion to Dyslexia*. London: Routledge.

Chinn, S. and Ashcroft, R. (2007) *Dyslexia and Mathematics* (3rd edn). London: Wiley.

Clayton, P. (1994) 'Using computers for numeracy and mathematics with dyslexic students'. In C. Singleton (ed.) *Dyslexia and Computers*. Hull: Dyslexia Computer Resource Centre.

Clements, J. (1987) *Severe Learning Disability and Psychological Handicap*. Chichester: Wiley.

Cline, T. and Reason, R. (1993) 'Specific learning difficulties (dyslexia): equal opportunities issues'. *British Journal of Special Education*, 20 (1), 44–49

Coffield, M., Riddick, B., Barmby, P. and O'Neill, J. (2008) 'Dyslexia friendly schools: What can we learn from asking the pupils?'. In G. Reid, A. Fawcett, F. Manis and L. Siegel (eds) *The Sage Handbook of Dyslexia*. London: Sage.

Cole, D. and Jordan, A. (1995) 'Competence and memory: integrating psychosocial and cognitive correlates of childhood depression'. *Child Development*, 66, 450–73.

Coltheart, M., Masterson, I., Byng, S., Prior, M. and Riddoch, J. (1983) 'Surface dyslexia'. *Quarterly Journal of Experimental Psychology*, 25 A, 469–95.

Connell, B. (1987) 'Families and their kids'. In J. Bastiani (ed.) *Parents and Teachers*. Windsor: NFER-Nelson.

Coopersmith, S. (1967) *The Antecedents of Self-Esteem*. San Francisco: Freeman Press.

Critchley, M. (1970) *The Dyslexic Child*. London: Heinemann.

Croll, P. and Moses, D. (1985) *One in Five: The Assessment and Incidence of Special Educational Needs*. London: Routledge & Kegan Paul.

Cunningham, A.E. and Stanovich, K.E. (1997) 'Early reading acquisition and its relation to reading experience and ability 10 years later'. *Developmental Psychology*, 33 (6), 934–5.

Cutting, L. and Denckla, M. (2003) 'Attention: relationships between attention deficit hyperactivity disorder and learning disabilities'. In H.L. Swanson, K.R. Harris and S. Graham (eds) *Handbook of Learning Disabilities*. New York: Guilford Press.

DA (2009) Dyslexia Action. www.dyslexiaaction.org.uk.

Darke, S. (1988) 'Anxiety and working memory capacity'. *Cognition and Emotion*, 2, 169–174.

DCSF (2007) 'The Inclusion Development Programme'. www.dcsf.gov.uk/pns.

De Fries, J. (1991) 'Genetics and dyslexia: an overview'. In M. Snowling and D. Thomson (eds) *Dyslexia: Integrating Theory and Practice*. London: Whurr.

DES (Department of Education and Science) (1978) *Special Educational Needs (Warnock Report)*. Cmnd 7271. London: HMSO.

Dewhirst, W. (1995) ' "Pushy parents and lazy kids: aspects of dyslexia". An investigation of the experiences of dyslexics and their families in the diagnostic process'. MSc thesis. University of Teesside.

DfES (Department for Education and Skills) (2005) *Learning and Teaching for Dyslexic Children*. CD-ROM. Nottingham: DCSF publications. www.dcsf.gov.uk/publications.

DfES (Department for Education and Skills) (2004) *Removing Barriers to Achievement, the Governments Strategy for SEN*. Nottingham: DCSF publications. www.dcsf.gov.uk/publication.

DfES (Department for Education and Skills) (2001) *Special Educational Needs Code of Practice*. Nottingham: DCSF publications. www.dcsf.gov.uk/publications.

Dockrell, J. and McShane, J. (1993) *Children's Learning Difficulties: A Cognitive Approach*. Oxford: Blackwell.

Donawa, W. (1995) 'Growing up dyslexic: a parent's view'. *Journal of Learning Disabilities*, 28 (6), 324–8.

Du Sautoy, M. (2008) 'I'm not very fast at my times tables'. *The Guardian*, 3 November, pp. 10–13.

Dutke, S. and Stoebber, J. (2001) 'Test anxiety, working memory, and cognitive performance: supportive effects of sequential demands'. *Cognition and Emotion*, 15 (3), 381–9.

Dyslexia Action (2007) www.dyslexiaaction.org.uk.

Dyson, A. and Skidmore, D. (1995) 'Provision for pupils with specific learning difficulties in secondary schools'. A report to SOED (Scottish Office Education Department). University of Newcastle.

Dyson, A. and Skidmore, D. (1994) 'Provision for pupils with specific learning difficulties in secondary schools'. A report to SOED (Scottish Office Education Department). University of Newcastle upon Tyne.

Edwards, J. (1994) *The Scars of Dyslexia*. London: Cassell.

Eisner, J.E. (1995). 'The origins of explanatory style: trust as a determinant of pessimism and optimism'. In G.M. Buchanan and M.E.P. Seligman (eds) *Explanatory Style*. New Jersey: Lawrence Erlbaum Associates.

Ellis, A.W. (1993) *Reading, Writing and Dyslexia: A Cognitive Analysis*. Hove: Lawrence Erlbaum Associates.

Elbaum, B. and Vaughn, S. (2003) 'Self-concept and students with learning disabilities'. In H.L. Swanson, K.R. Harris and S. Graham (eds) *Handbook of Learning Disabilities*. New York: Guilford Press.

Elmer, N. (2001) *The Costs and Causes of Low Self-Esteem*. York: Rowntree. www.jrf.org.uk.

Everatt, J. (2002) 'Visual processes'. In G. Reid and J. Wearmouth (eds) *Dyslexia and Literacy: Theory and Practice*. Chichester: Wiley.

Falik, C.H. (1995) 'Family patterns of reaction to a child with learning disability: a mediational perspective'. *Journal of Learning Disabilities*, 28 (6), 335–41.

Fairhurst, P. and Pumfrey, P. (1992) 'Secondary school organisation and the self concepts of pupils with relative reading difficulties'. *Research in Education*, 47, 325–331.

Fawcett, A. and Nicolson, R. (2008) 'Dyslexia and the cerebellum'. In G. Reid, A. Fawcett, F. Manis and L. Siegel (eds) *The Sage Handbook of Dyslexia*. London: Sage Publishers.

Fawcett, A. and Nicolson, R. (2004) *Dyslexia Early Screening Test* (2nd edn). San Antonio, TX: Pearson Education.

Fawcett, A. and Nicolson, R. (1994) 'Computer based diagnosis of dyslexia'. In C. Singleton (ed.) *Computers and Dyslexia*. Hull: Dyslexia Computer Resource Centre, University of Hull.

Finucci, J.M., Guthrie, J.T., Childs, A.L., Abbey, H. and Childs, B. (1976) 'The genetics of specific reading disability'. *Annals of Human Genetics*, 40, 1–23.

Fletcher, J. Morris, R. and Lyon, R. (2003) 'Classification and definition of learning disabilities'. In H. Swanson, K. Harris and S. Graham (eds) *Handbook of Learning Disabilities*. New York: Guilford Press.

Fogelmann, N. (1988) 'Continuity and change: lessons from the 1958 cohort'. Paper given at the ACPP conference, July.

Frederickson, N. and Jacobs, S. (2001) 'Controllability attributions for academic performance and the perceived scholastic competence, global worth and achievement of children with dyslexia'. *School Psychology International*, 22 (4), 401–16.

Frith, U. (1997) 'Brain, mind and behaviour in dyslexia'. In C. Hulme and M. Snowling (eds) *Dyslexia: Biology, Cognition and Intervention*. London: Whurr.

Frith, U. (1992) 'Cognitive development and cognitive deficit'. *The Psychologist: Bulletin of the British Psychological Society*, 5 (1), 13–19.

Fuchs, D. and Fuchs, L.S. (2006) 'Introduction to response to intervention: what, why, and how valid is it?'. *Reading Research Quarterly*, 41, 93–9.

Funnell, E. and Davison, M. (1989) 'Lexical capture: a developmental disorder of reading and spelling'. *Quarterly Journal of Experimental Psychology*, 41 A, 471–88.

Galloway, D.M. (1985) *School, Pupils and Social Educational Needs*. London: Croom Helm.

Garzia, R.P. (1993) 'Optometric factors in reading disability'. In D.M. Willows, R.S. Kruk and

E. Corcos (eds) *Visual Processes in Reading and Reading Disabilities*. Hillsdale, NJ: Lawrence Erlbaum.

Gates, A.I. (1992) *The Psychology of Reading and Spelling with Special Reference to Disability*. New York: Columbia University.

Geary, D. (2003) 'Learning disabilities in arithmetic'. In H.L. Swanson, K.R. Harris and S. Graham (eds) *Handbook of Learning Disabilities*. New York: Guilford Press.

Gersten, R. and Dimino, J. (2006) 'RTI (response to intervention): rethinking special education for students with reading difficulties'. *Reading Research Quarterly*, 41 (1), 99–107.

Gibb, B., Alloy, L. and Walshaw, P. (2006) 'Predictors of attributional style change in children'. *Journal of Abnormal Child Psychology*, 34 (3), 408–22.

Gilger, J. and Wilkins, M. (2008) 'Atypical neurodevelopmental variation as a basis for learning disorders'. In M. Moody and E. Silliman (eds) *Language Impairment and Reading Disability: Interactions Among Brain, Behaviour, and Experience*. New York: Guilford Press.

Gillis Light, J. and De Fries, J. (1995) 'Comorbidity of reading and mathematical difficulties: genetic and environmental etiologies'. *Journal of Learning Disabilities*, 28 (2), 96–106.

Gjessing, H.J. and Karlsen, B. (1989) *A Longitudinal Study of Dyslexia*. New York: Springer Verlag.

Goffman, E. (1968) *Stigma*. Harmondsworth: Penguin.

Goodnow, J.J. and Collins, W.A. (1990) *Development According to Parents*. Hove: Lawrence Erlbaum Associates.

Goswami, U. and Bryant, P.E. (1990) *Phonological Skills and Learning to Read*. London: Lawrence Erlbaum Associates.

Greenspan, S.I. (1981) *The Clinical Interview of the Child*. New York: McGraw-Hill.

Griffiths, C., Norwich, B. and Burden, R. (2004) 'I'm gad I didn't take no for an answer'. Research Report, Exeter University School of Education.

Gross, J. (1993) *Special Educational Needs in the Primary School*. Buckingham: Open University Press.

Gurney, P. (1988) *Self-esteem in Children with Special Educational Needs*. London: Routledge.

Hales, G. (1994) 'The human aspects of dyslexia'. In G. Hales (ed.) *Dyslexia Matters*. London: Whurr Publishers.

Hallgren, B. (1950) 'Specific dyslexia ("congenital word blindness"): a clinical and genetic study'. *Acta Psychiatrica et Neurologica Scandinavica*, Suppl. 65, 1–287.

Hampshire, S. (1990) *Susan's Story*. London: Corgi.

Hannavy, S. (1995) 'Able and willing'. *Special Children*, 15 (3), 38–41.

Hannavy, S. (1993) *The Middle Infant Screening and Forward Planning Programme*. Windsor: NFER-Nelson.

Hannon, P. (1995) *Literacy, Home and School: Research and Practice in Teaching Literacy with Parents*. London: Falmer Press.

Heiervang, E., Stevenson, J., Lund, A. and Hugdahl, K. (2001) 'Behaviour problems in children with dyslexia'. *Nordic Journal of Psychiatry*, 55 (4), 251–6.

Henderson, A. and Miles, E. (2001) *Basic Topics in Mathematics for Dyslexics*. London: Whurr.

Hinshelwood, J. (1917) *Congenital Word Blindness*. London: Lewis.

Hodge, N. and Runswick-Cole, K. (2008) 'Problematising parent–professional partnerships in education'. *Disability and Society*, 23 (6), 637–47.

Hodges, K. (1993) 'Structured interviewing for assessing children'. *Journal of Child Psychology and Psychiatry*, 34 (1), 49–68.

HCESC (House of Commons Education and Skills Committee) (2006) *Special Educational Needs*. Third Report of Session 2005–2006. Vol. 1. Norwich: The Stationery Office. www.tsoshop.co.uk.

Hulme, C. and Snowling, M. (1992) 'Deficits in output phonology: an explanation of reading failure?' *Cognitive Neuropsychology*, 9, 47–92.

Humphrey, N. (2003) 'Facilitating a positive sense of self in pupils with dyslexia: the role of teachers and peers'. *Support for Learning*, 18 (3), 129–36.

Humphrey, N. (2002) 'Teacher and pupil ratings of self-esteem in developmental dyslexia'. *British Journal of Special Education*, 29 (1), 29–36.

Humphrey, N. and Mullins, P. (2002) 'Personal constructs and attribution for academic success and failure in dyslexia'. *British Journal of Special Education*, 29 (4), 196–203.

IDA (2009) International Dyslexia Association. www.interdys.org/.

IDA (2007) www.interdys.org/ewebeditpro5/upload/Definition.

IDEA (2004) *The Individual with Disabilities Education Act*. http://idea.ed.gov.

Ingesson, S.G. (2007) 'Growing up with dyslexia'. *School Psychology International*, 28 (5), 574–91.

IRA (2002) *Summary of the (US) National Reading Panel Report: Teaching Children to Read*. Newark, US: International Reading Association. www.reading.org/resources/issues/reports/nrp.html.

Ireson, J. and Hallam, S. (2001) *Ability Grouping in Education*. London: Sage Publications.

Ireson, J. (1995) 'What do teachers do? Classroom activities used in the initial teaching of reading'. *Educational Psychology: An International Journal of Experimental Educational Psychology*, 15 (3), 245–56.

Johnson, D.J. and Myklebust, H.R. (1967) *Learning Disabilities: Education, Principles and Practices*. New York: Grune & Stratton.

Jordan, R. and Powell, S. (1992) 'Stop the reforms, Calvin wants to get off'. *Disability and Society*, 7 (1), 85–88.

Jorm, A.E., Share, D.L., Maclean, R. and Matthews, R. (1986) 'Cognitive factors at school entry predictive of specific reading retardation and general reading backwardness'. *Journal of Child Psychology and Psychiatry*, 27, 45–54.

Kame'enui, E. (2006) 'The teaching of reading: beyond vulgar dichotomies to the science of causality'. White House conference on preparing tomorrow's teachers. www.ed.gov/admin/tchrqual/.

Kavanaugh, D. (ed.) (1978) *Listen to Us!* New York: Workman Publishing.

Kelly, G.A. (1955) *The Psychology of Personal Constructs*. New York: W.W. Norton.

Korhonen, T.K. (1995) 'The persistence of rapid naming problems in children with reading disabilities: a nine year follow up'. *Journal of Learning Disabilities*, 28 (4), 195–213.

Kosmos, K.A. and Kidd, A.H. (1991) 'Personality characteristics of dyslexic and non dyslexic adults'. *Psychological Reports*, 69, 231–4.

Kunda, Z. and Olesen, K.C. (1995) 'Maintaining stereotypes in the face of disconfirmation: constructing grounds for subtyping deviants'. *Journal of Personality and Social Psychology*, 68 (4), 565–79.

Lackaye, T. and Margalit, M. (2006) 'Comparisons of achievement, effort, and self-perceptions among young students with learning disabilities and their peers from different achievement groups'. *Journal of Learning Disabilities*, 39 (5), 432–46.

Lawrence, D. (2006) *Enhancing Self-Esteem in the Classroom* (3rd edn). London: Paul Chapman.

Lawrence, D. (1985) 'Improving self-esteem and reading'. *Educational Research*, 27 (3), 32–9.

Lawrence, D. (1973) *Improved Reading through Counselling*. London: Ward Lock.

Lawrence, D. (1971) 'The effects of counselling on retarded readers'. *Educational Research*, 13 (2), 119–24.

Layder, D. (1993) *New Strategies in Social Research* (2nd edn). Cambridge: Polity Press.

LDA (2009) 'Learning Disabilities Association'. http://www.ldanatl.org/aboutld/parents/ld_basics/types.asp.

Lewis, J. (1995) 'The development of a unit for dyslexic children in a British comprehensive school'. *Dyslexia: An International Journal of Research and Practice*, 1 (1), 148–62.

Lewis, A., Davison, I., Ellins, J., Niblett, L., Parsons, S., Robertson, C. and Sharpe, J. (2007)

'The experiences of disabled pupils and their families'. *British Journal of Special Education*, 34 (4), 189–95.

Long, L., MacBlain, S. and MacBlain, M. (2007) 'Supporting students with dyslexia at the secondary level: an emotional model of literacy'. *Journal of Adolescent & Adult Literacy*, 51 (2), 124–34.

Lundberg, I. (1994) 'Reading difficulties can be predicted and prevented: a Scandinavian perspective on phonological awareness and reading'. In C. Hulme and M. Snowling (eds) *Reading Development and Dyslexia*. London: Whurr.

Lundberg, I. and Hoien, T. (2001) 'Dyslexia and phonology'. In A. Fawcett (ed.) *Dyslexia: Theory and Good Practice*. London: Whurr.

Lyon, R. (2006) 'Dyslexia'. In *Encyclopaedia of Disability*. Vol. 1. New York: Sage.

Macbeath, J. and Galton, M. (2006) 'The costs of inclusion: a study of inclusion policy and practice in English primary, secondary and special schools'. Faculty of Education, University of Cambridge.

Macbeth, A. (1989) *Involving Parents*. Oxford: Heinemann.

MacDonald, S. (2007) 'Dyslexia, class and the education system'. PhD thesis. Newcastle University.

McGee, R., Freeman, M., Williams, S. and Anderson, J. (1992) 'DSM III disorders from age 11 to age 15 years'. *Journal of the Academy of Child and Adolescent Psychiatry*, 31, 50–9.

McGee, R., Share, D. and Moffitt, T. (1988) 'Reading disability, behaviour problems and juvenile delinquency'. In D. Saklofske and S. Eysenck (eds) *Individual Differences in Children and Adolescents*. London: Hodder and Stoughton.

MacKay, N. (2001) 'Achieving the dyslexia friendly school – the Howarden approach'. Paper presented at the 5th BDA International Conference. www.bdainternationalconference-org/2001/presentations/wed_s3_c_2/htm.

MacKeith, R. (1973) 'The feelings and behaviour of parents of handicapped children'. *Developmental Medicine and Child Neurology*, 15 (4), 525–7.

McLoughlin, D. (2004) 'Dyslexia and the workplace: policy for an inclusive society'. In G. Reid and A. Fawcett (eds) *Dyslexia in Context*. London: Whurr Publishers.

McLoughlin, D. (1990) 'Adult dyslexia'. Masters dissertation. University of East London.

McLoughlin, D., Leather, C. and Stringer, P. (2002) *The Adult Dyslexic: Interventions and Outcomes*. London: Whurr.

Madge, N. and Fassam, M. (1982) *Ask the Children*. London: Batsford Academic.

Manis, F. and Bailey, C. (2008) 'Exploring heterogeneity in developmental dyslexia: a longitudinal investigation'. In G. Reid, A. Fawcett, F. Manis and L. Siegel (eds) *The Sage Handbook of Dyslexia*. London: Sage.

Marsh, H.W. (2005) 'Big fish little pond effect on academic self-concept'. *German Journal of Educational Psychology*, 19, 119–28.

Marsh, H.W. and Craven, R.G. (2006) 'Reciprocal effects of self-concept and performance from a multidimensional perspective: beyond seductive pleasure and unidimensional perspectives'. *Perspectives on Psychological Science*, 1, 133–63.

Marsh, H. and Hau, K. (2003) 'Big-fish–little-pond effect on academic self-concept: a cross-cultural (26 country) test of the negative effects of academically selective schools'. *American Psychologist*, 58, 364–76.

Marsh, H.W. and O'Mara, A.J. (2008) 'Reciprocal effects between academic self-concept, self-esteem, achievement and attainment over seven adolescent–adult years: unidimensional and multidimensional perspectives of self-concept'. *Personality and Social Psychology Bulletin, 34*, 542–52.

Marsh, H., Craven, R. and Debus, R. (1991) 'Self-concepts of young children 5 to 8 years of age: measurement and multi-dimensional structure'. *Journal of Educational Psychology*, 83 (3), 377–92.

Maughan, B. (1988) 'Reading problems: do they matter in the long term?'. Paper given at the ACPP conference, July.

Maughan, B. (1994) 'Behavioural development and reading disability'. In C. Hulme and M. Snowling (eds) *Reading Development and Dyslexia*. London: Whurr.

Melck, E. (1986) *Finding out about specific learning difficulties/dyslexia*. London: Academic Press.

Merrell, C. and Tymms, P. (2007) 'Identifying reading problems with computer-adaptive assessments'. *Journal of Computer Assisted Learning*, 23 (1), 27–35.

Miles, N. and Huberman, A. (1994) *Qualitative Data Analysis* (2nd edn). Beverly Hills: Sage.

Miles, T.R. (2007) 'Criteria for successful intervention'. *Dyslexia: An International Journal of Research and Practice*, 13, (4), 253–256.

Miles, T.R. (2006) *Fifty years in Dyslexia Research*. Chichester: John Wiley & Sons.

Miles, T.R. (1997) *The Bangor Dyslexia Test* (2nd edn). Oxford: Blackwell.

Miles, T.R. (1993) *Dyslexia: The Pattern of Difficulties* (2nd edn). London: Whurr.

Miles, T.R. (1987) *Understanding Dyslexia*. Bath: Bath Educational Publishers.

Miles, T.R. (1983) *Dyslexia: The Pattern of Difficulties*. Oxford: Blackwell.

Miles, T.R. (1982) *The Bangor Dyslexia Test*. Oxford: Blackwell.

Miles, T.R. and Miles, E. (2004) *Dyslexia and Mathematics* (2nd edn). London: Routledge Falmer.

Miles, T.R. and Miles, E. (1999) *Dyslexia: A Hundred Years On* (2nd edn). Milton Keynes: Open University Press.

Miles, T.R., Gilroy, D. and Du Pre, A. (2007) *Dyslexia at College* (3rd edn). London: Routledge.

Mittler, P. (1985) 'Approaches to evaluation in special education: concluding reflections'. In S. Hegarty and P. Evans (eds) *Research and Evaluation Methods in Special Education*. Windsor: NFER-Nelson.

Mok, M. (2002) 'Determinants of students quality of life: a path model'. *Learning Environments Research*, 5 (3), 275–300.

Mosely, D. (1989) 'How lack of confidence in spelling affects children's written expressionism'. *Educational Psychology in Practice*, 5, 185–9.

Muth, K.D. (1984) 'Solving arithmetic word problems: role of reading and computational skills'. *Journal of Educational Psychology*, 76, 205–10.

NCLB (2001) *No Child Left Behind Act*. US Department of Education. www.ed.gov/nclb.

Newson, J. and Newson, E. (1987) 'Both intermediary and beneficiary'. In J. Bastiani (ed.) *Parents and Teachers 1: Perspectives on Home–School Relations*. Reading: NFER-Nelson.

Nicolson, R. and Fawcett, A. (1999) 'Developmental dyslexia: the role of the cerebellum'. *Dyslexia: An International Journal of Research and Practice*, 5, 155–7.

Nugent, M. (2008) 'Service for children with dyslexia – the child's experience'. *Educational Psychology in Practice*, 24 (3): 189–206.

O'Brien, C. (2005) 'BDA Dyslexia Friendly Quality Mark'. www.liverpool.gov.uk/news/archives/2005.

Oka, E.R. and Paris, S.G. (1987) 'Patterns of motivation and reading skills in underachieving children'. In S.J. Ceci (ed.) *A Handbook of Cognitive, Social and Neuropsychological Aspects of Learning Disabilities,* vol. 2. Hillsdale, NJ: Lawrence Erlbaum Associates.

Oliver, M. (1981) 'Disability, adjustment and family life: some theoretical considerations'. In A. Brechin, P. Liddiard and J. Swain (eds) *Handicap in a Social World*. Sevenoaks: Hodder & Stoughton.

Olson, R.K., Wise, B., Connor, F.A. and Rack J.P. (1990) 'Specific deficits in component reading and language skills: genetic and environmental influences'. *Journal of Learning Disabilities*, 22, 339–48.

Oney, B. and Goldman, S. (1986) 'Decoding and comprehension skills in Turkish and English:

effects of the regularity of phoneme–grapheme correspondences'. *Journal of Educational Psychology*, 76, 557–68.

Opie, S.J. (1995) 'The effective teaching of reading: a study of the personal qualities and teaching approaches in a group of successful teachers'. *Educational Psychology in Practice*, 11 (2), 23–9.

Orton, S.T. (1937) *Reading, Writing and Speech Problems in Children*. New York: Norton.

Osmond, J. (1993) *The Reality of Dyslexia*. London: Cassell.

Owens, M. (2008) 'Processing efficiency in children: working memory as a mediator between trait anxiety and academic performance'. *Anxiety, Stress and Coping*, 21, 418–30.

PACFOLD (2007) *Putting a Canadian Face on Learning Disability*. Learning Disabilities Association of Canada. www.pacfold.ca.

Palombo, J. (2001). *Learning Disorders and Disorders of the Self in Children and Adolescents*. New York: W.W. Norton & Company.

Pavey, B. (2007) *The Dyslexia-Friendly Primary School*. London: Paul Chapman Publishing.

Peer, L. (1994) *Dyslexia: The Training and Awareness of Teachers*. Reading: British Dyslexia Association.

Peters, M., Seeds, K., Goldstein, A. and Coleman, N. (2008) 'Parental involvement in children's education'. Research report no. DCSF-RR034. London: Department for Children, Schools and Families.

Pianta, R.C. and Caldwell, C.B. (1990) 'Stability of externalising symptoms from kindergarten to first grade and factors related to instability'. *Development and Psychopathology*, 2, 247–58.

Plowden, B. (chair) (1967) *Children and their Primary Schools*. London: HMSO.

Pollak, D. (2005) *Dyslexia, the Self and Higher Education*. Stoke on Trent: Trentham Books.

Pollock, J., Waller, E. and Politt, R. (2004) *Day-to-Day Dyslexia in the Classroom*. London: Routledge.

Porter, J. and Rourke, B.P. (1985) 'Socio-emotional functioning of learning disabled children: a subtype analysis of personality patterns'. In B.P. Rourke (ed.) *Neuropsychology of Learning Disabilities: Essentials of Subtype Analysis*. New York: Guildford.

Pressley, M. (2006) *Reading Instruction that Works: The Case for a Balanced Approach*. New York: Guilford Press.

Price, L.A., Gerber, P.J. and Mulligan, R. (2003) 'The Americans with Disabilities Act and adults with learning disabilities: the realities of the workplace'. *Remedial and Special Education*, 24, 350–8.

Pumfrey, P.D. and Reason, R. (1991) *Specific Learning Difficulties (Dyslexia): Challenges, Responses and Recommendations*. London: Routledge.

Raskind, M., Goldberg, R., Higgins, E. and Herman, K. (2002) 'Teaching "life success" to students with LD: lessons learned from a 20 year study'. *Intervention in School and Clinic*, 37 (4), 201–8.

Ravenette, A. (1985) *Specific Reading Difficulties*. London: Newham Education Authority.

Rayner, K. (1993) 'Eye movements in reading and information processing: 20 years of research'. *Psychological Bulletin*, 124 (3), 372–422.

Reid, G. (2007) *Motivating Learners in the Classroom: Ideas and Strategies*. London: Sage Publications.

Reid, G. (2001) 'Biological, cognitive and educational dimensions of dyslexia: current scientific thinking'. In L. Peer and G. Reid (eds) *Dyslexia – Successful Inclusion in the Secondary School*. London: David Fulton Publishers.

Reid, G. (1994) *Specific Learning Difficulties*. Edinburgh: Moray House Publications

Reid, G. and Wearmouth, J. (2009) 'Identification and assessment of dyslexia and planning for learning'. In G. Reid (ed.) *The Routledge Companion to Dyslexia*. London: Routledge.

Reid, G., Green, S. and Zylstra, C. (2008) 'The role of parents'. In G. Reid, A. Fawcett, F. Manis and L. Siegel (eds) *The Sage Handbook of Dyslexia*. London: Sage.

Reid, G., Deponio, P. and Davidson-Petch, L. (2005) 'Identification, assessment and intervention – implications of an audit on dyslexia policy and practice in Scotland'. *Dyslexia: An International Journal of Research*, 11, 203–16.

Reynolds, D. (1995) 'Using school effectiveness knowledge for children with special needs: the problems and possibilities'. In C. Clark, A. Dyson and A. Millward (eds) *Towards Inclusive Schools.* London: David Fulton.

Ribbens, J. (1994) *Mothers and their Children: A Feminist Sociology of Child Rearing.* London: Sage.

Ribbens, J. and Kirkpatrick, S. (2004) 'Negotiating public and private: maternal mediations of home–school boundaries'. In: G. Crozier and D. Reay (eds) *Activating Participation: Parents and Teachers Working towards Partnership.* Stoke on Trent: Trentham Books.

Riddell, S., Brown, S. and Duffield, J. (1994) 'Parental power and special educational needs: the case of specific learning difficulties'. *British Educational Research Journal*, 20 (3), 241–9.

Riddell, S., Duffield, J., Brown, S. and Ogilvy, C. (1992) *Specific Learning Difficulties: Policy, Practice and Provision.* A Report to SOED, Department of Education, University of Stirling.

Riddick, B. (2009) 'The implications of students' perspectives on dyslexia for school improvement'. In G. Reid (ed.) *Routledge Dyslexia Handbook.* London: Routledge.

Riddick, B. (2008) 'Parents perspectives on receiving, searching for and evaluating information relating to autistic spectrum disorders: sorting the wheat from the chaff'. *Journal of Good Autism Practice*, 9 (1), 58–64.

Riddick, B. (2006) 'Dyslexia friendly schools in the UK'. *Topics in Language Disorders*, 26 (2), 142–54.

Riddick, B. (2001) 'Dyslexia and inclusion: time for a social model of disability perspective?'. *International Studies in the Sociology of Education*, 11 (3), 223–36.

Riddick, B. (2000) 'An examination of the relationship between dyslexia and stigmatisation with special reference to dyslexia'. *Disability & Society*, 15 (4), 653–67.

Riddick, B. (1996) *Living with Dyslexia: The Social and Emotional Consequences of Specific Learning Difficulties* (1st edn). London: Routledge.

Riddick, B. (1995a) 'Dyslexia: dispelling the myths'. *Disability and Society*, 10 (4), 457–73.

Riddick, B. (1995b) 'Dyslexia and development: an interview study'. *Dyslexia: An International Journal of Research and Practice*, 1 (2), 63–74.

Riddick, B., Wolfe, J. and Lumsdon, D. (2002) *Dyslexia: A Practical Guide for Teachers and Parents.* London: David Fulton Publishers.

Riddick, B., Sterling, C., Farmer, M. and Morgan, S. (1999) 'Self-esteem and anxiety in the educational histories of adult dyslexic students'. *Dyslexia*, 5, 227–48.

Riddick, B., Farmer, M. and Sterling, C. (1997) *Students and Dyslexia: Growing Up with a Specific Learning Difficulty.* London: Whurr.

Rix, J., Nind, M., Sheahy, K. and Wearmouth, J. (2006) 'A systematic review of interactions in pedagogical approaches with reported outcomes for the academic and social inclusion of pupils with SENs'. EPPI-Centre, London, Institute of Education. http//eppi/ioe.ac.uk.

Robinson, T. (1978) *In Worlds Apart.* London: Bedford Square Press.

Rogers, C.R. (1951) *Client Centered Therapy.* Boston: Houghton Mifflin.

Rogers, R., Tod, J., Powell, S., Parson, C. and Cornwall, J. (2006) *Evaluation of the Parent Partnership Services in England.* DfES Research Report RR 719.

Roland, E. and Galloway, D. (2004) 'Professional cultures in schools with high and low rates of bullying'. *School Effectiveness and School Improvement*, 15 (3–4), 241–60.

Rosenthal, J. (1973) 'Self-esteem in dyslexic children'. *Academic Therapy*, 9(1), 27–39.

Rose, J. (2008) www.dcsf.gov.uk/jimroseanddyslexia.

Rose, J. (2006) *Independent Review of the Teaching of Reading.* DfES. www.standards.dfes.gov.uk/phonics/report.

Rowe, K. (2005) *Teaching Reading: Final Report of the National Inquiry into the Teaching of*

Literacy. Canberra, ACT: Australian Government Department of Education, Science and Training.

Rudel, R.G. (1985) 'The definition of dyslexia: language and motor deficits'. In F.H. Duffy and N. Geschuimd (eds) *Dyslexia: A Neuroscientific Approach to Clinical Evaluation.* Boston: Little Brown.

Rutter, M., Caspi, A., Fergusson, D., Horwood, L., Goodman, R., Maughan, B., Moffitt, T., Meltzer, H. and Carroll, J. (2004) 'Sex differences in developmental reading disability'. *Journal of the American Medical Association*, 291 (16), 2007–12.

Rutter, M., Tizard, J., Yule, W., Graham, P. and Whitmore, K. (1976) 'Isle of Wight studies 1964–1974'. *Psychological Medicine*, 6, 313–32.

Rutter, M., Tizard, J. and Whitmore, K. (eds) (1970) *Education, Health and Behaviour.* London: Longman & Green.

Sanson, A. (2006) 'Reading disabilities with and without behaviour problems at 7–8 years: prediction from longitudinal data from infancy to 6 years'. *Child Psychology and Psychiatry*, 37 (5), 529–41.

Sawyer, D. and Bernstein, S. (2008) 'Students with phonological dyslexia in school based programmes'. In G. Reid, A. Fawcett, F. Manis and L. Siegel (eds) *The Sage Handbook of Dyslexia.* London: Sage.

Schumacher, J., Hoffman, P. and Schmal, C. (2007) 'Genetics of dyslexia: the evolving landscape'. *Journal of Medical Genetics*, 44, 289–97.

Scott, G. and Richards, M.P.M. (1988) 'Night waking in infants: effects of providing advice and support for parents'. *Journal of Child Psychology and Psychiatry*, 31, 551–67.

Scott, M.E., Scherman, A. and Phillips, H. (1992) 'Helping individuals with dyslexia succeed in adulthood: emerging keys for effective parenting, education and development of positive self-concept'. *Journal of Instructional Psychology*, 19 (3), 312–18.

Seligman, M. (2006). *Learned Optimism: How to Change Your Mind and Your Life.* New York: Random House.

Shakespeare, T. (2006) *Disability Rights and Wrongs.* London: Routledge.

Shankweiler, D. and Fowler, A. (2004) 'Questions people ask about the role of phonological processes in learning to read'. *Reading and Writing*, 17, 483–515.

Shaywitz, S.E., Shaywitz, B.A., Fletcher, J.M. and Escobar, M.D. (1990) 'Prevalence of reading disability in boys and girls: results of the Connecticut Longitudinal Study'. *Journal of the American Medical Association*, 264 (8), 998–1002.

Siegel, L.S. (2004) 'Schooling, socioeconomic context and literacy development'. *Educational Psychology*, 24, 867–83.

Siegel, L.S. (2003) 'Basic cognitive processes and reading disabilities'. In H.L. Swanson, K.R. Harris and S. Graham (eds) *Handbook of Learning Disabilities.* New York: Guilford Press.

Siegel, L. S. and Lipka, O. (2008) 'The definition of learning disabilities: who is the individual learner with learning disabilities?'. In G. Reid, A. Fawcett, F. Manis and L. Siegel (eds) *The Sage Handbook of Dyslexia.* London: Sage.

Siegel, L. S. and Smythe, I. (2006) 'Supporting dyslexic adults – a need for clarity: a critical review of the Rice Report "Developmental Dyslexia in Adults: A review of research"'. *Dyslexia*, 12, 69–79.

Singer, E. (2008) 'Coping with academic failure, a study of Dutch children with dyslexia'. *Dyslexia*, 14, 314–33.

Singer, E. (2005) 'The strategies adopted by Dutch children with dyslexia to maintain their self-esteem when teased at school'. *Journal of Learning Disabilities*, 38 (5), 411–23.

Singleton, C.H. (2002) *Lucid Baseline – Computerised Baseline Assessment.* Hull: Lucid Research Limited.

Smith, B. and Sparkes, A. (2008) 'Narrative and its potential contribution to disability studies'. *Disability and Society*, 23 (1), 17–28.

Smith, F. (2006) *Reading without Nonsense*. US: Teachers College Press.

Smith, F. (2004) *Understanding Reading: A Psycholinguistic Analysis of Reading and Learning to Read* (6th edn). Hillsdale, NJ: Erlbaum.

Smith, P., Pepler, D. and Rigby, K. (2004) *Bullying in Schools*. Cambridge: Cambridge University Press.

Smythe, I., Everatt, J. and Salter, R. (2004) *The International Book of Dyslexia*. London: Wiley & Sons.

Snowling, M.J. (2008) 'Specific disorders and broader phenotypes: the case of dyslexia'. *Quarterly Journal of Experimental Psychology*, 61, 142–56.

Snowling, M.J. (2005) 'Dyslexia is not a myth'. *Literacy Today*, 45, 7.

Snowling, M.J. (2002) 'Reading development and dyslexia'. In U.C. Goswami (ed.) *Handbook of Cognitive Development*. Oxford: Blackwell.

Snowling, M.J. (2000) *Dyslexia* (2nd edn). Oxford: Blackwell.

Snowling, M.J. (1980) 'The development of grapheme–phoneme correspondences in normal and dyslexic readers'. *Journal of Experimental Child Psychology*, 29, 294–304.

Snowling, M.J., Muter, V. and Carroll, J.M. (2007) 'Children at family risk of dyslexia: a follow-up in adolescence'. *Journal of Child Psychology & Psychiatry*, 48, 609–18.

Snowling, M.J. and Stackhouse, J. (2006) *Dyslexia, Speech and Language* (2nd edn). London: Whurr.

Solvag, P. (2007) 'Developing an ambivalence perspective on medical labelling in education: case dyslexia'. *International Studies in the Sociology of Education*, 17 (1), 79–84.

Speece, D., McKinney, J. and Appelbaum, M. (1985) 'Classification and validation of behavioural sub-types of learning disabled children'. *Journal of Educational Psychology*, 77, 67–77.

Spencer, K.A. (2002) 'English spelling and its contribution to illiteracy: word difficulty for common English words'. *Reading*, 36 (1), 16–25.

Spreen, O. (1987) *Learning Disabled Children Growing Up: A Follow Up into Adult-hood*. Lisse, Netherlands: Swets & Zeitlinger.

Springett, L. (2002) 'Dyslexia friendly schools'. In L. Peer and M. Johnson (eds) *The Dyslexia Handbook*. Reading: British Dyslexia Association.

Stace, S. and Roker, D. (2005) 'Monitoring and supervision in ordinary families: the views and experiences of young people aged 11–16 years and their parents'. Report published by the National Children's Bureau, London.

Stackhouse, J. (1991) 'Dyslexia: the obvious and hidden speech and language disorder'. In M. Snowling and D. Thomson (eds) *Dyslexia: Integrating Theory and Practice*. London: Whurr.

Stanovich, K.E. and Stanovich, P.J. (2006) 'Fostering the scientific study of reading instruction by example'. In K. Dougherty Stahl and M. McKenna (eds) *Reading Research at Work: Foundations of Effective Practice*. New York: Guilford Press.

Stanovich, K.E. (2005) 'The future of a mistake: will discrepancy measurement continue to make the learning disabilities field a pseudoscience?'. *Learning Disability Quarterly*, 28, 103–6.

Stanovich, P.J. and Stanovich, K.E. (2003) 'Using research and reason in education: how teachers can use scientifically based research to make curricular & instructional decisions'. Washington, DC: US Department of Education. http://www.nifl.gov/partnershipforreading/publications/html/stanovich/.

Stansfield, J. (1994) 'Using I.T. to support children with specific learning difficulties: an LEA approach'. In C. Singleton (ed.) *Computers and Dyslexia*. Hull: Dyslexia Computer Resource Centre, University of Hull.

Stein, J. (2003) 'Visual motion sensitivity and reading'. *Neuropsychologia*, 41, 1785–93.

Stein, J. (2001) 'The magnocellular system of developmental dyslexia'. *Dyslexia*, 7 (1), 12–36.

Stein, J. (1994) 'A visual defect in dyslexics?'. In A. Fawcett and R. Nicolson (eds) *Dyslexia in Children*. Hemel Hempstead: Harvester Wheatsheaf.

Stephan, W.G. (1985) 'Intergroup relations'. In G. Lindzey and E. Aronson (eds) *Handbook of Social Psychology* (3rd edn), vol. 12. New York: Random House.

Sternberg, R. and Grigorenko, E. (2004) 'Why we need to explore development in its cultural context'. *Merrill-Palmer Quarterly*, 50 (3), 369–86.

Swann, W. (1985) 'Dyslexia'. Unit 25 Block 4 E206 of *Personality, Development and Learning*. Milton Keynes: Open University Press.

Szasz, T. (1961) *The Myth of Mental Illness*. New York: Harper & Row.

Teachernet (2009) 'Specific learning difficulties'. http://www.teachernet.gov.uk/wholeschool/sen/datatypes/Cognitionlearningneeds/.

Thomas, D. (1982) *The Experience of Handicap*. London: Methuen.

Thomson, M. (1990) *Dyslexia and Development* (3rd edn). London: Whurr.

Thomson, M. and Hartley, G.M. (1980) 'Self-esteem in dyslexic children'. *Academic Therapy*, 16 (1), 19–36.

Todd, L. (2007) *Partnership and Inclusive Education*. London: Routledge.

Topping, K.J. (2001) *Thinking Reading Writing: A Practical Guide to Paired Learning with Peers, Parents & Volunteers*. New York: Continuum International.

Torgesen, J. (2004) 'Lessons learned from research on interventions for students who have difficulty learning to read'. In P. McCardle and P. Chabra (eds) *The Voice of Evidence in Reading Research*. Baltimore, MD: Paul Brookes.

Torgesen, J., Wagner, R. and Rashotte, C. (1994) 'Longitudinal studies of phonological processing and reading'. *Journal of Learning Disabilities*, 27 (5), 276–96.

Truss, C. (2008) 'Peter's story: reconceptualising the UK SEN system'. *European Journal of Special Needs Education*, 23 (4), 365–77.

Turner, M. (1990) 'Positive responses'. *Times Educational Supplement*, 19 January.

Undheim, A. (2008) 'Psychosocial factors and reading difficulties: students with reading difficulties drawn from a representative population sample'. *Scandinavian Journal of Psychology*, 49 (4), 377–84.

Vadasy, P. and Sanders, E. (2008) 'Repeated reading intervention: outcomes and interactions with reader skills and classroom instruction'. *Journal of Educational Psychology*, 100 (2), 272–90.

Van der Stoel, S. (ed.) (1990) *Parents on Dyslexia*. Clevedon: Multilingual Matters.

Wadswoth, S., DeFries, J., Olson, R. and Willcutt, E. (2007) 'Colorado longitudinal twin study of reading disability'. *Annals of Dyslexia*, 57 (2) 321–45.

Wagner, R.K. (2008) 'Rediscovering dyslexia: new approaches to identification and classification'. In G. Reid, A. Fawcett, F. Manis and L. Siegel (eds) *The Sage Handbook of Dyslexia*. London: Sage.

Warnock, M. (1994) 'Preface'. In L. Peer (ed.) *Dyslexia: The Training and Awareness of Teachers*. Reading: British Dyslexia Association.

Webster, A. and Ellwood J. (1985) *The Hearing Impaired Child in the Ordinary School*. Beckenham: Croom Helm.

Wearmouth, J. (2004) Issues in addressing children's difficulties in literacy development through family–school partnerships. *Curriculum Journal*, 1, 5–17.

Wolf, M. and O'Brien, B. (2001) 'On issues of time, fluency and intervention'. In A. Fawcett (ed) *Dyslexia: Theory and Good Practice*. London: Whurr.

Wolfendale, S. (2002). *Parents Partnership Services for Special Educational Need*. London: David Fulton Publishers.

Wolfendale, S. (ed.) (1997) *Working with Parents of SEN Children after the Code of Practice*. London: David Fulton Publishers.

Wolfendale, S. (1995) *Meeting Special Needs in the Early Years: Directions in Policy and Practice*. London: David Fulton.

Woolfon, R., Hasker, M., Lowe, D., Shields, M. and Mackintosh, H. (2007) 'Consulting young people who have disabilities'. *British Journal of Special Education*, 30, 40–9.

Yasutake, D. and Bryan, T. (1995) 'The influence of affect on the achievement of behaviour of students with learning disabilities'. *Journal of Learning Disabilities*, 28 (6), 329–44.

Zeleke, S. (2004) 'Self-concepts of students with learning disabilities and their normally achieving peers: a review'. *European Journal of Special Needs Education*, 28 (5), 574–91.

Index